LAST COPY

# GREENWICH LIBRARIES

N.N.

*Also by Richie Benaud*

BENAUD ON REFLECTION
WILLOW PATTERNS
THE NEW CHAMPIONS
SPIN ME A SPINNER
TALE OF TWO TESTS
WAY OF CRICKET

# THE APPEAL OF CRICKET

## The Modern Game

RICHIE BENAUD

Hodder & Stoughton

Copyright © Richie Benaud 1995

First published in Great Britain in 1995 by
Hodder and Stoughton
A division of Hodder Headline PLC

The right of Richie Benaud to be identified as the Author of
the Work has been asserted by him in accordance with the
Copyright, Designs and Patents Act 1988.

10   9   8   7   6   5   4   3   2   1

British Library Cataloguing in Publication Data
Benaud, Richie
  The Appeal of Cricket
  I. Title
  796.358

ISBN 0 340 63227 5

Typeset by Hewer Text Composition Services, Edinburgh
Printed and bound in Great Britain by
Mackays of Chatham PLC

Hodder and Stoughton
A Division of Hodder Headline PLC
338 Euston Road
London NW1 3BH

# CONTENTS

Acknowledgments     vii

1   The swirling mist on Table Mountain and the red mist
on the Australian cricket team     1
2   Shane Warne the magician and con-tricks with over-rates     15
3   Michael Atherton and the dirt, Illingworth and the bacon     27
4   Magnificent Michael Slater, the Australians devastate
Atherton     41
5   England go slow and pay dearly, captains and selectors     57
6   Darren Gough, Tufnell's catch of the summer and
May and Warne save the Ashes     69
7   England attack at last and win     83
8   A new ball game for television and Percy Sledge
makes his name     105
9   Nicklaus and Seve and chaos in the commentary box     121
10   A new structure for English cricket     135
11   The Adelaide Academy, the ultimate in cricket?     159
12   Shane Warne, the greatest young legspinner I've seen     189
13   Kapil Dev, Allan Border and a few other greats     215
14   Why I bet on horses and not humans     231
15   Darren Gough, Michael Slater and Mark Taylor, Bradman
and Australian cricket     239

Appendices     255
Index     273

# ACKNOWLEDGMENTS

Ten years is a long time between books but so much happens in cricket and in life these days that such a timespan flashes past. There have been changes in the game itself, in television and all forms of the media, and there are more to come. Certainly there have been changes in playing personnel, great players have gone and others have started to make their names, players' attitudes have changed.

Technology has been perceived by some to have taken over umpiring, sometimes match referees have been more publicised than the umpires themselves. Nothing has changed in one sense. Ten years ago I wrote that cricket, for me, remained the most controversial game of all. It still is! It is also a game with wonderful appeal for youngsters, the middle aged and the older generation.

Working in all areas of the media is a challenge made all the more enjoyable by the cricketers on the stage. As has been the case for the past one hundred and eighteen years, each international eleven taking the field provides an almost identical mix, the majority good players, a few very good and, if the captain and country happen to be lucky, a great player or even two!

To put everything into print is no easy task but one made considerably easier by Daphne's knowledge of cricket, the English language and sub-editing, the tireless efforts of Margaret Roseland in Sydney, the assistance of Clare Oldridge in London, and John Benaud in Valley Heights.

Charlie Wat provides me with excellent and imaginative statistics each year and Max Kruger's help was valuable in checking other matters.

The title was my publisher Roddy Bloomfield's, and if he has aged a little in the past year he won't be the first editor to whom I have done that.

Richie Benaud
Coogee, Australia
March, 1995

# PHOTOGRAPH ACKNOWLEDGMENTS

The author and publisher would like to thank Graham Morris for providing the majority of the photographs used in this book. Other copyright photographs are from AllSport, AllSport/Hulton Deutsch, the *Daily Sun*, Fairfax Photo Library/Golding and W. A. Rouch.

# 1

## *The swirling mist on Table Mountain and the red mist on the Australian cricket team*

The mist lay heavily across the top of Table Mountain, the edges of it swirled around the villas and the shops on the hillside and, at the end of Camps Bay beach, there were the first touches of another sea fret to match the one which had obliterated the street lights the previous evening. The waves would have been of little use to an Australian body-surfer; they started breaking thirty yards from the start of the soft, sandy beach and then they gouged into the sand leaving a ten-foot drop to the water as they quickly receded.

It wasn't an idyllic day but it was a far better place for me to be than up the road in Bophuthatswana where several hours earlier, the *Cape Times* noted, a woman had cracked a half-million-rand jackpot on the slot machines at the Sun City Casino, and she might be the last to do so if the looters and executioners of Bophuthatswana had their way.

This was twenty-four hours after the execution at point-blank range of three members of the AWB, the White right-wingers who had surged into Mmabatho in a bid to circumvent the toppling of the regime of President Lucas Mangope. Another fifty-seven people died the same day and almost four hundred were wounded. Television crews were fired on, beaten and kicked during the incidents and film of the executions was confiscated. But the *New York Times* correspondent, who was on the spot, was able graphically to describe how the paratrooper strolled casually up to the three men lying on the ground and shot them dead. Even more graphic was the South African *Sunday Times* front page picture taken by Cobus Bodenstein.

President F. W. de Klerk sent troops into the region to restore order and South African political analysts speculated again that the unrest was a preface to civil war.

It was the same day the Australian cricket team arrived in Cape Town for a three-day match against a Combined XI, as a run-up to the Second Test of the series. In the light of the other tragic events, their arrival was noted only on page three alongside another pertinent sports story that the possible cancellation of England's Rugby tour of South Africa later in 1994 would cost the South African RFU $A6,000,000. Lost revenue from tourism and other matters pertaining to the tour, scheduled just a short time after the elections, could take costs to a calamitous loss of $A8,000,000.

This was one aspect of South Africa in 1994 a month before its first democratic elections, while Australia and South Africa were celebrating their first cricket Test series in the country in twenty-four years.

South Africa came back into international cricket in 1991 when the Cricket Board representing Black players joined with the Cricket Board representing White players to form the United Cricket Board of South Africa. I was there at the historic moment, having been asked by Dr Ali Bacher to make the trip from London to speak at the official dinner and to be present at the signing. Also there, and officially representing Australia, was Bob Cowper, the former Test cricketer who is the Australian Cricket Board's representative in Europe.

It was interesting that after all the Australian government's noise about South Africa, their actual presence at this historic time was extraordinarily low key. It was poor reading by the government back in Australia and later it was to have an effect on various business happenings between South Africa and Australia.

India, on the other hand, had a party of seventeen officials led by Sunil Gavaskar who was in great form in a brilliant lunch-time speech he made at the Wanderers Club. The reason India had such a large delegation was that their government instantly realised the great cricket and trade advantages to be had from an early presence in a country where proper elections would be held in less than three years' time, and which had a considerable Indian population.

Mine was a slightly rushed visit since, having originally decided it was impossible to make the trip because of business commitments, I had an urgent call from Channel Nine to say Dr Bacher had phoned again to ask if I would reconsider, as it would be an interesting and historic weekend, and would I please pack and be on my way. I flew out of London on the Friday evening, into Johannesburg on the Saturday morning, where fog delayed the plane's arrival, straight to the Wanderers lunch where Sunil, as speaker, was in such good form. From there I went on to afternoon meetings, spoke at the official dinner on the Saturday evening in the Sandton Sun Hotel, had a cricket and business luncheon on Sunday with Joe Pamensky and friends and then caught the afternoon flight back to London, arriving at Wimbledon at noon on Monday to work for Channel Nine. It was something of a rush, but at the time, and, in retrospect, I see it was one of those unique events at which it was a good thing to be present. No good saying later, 'If only . . .'

India's seventeen-strong presence meant they had the well-deserved inside running for the first tour of South Africa which they duly received. There followed for South Africa other matches against the West Indies and Pakistan, and then there was the World Cup. At first it seemed South Africa would be excluded from that because the United Cricket Board had come into being mid-way through 1991, with the World Cup draw already made and agreed.

This World Cup was being played in Australasia and expenses were enormous. Travelling and accommodation around Australia and across to New Zealand and back for the various teams ate deeply into any possible profit for the host nations, even before a ball was bowled. South Africa eventually were included, beat Australia in their first encounter, moved on to the semi-finals, where they were beaten on an inferior run-rate after rain interfered with the match, and England and Pakistan fought out the final.

There was a very interesting happening the evening prior to the final where the official farewell dinner was held in the Royal Exhibition Building in Melbourne. The Pakistan and England teams were present but were to leave early, perfectly natural with the final the following day, therefore strict timetables were the order of the night. I was the main speaker and had been asked to speak for precisely fourteen minutes. That side of it suited me, but what didn't suit me quite as well was the fact that I had to do a very fast rejigging of my speech because of what happened on the floor of the auditorium. All 1,526 of us were sitting listening to a speech by Sir Colin Cowdrey and I was to follow him after a short item by an entertainer. This entertainer turned out to be someone impersonating Her Majesty The Queen, and in the course of this little interlude, Graham Gooch, the England captain, and Ian Botham walked out in protest at the content of the comedian's act.

I watched them storm out past my table, three feet from where I was sitting, and I showed no emotion, which is more than I can say for Mrs McDermott, the wife of the New Zealand Cricket Council member, Peter McDermott, who was responsible for organising the dinner. She had hold of my arm in what could conservatively be described as a vice-like grip and she said, 'They couldn't, they just couldn't, could they?'

They certainly could! The reason I was showing no emotion was that I was trying to get my brain into gear. Fifteen hundred and twenty-six people present, the comedian is coming to the end of his performance, and only about half the people in the auditorium know that Gooch and Botham have done a bunk – certainly the MC doesn't know because the television arc lamps are shining in his eyes. And I now had major changes to make to my fourteen-minute speech, in which I had planned to focus on three men – Imran Khan, the Pakistan captain, Graham Gooch and Ian Botham – and two of them had now disappeared. As soon as the comedian finished, the MC was moving into gear, but not as fast as Bob Bennett, the England team manager, who was across in a flash. 'Richie, just to say that the rest of the team would have gone as well but they have stayed out of respect for you and the fact that you are the main speaker.'

When I said, 'Thank you, Bob, do you have a little seven-minute filler I could use up there?' I wasn't joking. The material I had intended to use needed Gooch and Botham to be present, not having a relaxing beer back at their hotel.

I'm told the speech went well, the speaker is never sure about those things, but it lasted thirteen minutes and fifty-three seconds so at least my brain-timer hadn't seized up!

The following day the Australian Prime Minister, Mr Keating, called Botham 'precious' for having walked out believing the Queen to have been insulted, but somehow he didn't bother mentioning Gooch. Not all Prime Ministers of Australia have an inbuilt memory-bank for cricket, some even dislike it, but 'Goochie' holds no grudges against that kind of thing. He even graciously came back to Australia and shook Mr Keating's hand at the start of the 1994–5 Ashes battle and then announced his retirement from Test cricket, although the two are not necessarily connected.

Just to keep the record straight, and to show Botham was nowhere near as worried as I was about the 1,526 people, this is what *he* had to say about the evening. He introduced it by saying he rarely saw eye to eye with Graham Gooch on quite a number of things.

'But Gooch and I did see eye to eye the night before the World Cup Final in Melbourne when we both stormed out of the official banquet. It began pleasantly enough. The mood was good, we had a few glasses of wine and enjoyed ourselves. When the meal finished we sat back ready for the cabaret. Then, to our horror, we were treated to a stream of abuse in the name of entertainment.

'Some grotesque drag artist took to the stage and started to take the mickey out of the Queen. It was coarse and crude. If they had put a turban on the man's head, blackened his face and let him tell gags about the Indians or Pakistanis, he would have been lynched. Yet for some reason the monarchy was fair game.

'For ten minutes I sat there thinking this could not possibly go on much longer. Then I snapped. I pushed back my chair, fixed my eyes on the exit sign above the door and headed straight for it. On the way out I was joined by 'Goochie'. I was not going to sit around and listen to this rubbish and I made my protest in the only way I know how.

'Of course I knew there would be fireworks the following day and, sure enough, the hotel was besieged by the press. Bearing in mind the comments of Paul Keating, the Australian Prime Minister, who when told I had left the banquet described me as 'precious', I decided to have a go myself. The press boys were falling over themselves to get a quote, so I gave them one. I said, "I'm very, very proud of my heritage – and, unlike Mr Keating, I have one."'

Pakistan won the final the next night, and a brilliant win it was too. They were superbly led by Imran, they played wonderfully well and the celebrations went on long into the night, not just for them but for all those associated with the World Cup.

Three balls which will remain in my memory for a long time were the ones which accounted for Graeme Hick, Allan Lamb and Chris Lewis in that World Cup Final. England needed 250 to win after Pakistan had thrashed 102 from the last 12 overs of their innings, in one of the better entertainments of the season. Mushtaq put Hick through hell for a time and then did him with a wrong 'un to have him lbw. Wasim Akram, who is one of my favourite cricketers, bowled both Lamb and Lewis with what were close to unplayable deliveries. As he had also made 33 in that 102-run blast, it's no wonder the performances are not difficult to recall.

The South Africans had the seal put on their return to international cricket by those matches in Australia and New Zealand, a preface to the

1993–4 tour of Australia which had as its second stage the three Test matches and eight limited-overs games in South Africa.

It was great to see how well the South Africans did in Australia and at home after being so long out of the international scene. There is a vast difference between playing at levels of Sheffield Shield, county cricket, West Indian Red Stripe cricket and what used to be the Currie Cup, when compared with limited-overs Internationals and Tests. South Africa bridged that gap faster than I would have believed possible and it was even more meritorious when you consider that for twenty years they had only experienced competition at what amounted to Currie Cup level, even though there had been some unofficial tours played.

When they came to Australia for the three-match Test series and the World Series limited-overs Internationals, it was as a country which had been rushed back into international cricket and had undertaken, in a relatively short time, a full tour by India, four Tests and seven limited-overs Internationals, followed by a triangular one-day series with the West Indies and Pakistan.

A few months earlier, in April 1992, an historic Test in Barbados against the West Indies showed just how long they had been off the international scene. One of the vital things at that level is not just winning but knowing how to win. Needing only a handful of runs on the final day, they found themselves up against a team which knew how not to be beaten, which hated being beaten and, more important, knew how to win. The South Africans were bowled out but it was a good lesson for their inexperienced players on just how tough Test cricket can be and what a gap there is to be made up if you have been off the scene for so many years.

They showed against the Australians in 1993–4 that those lessons had been quickly assimilated when, after rain had marred the opening Test of the series in Melbourne, they won the Second Test in Sydney in a manner reminiscent of the run of play in that Barbados Test mentioned above.

They fought and clawed their way back into the game, after looking well beaten on several occasions, and finally set the Australians just 117 for victory. It turned out to be too many. It's not the first time in recent years Australia have collapsed when chasing a target, a point made by Allan Border when he was congratulating Kepler Wessels on their victory, and one to be underlined a year later when, under Mark Taylor, Australia collapsed against England in Adelaide.

The Australia–South Africa SCG Test match in 1994 rose to great heights for excitement though played on a poor pitch where runs were very hard to come by and strokeplay was the exception rather than the norm.

After the happenings of Barbados, the South Africans would have been hard pressed to forgive themselves if they had failed to win at the SCG. On the other hand, the Australians who took part in that game will go to the end of their careers unable to forgive themselves and wondering how on earth they could have failed to make 117 for victory, against a team with its captain batting with a broken hand and about to fly home, and a fledgeling stand-in captain, Hansie Cronje, who, theoretically, should not have been able to match Border from the tactical point of view. The victory was one of the greatest I had seen in forty-one years of playing and commentating on the game and it was precisely what South Africa needed to reassure themselves they were back where they belonged.

The Australians did well to square that series in Adelaide, in a welter of controversy concerning some of the umpiring decisions, and the second part of the six-match series then took place in South Africa with Kepler Wessels' team taking out that opening Test at the Wanderers ground in Johannesburg. It was a match of contrasts, South Africa bowled out for 251 the first day, Australia 34/0 and looking good. They then threw away their first five wickets on the second day, two to run-outs and three simply to indifferent shots which came about because of pressure applied by Wessels and his bowlers. They lost the match by a massive 197 runs after squandering one of the best victory opportunities I had seen for many years.

From that point everything went downhill for the Australians. Shane Warne and Merv Hughes were cited and fined for bad behaviour and bringing the game into disrepute, after incidents involving foul language, and provocative actions on the field and against a spectator. Hughes and Warne were initially fined $A450 by match referee Donald Carr, to which the Australian Cricket Board added their own fines of $A4,000, far more in keeping with the scale of the offences. Hughes, on the spectator charge matter, was handed an additional $A2,000 as a suspended sentence.

One of the more quaint aspects of the spectator incident with Merv was that he was said to have been upset at something the spectator said to him. It even appeared the spectator may have used crude language. Now I believe in Alice in Wonderland, as well as the Tooth Fairy, but it is stretching things a bit far to suggest Merv might have been upset by a verbal. At least he was lucky only to get a word or two in his ear – his team-mates have been known to have had a tongue in theirs!

It's not often in the past forty-seven years the Australian Cricket Board have moved swiftly but Alan Crompton, the Chairman, wasted no time. Nor should he have done because during the Adelaide Test, following the Warne–Cullinan confrontation in Sydney, he had warned the Australian team that their actions in giving a 'send-off' to players who had just been dismissed were 'cowardly'.

This sending-off gesture was to have more publicity after the 1995 Adelaide Test when Chris Lewis was fined $A1,600 for pointing Craig McDermott to the pavilion after dismissing him. Match referee John Reid described Lewis's actions as 'cowardly', precisely the same word used by Crompton a year earlier.

For Warne to act as he did to Andrew Hudson in Johannesburg was very strange. He might have done several other things. He could, instead, have said to Hudson something along the lines of 'well played', Hudson having made 60 and, in fact, played an innings as classy as the ball with which Warne dismissed him, bowling him behind his pads. He could have had a quick conference with Ian Healy to find out just where the ball had pitched, into the rough or on to the clean part of the pitch. He might have talked with his captain about field-placings. What he did though was to scream abuse at Hudson as the batsman walked from the crease. Now, why would anyone even think of doing that, let alone actually do it?

It was here the two umpires received ten marks out of ten for the way they addressed the matter. Umpire Barry Lambson at square-leg instantly reported to colleague David Shepherd what Warne, whose back had been to Shepherd, had said and done to Hudson. Shepherd immediately called Allan Border over and his body language was unmistakable, holding Border responsible for the actions of his team. This is quite rightly written into the ICC Code of Conduct. I was always responsible for the actions of all my team members and I see no reason why that should have changed in the years between my retirement and the present day. In fact, I would be very annoyed if it were to be any other way.

The relevant reminder is Law 42.1 which states: 'Responsibility of Captains. The Captains are responsible at all times for ensuring that play is conducted within the spirit of the game as well as within the Laws.'

The next step was that Border spoke to Warne at the end of the over and again the body language was unmistakable: Border was telling Warne in firm language that he, Border, was being held responsible for what his players did. No problem there either. The problem came when the match referee, Donald Carr, sat down with the umpires and captains and the television replays and worked out what, if any, the penalties should be.

There are few more pleasant people in the cricket world than Donald but, for his $A450 fines of the two players, I would have fined *him* eighty per cent of his match fee. It was at this point that the ACB correctly stepped in and issued their own fines. There were however some strange aspects of the whole affair. The reading of the scenario by the Australian team management was extraordinarily naive. Their reaction was that the matter was over once Donald Carr had slapped them on the wrist with a dry feather. Allan Border, Bob Simpson and the team manager, Cam Battersby, should have had enough common sense to stretch their memories back to the Adelaide Test and to what Alan Crompton had said about player behaviour. They either ignored that or simply didn't believe anyone on the Board would follow it through. Mind you, the odds were very much in their favour for thinking that, but full marks to Crompton for straightening a few backs. Test cricket is a hard business and no one wants it to be played by people who make wimps look aggressive, but a bit of common sense never goes astray in cricket and the team management weren't leading in the common sense stakes on this occasion.

Bob Simpson has for several years been at pains to tell the Australian cricketing public that perceived or imaginary excesses in Australian cricket have been well and truly eradicated in the time between him taking over the coaching job and the present day. I'm sure Bob believes he is a hundred per cent right but it's not as I have always seen it, with niggling little matters cropping up and players being cited and fined. There's a certain amount of wishful thinking in believing that in 1995 all is now sweetness and light, though I am impressed by Mark Taylor's genial but steely attitude to the matter.

One such niggling little matter in the team management system was that, in 1991, captain Allan Border didn't actually turn up to his own disciplinary hearing instituted by Raman Subba Row, the match referee at the 'Gabba when Australia played the West Indies. An absence of gross discourtesy. Other cricketers around the world have been fined more than once – Border joined them in the Fifth Test of that series – and there has always seemed to me to be a lack of awareness in cricket teams over what the public might think about all this.

In South Africa, after Mr Crompton turned up in Cape Town, it was said by the management that there would definitely be an unofficial meeting between the players and the representatives of the Board. I hope it was explained to the two players concerned and, even more, to the three members of the team management in South Africa, that in Australia there had been widespread dismay over what had happened and that nothing like it would again be tolerated. I also hope that meeting did actually take place, otherwise the Board would only have themselves to blame for any further breakdown in communications with the team.

When writing in the *1993–4 Channel Nine Wide World of Sports Yearbook*, I was critical of Allan Border's actions in not having the courtesy to appear at Raman Subba Row's hearing, and was also critical of other team management actions connected with Border and with Australia's loss against India in Perth in a limited-overs International. What I wrote brought bitter recriminations from sensitive administrative souls, which I can handle okay, although I did think at the time it might have been better if they paid more attention to making correct decisions and less attention to taking umbrage where none was needed. It may also have been better had the sensitivity been expressed directly to me rather than to a third party.

There was one other aspect about which no one seemed to bother. Cricket is very much a team game, although individual performances are what enable the players to hold their places in the teams, and a combination of the two allows them to hold their heads high. What about the other players in the team who came under the lash because of Warne's and Hughes's actions, and the subsequent fining and awful publicity back in Australia and the rest of the cricket world? Steve Waugh had nothing to do with it; Craig McDermott was blameless; David Boon, as he sat quietly having a beer or two a few days later might have wondered what he had done to deserve all this; Michael Slater had every reason to feel bewildered; so too Matthew Hayden.

Matthew Hayden. Here was a young player in his debut Test hoping for great things, having waited two years for recognition and finally getting it, but only because Mark Taylor fell ill on the morning of the match. Before that game was over he had failed twice with the bat, his finger had been broken by Allan Donald and he was part of a team labelled in Australia, in an over-the-top reaction, as a bunch of jerks. Did anyone ever stop to think of what the players in the team, other than Warne and Hughes, thought about all this?

I know the game has changed a lot. I have seen the changes through playing sixty-three Tests, twenty-eight as captain, and in commentating on more than three hundred Tests and three hundred limited-overs Internationals and, as a piece of trivia, travelling by ship and aeroplane more than a million miles to do all that. Hopefully, I have applied to the job a certain amount of common sense. I've certainly had a lot of fun and seen some interesting happenings.

Let's go back for a moment to that Law of the game which talks about the responsibility of the captain of a team. It is a good Law because it says, 'The captains are responsible at all times for ensuring play is conducted within the spirit of the game as well as within the Laws.'

That wording should stay; it is explicit. To it now should be added as a Law of the game the words, 'The captains are also totally responsible for the behaviour of the players in their team and they must not in any way bring the game into disrepute.'

Only twenty-seven words but, when the next edition of the Laws of the Game, or the ICC Code of Conduct, is produced, I hope to see them there on page forty-four under the heading of 'Unfair Play'.

With all this as the background to their efforts, the Australians prepared themselves for the Second Test with their normal practice schedules at Newlands, a ground which has greatly changed over the past eighteen years. While they were doing that, I sat down at the magnificent Bay Hotel at Camps Bay and reflected on the fact that the next week would show a lot about the character of this Australian team and each individual member. Shane Warne certainly was remorseful – hopefully the pressure of that and the match itself would not be too great for him – and Merv Hughes would be an interesting proposition. Hughes had finished the 1993 Ashes series in England on 999 runs and, when he made his first run at the Wanderers, he became only the eighth Australian cricketer ever to make 1,000 Test runs and take 100 wickets and the third to have scored 1,000 runs and taken 200 wickets. When you think that more than 350 Australian cricketers have played at Test level, it is quite an achievement.

Australians who have 1,000 runs and 100 wickets in Tests:

| Name | Runs | Wkts | Tests No. |
|------|------|------|-----------|
| R. Benaud | 2201 | 248 | 32 |
| A. K. Davidson | 1328 | 186 | 34 |
| G. Giffen | 1238 | 103 | 30 |
| M. G. Hughes | 1006 | 211 | 53 |
| I. W. Johnson | 1000 | 109 | 45 |

| R. R. Lindwall | 1502 | 228 | 38 |
| K. R. Miller   | 2958 | 170 | 33 |
| M. A. Noble    | 1997 | 121 | 27 |

Australians who have 1,000 runs and 200 wickets in Tests:

| R. Benaud      | 2201 | 248 |
| M. G. Hughes   | 1006 | 211 |
| R. R. Lindwall | 1502 | 228 |

There was still no shortage of publicity concerning the Warne–Hughes incidents but, like life itself, many of these things have happened before. I've seen them. There was a moment some years ago, at the time of the stoush between Dennis Lillee and Javed Miandad, when the Australian Cricket Board, unofficially, made it clear they thought I was leaning to the right of Genghis Khan.

Lillee, in the green and gold corner, was penalised for what happened at the WACA, Perth, but the Pakistan team manager and Cricket Board did nothing about Javed.

At the time I said I would like to see escalating penalties in serious matters of this kind which brought the game into disrepute. Nothing I have seen in the intervening years has changed my mind in the slightest.

The Warne–Hughes incidents at the Wanderers ground in Johannesburg have been well documented. The Australian Cricket Board fined them $A4,000 and that's where we can begin.

If my system were to be used, the ACB would have announced that the next penalty issued by them would be $8,000. The one after that $16,000 and a one-match suspension in the same type of cricket in which the incident took place. The next penalty would be $32,000 and two matches.

It is my opinion that you would stamp out the problem overnight!

With any suggestion of this kind it is necessary to think through the consequences. It would mean the players concerned would be out of pocket, they would possibly be deprived of playing in a match, and they would be subjected to close public attention. Would that really be a downside?

There would also be, in some quarters, great sympathy for players so penalised and it would be said, quite possibly by the same Australian voices which so castigated Hughes and Warne, that the penalties are too severe.

The upside would have been that Australian players of the future, that is from Johannesburg onwards, would have had a clear idea of exactly what was in store for them if they were to transgress in the same way as happened at the Wanderers.

In my view the ACB would be doing the players of the present and the young players of the future in Australian cricket a great service by including such a rule in their contracts or in their own code of conduct. *The proviso now would be that the players so charged were found guilty by the ICC Match Referee of bringing the game into disrepute, which I believe should bring the harshest penalty.* The ACB would need to make very clear to the team managements of the future that it is their responsibility that players completely understand the situation.

After the Wanderers incidents there appeared in Australia an agency story quoting Shane Warne as burning up with remorse over what happened. Young cricketers have room for remorse, even in these hectic days, and for Warne to show regret was definitely along the right lines. He went on to say he hoped he wasn't going to be pilloried for the rest of his career for something he had done once. It was twice actually. We need to take into account, and should do so, what had happened at the Sydney Cricket Ground on the first occasion with Daryll Cullinan, the young South African batsman who was given a send-off by Warne.

The story went on to quote Warne as saying that at the crucial moment at the Wanderers he felt as though he was snapping, that he had a very short fuse that day, that he was letting pressure from barrackers get to him and hadn't been able to relax away from the game at all. That didn't surprise me. He said he was stung that Australian Cricket Board Chairman, Alan Crompton, said, 'Warne had been a poor role model for the youth of Australia to follow.' He was right to be stung. What the Australian Cricket Board Chairman could have said, in order to be more accurate, was that '*in the Wanderers incident* Warne had been a poor role model for the youth of Australia to follow.' For the rest of his time, again excepting the Cullinan incident, Warne has in fact been an excellent role model for the youth of Australia to follow. He is an extremely pleasant young man, completely unspoilt by fame, which has been instant, and is popular wherever he goes, except with opposition batsmen.

The remorse and the good vibes mentioned above apparently came about because Warne had a long talk with Mark Taylor, the team vice-captain. In the story Taylor was said to have been brutally frank with Warne, which, if reported correctly, is exactly what was needed. It was also a comforting indicator of the manner in which Taylor intended to approach the responsibilities of captaincy.

Welcome back to the real world of cricket, Shane!

# 2

## *Shane Warne the magician and con-tricks with over-rates*

When the Newlands match began at Cape Town Shane Warne turned in a wonderful performance. I have never seen him bowl better than in the first innings of that Test and it was a bowling performance he was able to use as a benchmark for his future as Australia's legspinner.

Despite his immense talent, there was always a chance he wouldn't bowl well in Cape Town, an aftermath perhaps of the Wanderers citing and fining. Spectators had the impression he could be flustered and quite deliberately set out to fluster him; South Africans said he had been mastered.

Right from the first over he bowled with skill and intelligence, and above all with patience. It is easy to become impatient in circumstances of this kind; success comes through mental strength as well as the physical attributes.

Warne's great strength lies in his ability to bowl the hard-spun leg-break as his stock ball, a match-winning delivery on many occasions, and on others, when he and the team might be in trouble, a basic delivery which can slow the batting carnage. He came out and bowled at Newlands on the first two days like the champion he is. Faced by a swirling breeze something like he encounters on the MCG, he flighted the ball, spun it sharply and used his variation in subtle fashion.

My count of the number of times he went past the outside edge of the bat was seventeen. That can happen to a lot of bowlers but the answer is not to become upset by it and to retain your patience. He did that. He bowled with great control and it was a tribute to his skills that the South Africans decided he was such a threat that they played him totally defensively until he bowled a rare loose delivery. That made for the possibility of some tedious South African batting but Warne's answer, in the face of this, was to develop even more patience without sacrificing even a fraction of his great attacking ability.

There are a lot of things which go to make up an outstanding bowler who has the brilliant natural ability to be top class. The first of these things is using your brain. In years to come I shall recall the Newlands Test for being the match when a young Australian cricketer learnt more about slow bowling in two days than in the previous two years of his career and where I saw the art of legspin bowling at its very best.

The Australians won brilliantly in Cape Town to square the series, with Steve Waugh turning in a magnificent exhibition of batting, bowling and fielding. His 86 at a crucial time, which he followed with 5/28 from 22.3 overs, was one of the best all-round doubles I have seen.

In theory, this should have set up the series for a great finish, but it was one of those situations where it was unwise to assume anything and the next five Test match days turned out to be a lacklustre anti-climax. With the elections drawing closer, there was more activity off the field than on it and everyone, in the end, had to be satisfied with a 1–1 series.

The Newlands Test was responsible for something I shall always remember, and something of which cricket followers should be aware. It's the con-trick being played on them by an International Cricket Council ruling to do with the adjustment of the number of overs to be bowled in a day.

In the past thirty-five years I have been one of a small number of people who have protested at the quite deliberate reduction in the number of overs being bowled in a day's play in a Test match. I emphasise the words 'Test match' because, in a limited-overs match, where the game is played out to its full number of available overs, there will most times be 100 in the day. There might be 110 in a Benson & Hedges match in England, 120 in a NatWest match. A lot depends on weather conditions and how much light is available in a day, sometimes for example a fast closing twilight can pose problems. In Australia because of light problems it is impossible to run a limited-overs competition of more than 50 overs each side between the states or international teams.

Test matches are different. Generally there is an 11 a.m. start and the game will end at 6 p.m. Supposedly, there will be 90 overs provided in a scheduled day's play, which is the very least which should apply. You have twenty-two grown men out in the centre of a ground and if they are unable to bowl at least 90 overs in the day, then there is something radically wrong with them. The ICC made great play with the fact that at last they were doing something about captains and players who were deliberately slowing down the game and refusing to allow the opposition batsmen the chance to score a reasonable total in the scheduled playing hours. I have not said teams are being denied the chance to score at a reasonable rate per over. They do that. In fact, the actual scoring-rates these days in Test cricket are excellent, quite often something like 50 runs per 100 balls, and that is as good as or better than the very best scoring-rates we have had, even in what the older cricket watchers will call 'the golden age of cricket', back in the 1930s.

The simplest way to look at it is that if you have only 90 overs in the scheduled playing time and the scoring-rate is 50 runs per 100 balls, or three an over, the total runs in the day will be only 270. Ninety-six overs at the same rate would produce 290 runs, 102 overs more than 300 runs.

Where the con-trick comes in is in the wording of the Playing Condition regarding minimum over-rates for Test matches which is agreed between the countries. Fortunately, it is not a Law of Cricket. It says:

> Play shall continue on each day until the completion of a minimum number of overs or until the scheduled cessation time, whichever is the later. The minimum number of overs to be completed, unless an innings ends or an interruption occurs, shall be:
>
> (a) On days other than the last day, a minimum of 90 overs.
> (b) On the last day, a minimum of 75 overs up to the start of the last scheduled hour, from which time a minimum of 15 shall be bowled.
>
> Penalties for not reaching those over targets during the match will produce a calculation at the conclusion whereby, for each over short of the target of 15 overs an hour, each member of a team will be fined 5 per cent of the applicable match fee.

On the surface, this would seem to mean that a team deliberately slowing things down so that the batting side might be forced to bat in bad light, or so that a game might be won or saved, and bowling only 86 overs by the scheduled close of play, could have each player up for a penalty of $400. Cricket administrators have been congratulating themselves on this for some time now, but hang on a second.

There are deductions all right, not from the players' fees but from the penalties. Two minutes are allowed for each incoming batsman other than the opening pair, or one who comes in at an interval or a break in play, medical treatment on the field is deducted and also four minutes for a drinks break.

What is happening is that in an innings where all wickets fall in the day, only 85 overs in six hours need be bowled. Of all the weak legislation produced in recent years, this is one of the classic examples. Test cricket is fighting to keep its popularity and its attendances, and it is winning only in a country like England where the grounds are small and there is a necessity to book seats months in advance at high prices in order to be able to attend the game.

That the ruling body of cricket should introduce a playing condition that only pretends to insist on at least 90 overs in a day is doing a disservice to the game. The total required figure should be 102 but apathy and crass political overtones will ensure it stays at 90, which, in reality, can mean something well below that figure.

The Playing Condition goes on to say that: 'When an innings ends a minimum number of overs shall be bowled from the start of the new innings. The number of overs to be bowled shall be calculated at the rate of one (1) over for each full four minutes remaining from the commencement of the new innings to the scheduled time for the close of play.'

This can lend itself to a combination of con-trick and cheating. Cheating, I hear you cry, and you may even ask how that can come about. Well, take the case of a captain in the field who is in the position of wanting to waste time because it is possible he will be on the big end of a Test match hiding. The day is scheduled to finish at 6 p.m. and the batting side is going to close its innings or may even be bowled out in mid-afternoon. Ninety overs are to be bowled in the day. Right? Wrong! The fielding captain 'A' slows things down so that his team is nine overs in arrears of what it should be when the innings of side 'B' ends at 2.50 p.m. From the start of play at 11 a.m. to 2.50 p.m. they have bowled 38 overs and they should have bowled 47. All that will be made up when the recalculation is made for the number of overs side 'A' will face. Right? Wrong again! With three hours to play, 45 overs will be bowled at side 'A', who have just been wasting time. This is distinctly to their advantage because they wish to face as little bowling as possible as they are intent on a draw. In all, 83 overs bowled, not 90! That's why they wasted time. You might say, 'Well, does it really matter how many overs there are in a Test day?' It doesn't matter at all to the spectators who are sitting back in their living-rooms watching television. It does to those who have to fork out a hundred dollars or more to take a family to watch six hours of a Test match.

Whether Sir Clyde Walcott and David Richards at the ICC are able to change that is a matter of some conjecture. They know there is a problem but will the various delegates and the lobbyists be in the slightest bit interested in the people paying their money at the gate for a Test match? Or will those people instead have their minds concentrated on how much the television rights will bring in for the various World Cup and other future limited-overs competitions, as well as the Tests?

Match referee John Reid, a former New Zealand captain, was under no illusions when he was in Australia. He was of the opinion that the paying public often receive a raw deal, which is a pity as they are the ones who assist in paying players' match fees. When I asked him, only half in jest, at the 'Gabba Test what the number of overs in a day should be, he said, 'Ninety, but a proper ninety.' He added, 'What's more, they should be bowled in the scheduled playing hours, finishing at six o'clock, not ten past or a quarter past. And, the allowances should be cut out.' That deliberate time-wasting at Newlands caught the attention of many people, and no one to whom I spoke had even one good word to say for it.

There is no shortage of ideas floating around on how to improve over-rates in Test cricket so that the spectators at the ground will not be cheated of value for their money. The teams and the players can be fined these days, but it's only drinking money to them. Another idea is to fine the offending team in runs. The scale of penalties suggested ranges from three to ten runs for each over not bowled. I receive a lot of correspondence on the matter and my reply generally is that I'm not in favour of run penalties because I believe it would affect the ethos of the game. But has the idea of run penalties been thought through?

Scenario: It is the Fifth Test of an Ashes series being played in Australia, the match is at the MCG, Australia holds the Ashes, the series at the moment is tied at 2–2, it is the final day of the last Test, there are 95,000 spectators present, a new record attendance for Test cricket, and there are hundreds of millions of television viewers watching around the world.

England need 250 to win to regain the Ashes.

They are 247/9 when stumps are drawn, and Australia hold the Ashes

in a thrilling contest much applauded by everyone. But then, as
spectators are filing out of the ground, it is calculated and announced
that the Australians have been penalised three runs for a slow over-rate.

England have won the series and regained the Ashes!

Sounds a bit dodgy to me.

When we moved to Durban for the Test it was to a climate not unlike
Brisbane where humidity is high and the twilight is very short. John
Woodcock, who had joined us, and who first covered a Test tour in
1950–1 and has covered more Test matches than anyone in the media, is
generally known as 'Wooders' or 'the Squire of Longparish'.

He and I had been chatting about the forthcoming South African
elections but hadn't been able to come to any conclusions, probably
because we were both very short on information other than from the
newspapers. Next evening, out with Jack Bannister, Woodcock decided
at the end of a very good dinner to solve that and to become better
informed about the elections, so he gave the taxi driver the third degree,
but all in one series of questions. Was he going to vote, which way
would he vote, was he worried about the threat of violence, which party
did he think would win, would the ANC reach its hoped-for sixty-six
and two-thirds per cent of the vote, how many political parties were
there and how many different languages?

The taxi driver turned and looked long and hard at him, which in
itself can be slightly dangerous if allied to travelling at 50 mph in a
Durban taxi at night, and said it was nice of him to be so interested. He
then launched into his own question of why on earth Woodcock
expected him to say which way he intended to vote, when after all it
was supposed to be a secret ballot and Woodcock might be an *agent
provocateur*, when Jack sneaked a look to his left to see what effect this was
having on the 'Squire'. The taxi driver needn't have minded: the
inquisitor was fast asleep. Jack had the answers and the conversation
all to himself the entire way back to the Elangeni Sun!

Sleep would have been a merciful release for some of the paying
spectators at Kingsmead, Durban during that final Test of the three-
match series. It took five days to finish three innings and, although I can
find something good in every day's cricket I watch, I was really
struggling there.

Despite that, overall it was one of the best six-match Test series I've
seen; if you can have four great Test matches out of six, then you've
done well. I thought the one at the Wanderers and the Second at

Newlands were in the top twenty Tests I've seen, although the South Africans need to get out of what seems to me to be a bunker mentality. In Durban I had the feeling they desperately wanted to go on tour to England having finished the South African leg of the series no worse than 1–1. That's also how they finished the series in Australia. It was a matter of the *prestige* of not being beaten more than anything else, and they might have won in Durban had they done things differently.

During the series the ICC attempted to improve the game with the introduction of match referees. My thoughts *at the time* were why do you want match referees when you have umpires of the quality of David Shepherd of England who, with Barry Lambson, handled the problems at the Wanderers calmly and well, and the likes of Dickie Bird and Steve Bucknor currently umpiring in the West Indies?

The idea of an international panel of umpires – four from England, two from every other country – creates problems for me, since some umpires in a home country are denied the opportunity to stand in a Test match and I see no reason to take away what is the ultimate in an umpire's career. It's like a cricketer wanting to play for his country. An umpire wants to go out there and umpire in a Test match between two countries and I think what the ICC have started doing is purely cosmetic. I'd rather put all the money they're spending in this way into a very large fund to improve the standard of umpiring in every country.

When the World Cup was held in Australasia in 1991–2, there were what you might loosely call 'neutral umpires'. There were also just as many mistakes made by those same umpires as would have been the case had they been umpiring with a team from their own country taking part.

Then we had the ultimate in stupid administration. The best umpire, without doubt, in the World Cup was Englishman David Shepherd, the roly-poly ex-Gloucestershire batsman. When England made it to the World Cup Final at the MCG, Shepherd was not allowed to umpire, nor was the Pakistan umpire permitted to stand. There is something wrong, even slightly crazy, with a system which on the one hand wants the best umpires, but then debars the best man.

By the time we left South Africa in 1994, there had been several occasions in the preceding sixteen months where there was a problem with a player or an umpire getting in the way of the television camera, and bear in mind it was, until 1994 in South Africa, very strictly the television camera. The classic, if that is the word, was in Durban when Andrew Hudson ran wide and, as an added problem, the popping creases hadn't been extended past the minimum of six feet. The one camera

under the scoreboard at Durban was trying to cover both ends and a
player got in the way. The third umpire, Barry Lambson, gave Hudson
the benefit of the doubt because the TV replay was so bad. What made it
all the more interesting was that, because of the poor picture, the
television crew was in touch with the third umpire telling him what the
run-out looked like. The ICC have a lot of work to do on this question.

Thankfully the United Cricket Board of South Africa, with the help
of Dr Ali Bacher, and showing imagination and a will to do the right
thing, have now introduced four new cameras at point and square-leg
for all international matches in South Africa. Panasonic devised and paid
for the equipment and it is brilliant. This was the press release at the start
of 1995:

> South African cricket breaks new ground on Sunday with what is
> described as a foolproof system for resolving umpiring disputes. For
> the Mandela Trophy match between Sri Lanka and Pakistan at
> Centurion Park, Pretoria, four automatic television cameras are
> being installed at a total cost of one million rand, giving the third
> umpire a perfect view of the action. The new cameras, two on each
> side of the pitch and in line with the crease, are all on fixed positions
> and will automatically video the entire match. Previously just two
> cameras, operated manually for television coverage, have been
> available to help the umpires.
>
> Problems under that system were highlighted on Friday when
> Pakistan captain, Salim Malik, escaped a stumping chance against Sri
> Lanka in the Mandela Trophy match simply because the cameraman
> missed the action.
>
> This is a first in world cricket. Up until now there has been a
> weakness in the system in that it depends on the competence of the
> cameraman and there can also be obstructions.
>
> The South African Broadcasting Corporation reckons they have a
> 90 per cent success rate, but we want to make certain that this last
> phase is foolproof and a hundred per cent correct, so that umpires can
> make decisions with total assurance.

The Australian tour of South Africa showed also that authorities need to
be vigilant about the standard of lighting on various grounds if they
expect day-night cricket to continue to flourish.

'Let there be light' was the cry at East London and Port Elizabeth
when the Australians played there, but there was very little light

available. The match at East London was first and it wasn't a total disaster because Steve Waugh hit a brilliant 60 and the match was over early. The lights though were poor. Port Elizabeth was quite different, where South Africa made 227 and the lights were not switched on until twelve minutes before the start of the Australian innings. They were also switched on at thirty per cent of capacity, although the error was quickly noticed, but astonishingly the umpires took the players out on to the field with the lights still not at full capacity. Later Allan Border was to say he didn't think it had made all that much difference and the Australian defeat was more to do with the excellent South African seam bowling. Shane Warne and Paul Reiffel shared a world-record limited-overs stand and the Australians, though not really threatening to win, made it an exciting evening for the 19,000 spectators who went home deliriously happy.

Not so happy were those thinking forward to the time the South Africans might stage the World Cup, and, believe me, the ICC will have to ensure the lights on all grounds are of international standard, otherwise no World Cup. You simply can't have one team batting second at Port Elizabeth in poor lighting conditions and another batting second at Newlands in splendid lighting conditions. It won't work. The game following that Port Elizabeth match in the limited-overs series was played at Newlands under excellent lights.

Cricket tours can be great, sometimes they can also jangle the nerves on and off the field. It was certainly the case in South Africa where we were in the situation of having those first-ever free elections coming up a few weeks after the tour was due to finish.

When we went to East London for the first of the day-night matches Ian Chappell and I played as Australia in a golf match against Jack Bannister and Trevor Quirk of the South African Broadcasting Corporation. They represented the Rest of the World.

Grandiose names, but the competitive aspect of the matches almost justified the description. We couldn't play at the East London Golf Club as it was closed for use by the Black caddies from a neighbouring course, who were playing their annual championship, so Quirk managed to organise a game at King William's Town, a round trip of 104 kilometres. All motorway, and only one slight hiccup when we came over a rise in the road 30 kilometres from East London to find a truck blocking the way. Even in a peaceful atmosphere this need not be the most comforting aspect of a car trip. In East London, South Africa, just down the road from Natal where 126 people had been murdered in the last eleven days, to be stopped in this fashion was not at all comforting. As we came closer to the truck we saw it looked like a police or army vehicle – it is difficult to distinguish between the two in South Africa these days because they are painted with camouflage colours and so are the occupants. We stopped. Trevor was driving and, as he pulled up, he wound down his window. I did the same thing. Always follow the locals, I reckon. I didn't want the guy with the machine-gun thinking I had something to hide. Trevor then proceeded to speak in Afrikaans to the leader of the group who had a hard face and very big hands which were resting idly on the gun.

After a moment Trevor switched to English and said we were all English. That was not strictly true because 'Chappelli' and I had just been expressing the hope and belief that Australia would that day stuff the lousy opposition out of sight on the golf course. Then came one of the strangest questions I had ever heard in my life.

'Have you any guns or ammunition in your vehicle?' the sergeant asked. I awaited the answer with considerable interest.

'No,' said Trevor.

That was a relief, I can tell you, and we were waved on. My immediate thought was how extraordinary it was to ask such a question and then not to request at least that the boot of the car be opened. There were plenty of white gunmen in South Africa at the time: it wasn't only Zulus and ANC members who were knocking off the opposition.

We made it to the golf club, played eighteen holes, with Australia winning, and when we came back into the locker-room the Secretary-Manager confirmed that this indeed was the club where some members had recently been murdered when two terrorists burst into the room above with grenades and machine-guns. He pointed to the ceiling.

'See the plastering that's been done up there?' he said. 'That's where one of the grenades blew a hole in the foot-thick solid concrete floor.'

It was a sudden bringing back to earth for us all despite what had been a pleasant day on the golf course, a realisation that in what is a beautiful country there were still a lot more people who would lose their lives.

A lighter note came when we went to the bar to buy our host a drink. Normally in a golf club there will be a sign restricting anyone taking golf clubs and perhaps bags into the bar. Wearing spikes into a bar is banned unless it is a 'Niblick Bar'. 'No Spikes' is the usual sign. Here the sign merely said, 'Spikes welcome: 1 rand each spike.' It was the idea of the

Secretary-Manager who said it had been shown to be an enormous deterrent at twenty-four rand a time.

I was still in East London at the beginning of April but I had not actually put the date in my memory-bank. Sitting in my hotel room, I was browsing away on the meaning of life and whether my right hand should be over a little more in the golf swing, when on to Sky News came David Gower. He was batting in the nets in Trinidad where the England team had just been bowled out for 46 in the Third Test and, from what I had seen on other Sky News bulletins, they were lucky to make that many. The feature said Gower was thinking about making a comeback, and that caught my attention.

The gist of the story was that Hampshire and Gower had been in touch with one another and there was a chance he would be playing with them again in the 1994 summer and, therefore, would be available for the Test series between England and first New Zealand then South Africa, and for the tour of Australia. This was an intriguing thought. Then Geoff Boycott came on the screen and gave his opinion that Gower should definitely make a comeback, and it was at that instant the first real seed of doubt was sown.

I wondered also about Raymond Illingworth, who had recently been made Chairman of the England Selection Committee. Had he, from Spain, been in touch with Gower to persuade him to play county cricket again? If so, that certainly might lead to playing cricket for England and therefore, perhaps, being vice-captain to Australia under Michael Atherton. A very big story. The 'bring back David Gower group' in England would be breaking out the champagne, and if left out on the lawn for half an hour in St John's Wood, it would have been beautifully cold. The Sky weather map had just shown it to be one of the coldest days of the year in England, with a wind-chill factor of minus ten degrees.

Sky cut from Gower to the next item concerning the breeding of a strain of rabbit with wings which was certain to be a real hit with tourists visiting England in the coming year. The wings allowed it to fly over the top of cars on the motorways of England. Conservationists interviewed were in raptures. Suddenly I realised it was April 1st and I knew I had been 'done', but I was very sorry the Gower story was a hoax – I'd have enjoyed seeing him come back. Didn't mind about the bunnies.

Later that day my attention was called to a dangerous sporting hazard. In cricket, umpires and players never appear to pay the slightest attention to lightning, and on golf courses amateur golfers seem to adopt the same attitude. Professionals though, sensibly, are off that golf course at the first hint of lightning. Perhaps it is to do with the fact that the pros know they will be back tomorrow whereas the amateurs, who have taken the afternoon off from work, know they will be behind their desks the next day.

We were happily walking along a fairway when our opponents called our attention to a large split tree on the edge of the rough. I thought it a bit suspicious because we were one up on them at the time. When we were all gathered under the tree, two of us having no idea why we were there, our opponents announced that this was the tree where one of the members had been standing when he and it were struck by lightning. As golfers are generally meticulous, other members had come flocking from the bar, one with a tape measure. The information was that the poor guy had been driven six and a quarter inches into the ground. The good news was that he recovered after emergency treatment and a year later continued to play a lot of golf. One of his mates at the club said to me, quite seriously I think, that his putting never seemed to be the same after he had been struck. I wasn't surprised.

Everyone wants South Africa to flourish as a country and they have a great deal to look forward to in years to come, and no doubt many problems as well. When they win the ballot to hold an Olympic Games of the future there is one thing I'd quite like to see: the Olympic flame burning on Robben Island, now that would be something!

As a prelude to the English summer when South Africa would tour the United Kingdom in the second half of the season after New Zealand had toured, this Australian tour of South Africa could hardly have been better. The cricket was often brilliant, rarely indifferent, life was sometimes scary off the field, on many occasions delightful. Brave cricket and cricketers, sensational fielding and, as is always the case with cricket, not too many dull moments. It was to be so in England for the next six months as well.

# 3

# Michael Atherton and the dirt, Illingworth and the bacon

The problems for Michael Atherton began on the Saturday afternoon of the Lord's Test of that summer with a BBC Television camera zooming in as the ball was passed to him on its way back to the bowler. I was sitting at my desk in the commentary box typing a story for the *News of the World* first edition for the next day. Tony Lewis, the former England captain who was commenting at the time, said later, 'On the screen I saw Atherton appear to take something from his pocket and put it on the ball. I thought, "I can't believe what I'm seeing." '

Those pictures had automatically been recorded and Lewis asked Keith Mackenzie, the producer, to show the sequence at the end of the over. 'I had to think carefully about what I should say,' said Lewis. 'There were legal implications and I could see writs flying in the direction of the BBC. I had a few balls to think it over and during that time I decided, when the replay appeared, to say, "It looks as though he's giving it the Aladdin's Lamp treatment." '

As it happened, it didn't need to be replayed because at the end of the next over Atherton did precisely the same thing. It appeared as though he took something from his pocket and rubbed it on the ball; it also appeared that some of whatever had been rubbed on the ball was then falling off the ball on to the ground. It was at this point Lewis made his 'Aladdin's Lamp treatment' remark and no one at that stage had the slightest idea of the momentous events which were about to be put in train. Those events will remain part of cricket history and, because of that, it is important to know what was said at the time, not merely with hindsight, and I have endeavoured here to paint the picture of the match. That afternoon at

Lord's, time constraints meant I only had a few minutes to rewrite the opening paragraphs of my first edition story to say:

> Mike Atherton yesterday managed to catch the attention of millions of television viewers around the country when sighted rubbing his fingers over the ball.
>
> Nothing against that in the Laws of Cricket, but the method of doing it certainly brought eyes raised to the heavens and several heart-flutters around the corridors of power at the home of cricket.
>
> It looked very odd to me and I am now intensely interested in what match referee Peter Burge thinks about it; what Dickie Bird and Steve Randell say about it; and what Raymond Illingworth and Atherton do about it!
>
> The match? It was slaughter! The South Africans in this historic Lord's Test have demolished England and given them a taste of the 'Pace like Fire' they can expect in Australia in a few months. I told you last week these South Africans are tough and they have confirmed it with a magnificent display over the past three days . . .

Nothing sensational about that. It was a story on the game itself, with the leading paragraphs changed and alluding to the fact that there was a possibility something unusual may have happened on the field. A perfectly normal afternoon with a first edition story going to press, a story which, as always, would be completely replaced with whatever occurred between tea and stumps.

However, at the close of play on that Saturday, the match referee Peter Burge asked to see Atherton who was reported to have offered to produce the trousers he had been wearing on the field. He answered a series of questions through which Burge was trying to ascertain exactly what had happened. I imagine it wasn't at all easy. There was an ICC 'form letter' statement issued by Burge after the hearing but it said little and I was uneasy about it. The statement said:

> The Match Referee has investigated, under 4(a) of ICC procedures, unfamiliar action taken by the England Captain when handling the ball during the afternoon session.
>
> Consultation with the umpires and inspection of the ball confirmed that there was nothing untoward. I also confirm that no official reports were lodged by any parties.
>
> I have accepted the explanation given and no action will be taken.

Just goes to show one should assume nothing, particularly if you happen to feel uneasy. What had actually happened was that Burge had issued his statement on the basis of what he had been told at the hearing. It turned out later he did not have the full facts at his disposal.

It was impossible to glean further information and I sent through a complete replace story for the later editions of the *News of the World*. It was based on the fact that the administrators seemed to have clammed up on the matter:

Has everyone in this cricket world gone bonkers? We have had controversy after controversy and for most of the time cricket authorities seem to live behind a veil of secrecy. And these are matters about which the world's cricket lovers are entitled to be told.

Now we have the England captain hauled before the match referee to watch videotape of the incident yesterday when, in mid-afternoon, with South Africa steaming towards a big lead, it appeared that something was transferred from his pocket to the ball.

When the statement was issued by the match referee two and a half hours after close of play, it said nothing. Or nothing of any consequence anyway. The telling phrase was, 'I have accepted the explanation given and no action will be taken.'

What was the explanation given by Mike Atherton? We don't know, because Atherton was instructed by England's cricket authorities not to say anything.

Why on earth would they tell him that? There are two possible reasons. The first that it was such a boring excuse or explanation that by the time readers of this newspaper had got to the end of the first line they would have been dozing off.

The second reason is that it might be potentially embarrassing to those who are running English cricket.

When the Pakistan ball-tampering allegations involving Wasim Akram and Waqar Younis were made, the ball mysteriously disappeared to a vault remarkably close to Thomas Lord's old ground in St John's Wood.

I said then that the cricket authorities should know better than to think they would be able, deliberately, to deprive the cricketing public of such knowledge. I say it again in this Atherton matter. If there has been an explanation given *and* accepted by the match referee, then the cricket authorities have a duty to their public to make that explanation for the benefit of this and other cricket countries.

People paying their money at the turnstiles, watching on television and buying newspapers keep the game going, along with all those who play club cricket and engage in other aspects of the game.

The system of having match referees may have been set up with good intentions, but so far I haven't seen it work. So far as I am concerned, it certainly hasn't worked this time. If the explanation is given and accepted, then the match referee must have been completely satisfied. If he is completely satisfied then everyone should know about it.

By sewing tight the lips of the referee and refusing to allow cricket followers to know the facts, the cricket authorities are doing a grave disservice to the game.

Ray Illingworth reads every Sunday paper as a matter of course and I imagine that Sunday at Lord's he was a very early riser. The previous evening when Atherton had gone to dinner, reportedly with A. C. Smith and D. J. Insole, Illingworth was having a quiet drink in the sponsors' marquee when, in a perfectly casual conversation with someone connected with the BBC, he gained a clearer knowledge of the exact sequence of events seen by millions on television earlier in the afternoon.

The next morning, with knowledge that some administrators might have hoped the incident would go away of its own accord, he had a decision to make. His decision was that action, not silence, was needed.

What he had read in the *News of the World* and other newspapers that morning, concerning cricket's refusal to let the public know what was happening, would have been unlikely to dissuade him from that view. Illingworth had said, at the end of the hearing held by the match referee, that the Atherton matter was closed. I don't think there is any doubt on the Sunday morning he would have regretted making that statement, although it was done in perfectly straightforward fashion, but not with the full facts at his disposal.

It was later said Illingworth and Atherton had a Sunday morning breakfast together at the ground and it is unlikely they failed to touch on what had happened the previous day on the field and what should now be done.

While Atherton then took his men on to the field against the South

Africans, Illingworth had a meeting with Test and County Cricket Board officials. He said, if the truth came out at a later date, England's administrators might be shown in a very poor light. The facts had to be stated now, and appropriate action taken.

Illingworth fined Atherton £2,000, not a great amount of money in some sports but quite a sizeable figure to a cricketer, and Atherton and Illingworth then issued respectively the following statements on July 24th.

You all know I do not normally attend media conferences during Test matches; however, having spent some time looking at television footage and discussing with Ray Illingworth I felt that the sooner I explained the situation the better.

Yesterday evening I was asked to attend a meeting with the Match Referee, Mr Burge. After that meeting he issued a statement that he accepted the explanation I gave and that no action would be taken. In my explanation I did not present all the facts.

I am here to explain what I did and to answer any questions you wish to ask. As you are aware, we use sweat to get the bruises out of the ball and then rub it to maintain the shine. It was very hot and humid out there yesterday, your hands get wet and this in turn dampens the ball when you handle it. You all saw me reach into my pocket, dry my fingers with some dirt in order not to dampen the ball. Whilst I told Mr Burge that I put my hand into my pocket to dry my fingers, I did not tell him that I used the dirt to dry them; therefore, my response to his questioning was incomplete.

I would like to add at no stage during my career have I ever used any substances to alter the condition of the ball.

I would apologise to the Match Referee, Mr Burge, and the South African team. I hope everybody will accept my apology.

On discussing this incident with Michael Atherton this morning he told me that he had dried his fingers with some dirt in order not to dampen the ball. After giving this some consideration I decided that this matter should be resolved, put to rest, as quickly as possible.

I took account that the Match Referee, Mr Burge, was unaware of the full facts, that there had been no alteration to the condition of the ball and that no artificial substance had been used. He used dirt to dry his fingers. Taking this into account I have decided to fine Michael on two counts.

Firstly, for using dirt. Secondly, for giving incomplete information to the Match Referee.

He is to be fined £1,000 for each count. £2,000 in total.

As far as I am concerned this matter has been dealt with and is now closed.

The Test finished on Monday with an overwhelming South African victory, and on Tuesday BBC Television went to Swansea to cover the NatWest quarter-final between Glamorgan and Surrey. I went to stay with Tony and Joan Lewis at Castellau that night, and had a delightful dinner, with guests including opera singer Gwynne Howell. He has sung with Pavarotti and Dame Kiri, knows and has worked with Australian opera singers like John Shaw and Neil Easton, the latter against whom I used to play cricket in Sydney, and his stories were a delight. There was little time to think about the happenings at Lord's, other than in a general way, although they surfaced again when we arrived at the ground the next morning because it had been raining for much of the night and the game was to be first of all delayed, and then abandoned for the day.

Keith Mackenzie is a very good cricket producer with an excellent eye for news, and for what might be making the news later in the day or the following day. He also keeps a level head on how a variety of matters should be approached, bearing in mind time constraints, the requirements of the game itself and of the television viewers who have every right to be informed on those matters.

The belting rain provided the perfect opportunity for him to stage a discussion on the Atherton affair, first of all to set out for viewers a reminder of the precise sequence of events at Lord's on the Saturday and Sunday of the Test and to take into account various other matters which had occurred since, including some calls for Atherton's resignation, and others for his retention.

The programme provided viewers with a chronological sequence of the events in a perfectly straightforward fashion. The live telecast was thoughtfully chaired by Tony Lewis and, at the end, David Gower and I provided a summing-up.

In the light of what was being said in the media that day, the final question posed by Lewis to each of us was, 'Should Michael Atherton resign, or should he stay?'

David said that in his opinion it seemed there were still one or two points outstanding. Until those points were cleared up, he felt the jury would remain out.

I said, so far as I was concerned, there was only one thing that mattered, and that was what had been in Atherton's mind on the Saturday of the Test when he rubbed the dirt on the ball.

*If, in his own mind, he knew he had done nothing wrong, if he was able to look in the mirror when shaving the next day, then there was certainly no question of any thought of resignation. He should captain England at Headingley.*

I drove back to London that evening ready for a relaxing game of golf the next day, if the annual game of golf against Mark Wilson and John Spurling could ever be regarded as relaxing. The captain of our two-man side, Renton Laidlaw, television, radio and newspaper man in professional golf, is a stickler for discipline and for winning. There is a very good reason for this, as the losers of the battle each year find themselves in the costly position of buying dinner and wines for the opposition and wives, plus other nearest and dearest of both teams. This time the clash was at Sunningdale and Laidlaw and Benaud later hosted the dinner at the splendid Shepherd's restaurant in Westminster.

I needed the relaxation of golf, and the dinner at Shepherd's was a convivial evening. I mused on the way to France the following morning that if I, as a merely peripheral player, found a break from the Lord's affair to be advantageous, then the main participant might also be keen to get away from it for a day or two. Reading all the newspapers during the flight, I still found headlines concerning Atherton, and they continued every day for the rest of the week.

One valid point made by Alan Lee of *The Times* was that the curiosity of the Atherton incident was its anonymity and that anyone who attended Saturday's play and returned to the cricket on Sunday without reading a newspaper would have been unaware of the imbroglio. Here was a story created entirely by television.

Even if you kept your concentration in go-mode, it was difficult to follow all the nuances of the Atherton–Illingworth affair at Lord's over the three days. Spare a thought then for Jacob Malao, a young South African who was cheering for the touring team and who knew something about cricket, but not a lot, if anything, about ball-tampering.

Malao had been part of the Lord's ground staff for several weeks, doing all the usual things that have been done since the days when Denis Compton was on the same staff: selling scorecards; working in various areas around the ground wearing the MCC ground staff blazer; taking part in the ground preparation and bowling in the nets. It is said the ground staff boys eat, sleep and dream cricket, which can only be good for someone who desperately wants to make it into big-time cricket.

There was a difference with Malao, however, because he is from
Soweto in South Africa and is the first young Black cricketer from that
country to be given a place on the Lord's ground staff. Malao is a left-arm
spin bowler who used to be a medium-pacer, and he bowled to the
South African touring side in the nets prior to the Test. He was also on
the South African balcony during the match and is one of the young
players coming through South African cricket in the aftermath of
apartheid. He took the wickets of Mark Waugh and Matthew Hayden
when the Australians played one of their tour matches near Johannesburg in February 1994.

He flew back to Johannesburg straight after the Test and I liked his
quote about how much he enjoyed the South African win, even if he
seemed to be one of the few people supporting them. It was a Test to
remember for him from that point of view, and certainly for the blaze of
publicity which accompanied the dirt on the ball incident.

I have briefly listed the sequence of events but one aspect of the whole
business kept nagging at me. All these and earlier problems with the ball
and things being done to it could be avoided if the cricket authorities
were to bring in one simple Playing Condition. The suggested regula-
tion could have spared Michael Atherton his week of agony and I hope
to see it introduced as soon as possible.

*Allow only the bowler to shine the ball.*

Ball polishing, and its attendant controversies, is seriously detracting
from the game itself and the whole thing should be sorted out as quickly
as possible.

At the end of each over, toss the ball to the umpire, who can have a
look at it – as is laid down now under the ICC clause covering regular
inspection of the ball. The umpire tosses the ball to the bowler, who has
precisely six balls in which to work on it legally. The remainder of the
fielding team are banned from doing anything to it.

This would save considerable time, when you think of the ridiculous
posturing and polishing that goes on at the moment: the ball is returned
from the 'keeper to gully, who polishes, to cover, who polishes, to extra
cover (more polishing), to mid-off, who polishes madly – often bending
double to do so, as though stricken by some muscular affliction.

Then the bowler has a go, sometimes doing it for twenty seconds at
the top of his run while the batsman waits. Spectators at the ground are
thoroughly bored by this. Millions of television viewers hardly ever see it
because the TV producer knows how boring it looks and cuts away to
something more interesting. Allowing the bowler to be the only one to

polish would solve the matter. Anyway, why on earth – if that is the phrase to use in a matter stemming from Lord's 1994 – should fieldsmen be allowed to polish?

It has become a modern fetish, it wastes time, and if the International Cricket Council want to do something constructive in the game, here's their chance.

Many years ago this *was* an experimental Law. It was dropped because of extremely misguided pressure from certain administrators. Bring it back, put it on the next ICC meeting's agenda now, and vote it in. And when bowlers start whingeing about restrictions on letting the whole team shine the ball, tell them to get on with it and pay more attention to the spectators and the TV viewers. Those who watch Test cricket deserve better than they receive at the moment.

The whole Atherton affair was extraordinary, and there were still some little twists and turns to come. It resulted in more publicity than I can recall in the seventeen years since World Series Cricket, mainly because it involved the England captain, someone who had risen to hold the highest sporting title in the land.

I am able to assure you not everyone could have come back mentally from a sequence of events which might have seemed to the England captain to be never-ending. Michael Atherton managed it and deserves great credit, particularly in view of the ill luck his team endured in Australia with injuries and illness. He wasn't able to win in Australia but he will be back.

Atherton was now trying to get himself organised for the Headingley Test, a game where he would be under a certain amount of pressure. In fact, he countered that pressure magnificently, making 99 before being caught and bowled and then, at his press conference that evening, he had his say about the media's coverage of the Lord's incidents. Fortunately we live in a democracy, or at least we say we do, and therefore free speech is one of our rights. No reason why Atherton shouldn't talk as he did of the 'gutter press', no reason either why anyone in the media shouldn't make a mild reply in defence, which I did in this manner:

England skipper Michael Atherton's leadership qualities impressed me greatly yesterday. But there is one area where he leaves a lot to be desired. Forty-six years' experience in cricket and the media has underlined for me that the two imposters, success and failure, have strange effects on different people. Some are able to handle both, some find it difficult to handle either. Arrogance can be one of the main problems.

Self-confidence is a great attribute, but arrogance is only a tiny step away and it needs to be measured with great care if common sense is not to become a forgotten item on the agenda. Atherton's arrogance was making 99 in a Test match and then expressing the view that making those runs, in the aftermath of the dirt-in-the-pocket controversy at Lord's, was the best possible answer to the 'gutter press'. What gutter press? The writers, both broadsheet and tabloid, who recorded the facts and offered opinions on what had happened at Lord's? Or perhaps the BBC, whose commentators did the same thing?

BBC Television's role in the episode was impeccable. The facts were produced on the Saturday for examination by the public and other areas of the media, then came the press conference and on the Tuesday following the Test, there was, at Swansea at the NatWest quarter-final, a perfect chronological account of the whole thing.

I'm delighted Michael made 99 at Headingley. In the course of that innings he confirmed he has courage, can bat in determined fashion, is able to set goals for himself and is a great fighter. He then went on to confirm also, with his 'gutter press' remarks, that it is still possible to open one's mouth without the brain being in the proper gear!

I've been a player, captain and commentator on cricket for the past forty-six years and a working journalist over the last thirty-eight of those. And I take the greatest possible exception to being labelled as part of a 'gutter press'. Especially by someone who had the cricket world, not just England, talking for a week about whether or not he was a fit person to hold one of the greatest of sporting honours – to captain your country at cricket.

The matter of the press and a form of censorship wasn't done with yet. Peter Hayter of the *Mail on Sunday* had written an article for the TCCB Headingley Test match programme. He had been assured the copy he had written on Atherton and the controversial Lord's Test had gone into print, with only a few words in the thousand altered. Hayter said however that the following day he was told the TCCB public relations department had insisted the reference to Atherton should come out. Later, when he received a print-out of the Board's amended version, other passages had been substantially altered or removed.

Because of that, Hayter said he had immediately withdrawn the article, on the basis that the Board's action amounted to unwarranted censorship and that in four seasons of submitting similar articles, not one word of the substance of these had been changed.

One point made by Hayter was that contentious issues, such as the fine imposed on Aqib Javed after his excessive use of the bouncer during the Third Test between England and Pakistan at Old Trafford, had been accepted without comment, and certainly without any form of selective editing.

'Only now,' he said, 'with the England captain the subject of controversy, have the TCCB changed their stance.'

Pakistan cricket had been in the news at different times concerning alleged ball-tampering and reverse swing. Scientists had written articles about reverse swing, some of them illuminating, some extremely difficult to understand. Quite involuntarily I had involved myself in this with the remark I made at The Oval in 1992 on the final day of the Test where Aqib Javed was shown on television to be doing something with the ball, or to it, and I invoked the name of the founder of Christian religion. It was an exclamation which found its way into the Allan Lamb–Sarfraz Nawaz court hearing in London.

The plain fact was as stated in court that, despite whatever efforts were made to prevent publication of the details, the ball at Lord's had been changed because, in the opinion of the umpires, illegal methods had been used to change its condition. It took slightly over two years for that to emerge, and then only in court when the contest was Sarfraz versus Lamb.

Pakistan cricket took some stick at the time and this wasn't helped by Imran Khan's revelation that he had used a bottle top on a ball to roughen one side of it so that reverse swing could be used. Now, though, the Atherton affair offered a chance for Pakistan media outlets to compare two different allegations of ball-tampering.

It says much for the interest in cricket on the sub-continent that Pakistan newspapers were said to have doubled their circulation at the height of the Mike Atherton business. Anger and indignation were the most common feelings voiced at what was regarded in Pakistan as a lenient punishment for the England captain.

I didn't blame Pakistan for being upset. Two years earlier, cricket balls used in matches had found their way into locked safes, and the Sarfraz–Lamb court case had produced some interesting information from Don Oslear who was the reserve umpire in the game in question at Lord's where the ball was changed. They had every right to have their own say on a similar matter involving England. They may even have enjoyed it!

Not least of the bizarre happenings to do with ball-tampering came in February 1995 with a wire service report that Sir Richard Hadlee had advocated it should become legal practice for bowlers. I thought as I read this that Richard had lost his marbles, particularly as he had been livid when Imran had talked about bottle tops being taken to balls, and had made a point of saying so in print.

It must have been a slow day on the computer for column writing. Legalised ball-tampering; cricketers on steroids, pumped up and bowling fast because of a few sniffs of whatever takes your fancy, and using a ball brilliant red on one side and on the other looking like something just rescued off Waikuku Beach. An exaggeration? Perhaps. But why on earth start talking about legalising scuffing of a ball in a Test match?

By the time Atherton arrived at The Oval for the final Test of the three-match series against South Africa, he might have thought most things that could happen to him had happened. Wrong. When given out lbw he incurred the wrath of the match referee, Peter Burge once again, this time for showing dissent, and was fined fifty per cent of his match fee.

This was something quite different from what had happened across at St John's Wood a few weeks earlier. In my *News of the World* column I commented on the dissent which brought some suggestions that Atherton's captaincy might again be under scrutiny. I thought this new incident to be of minor importance, but recalled there had been similar ones at Leeds on the part of other players. I also pointed out yet another blatant example of spectators at the ground being conned.

Michael Atherton must remain England's cricket captain. Atherton, slugged half his match fee on Friday for dissent by match referee Peter Burge, led the side brilliantly in the field and with the bat yesterday. He handled the bowlers in splendid fashion and inspired Devon Malcolm to the second-best bowling figures by an Englishman this century.

It was a superb spell and will have caught the attention of the Australians, who will be Malcolm's next opponents in the Ashes battle at the end of the year.

I've always held the opinion that Malcolm is appallingly under-used by England's various selection committees and this brilliant effort has done nothing to dissuade me from that view. I have now seen three nine-wicket or better innings hauls in Test cricket – I was on the receiving end of two of them from Jim Laker in 1956 – and now have watched Malcolm's magnificent performance.

Atherton, as well as inspiring the team, also batted brilliantly. He was under enormous pressure following the latest fine and resultant publicity, which itself came after the Lord's controversies where Burge caned him for being economical with the truth and Ray Illingworth fined him for the same thing and for having dirt in his pocket.

I thought Burge's £1,500 fine for dissent at Ken Palmer's Oval decision was harsh but not necessarily unfair. It did though seem to show inconsistency in judging what is dissent.

At Headingley, for example, I was astonished Jonty Rhodes was not admonished after what was clearly the equivalent dissent when he was caught at the wicket off his arm. For Rhodes and Atherton, being given out was bad luck. Atherton's performance on Friday was not a hanging offence and not in a zillion years something where administrators should again get their knickers in a twist over the England captaincy.

*What I will be interested in seeing is what administrators and Burge do about the appallingly cynical displays that are robbing cricket's spectators from receiving the value to which they are entitled when they pay £35 ($A80.00) for a Test match ticket to watch a day's play.*

South Africa's attitude on Friday was breath-taking in its audacity. There should have been 85 overs but there were 71. Spectators were deprived of 14 overs.

Yesterday England also managed to lose 14 overs. Perhaps we need to start playing six-day Tests so the players are able to get through the 450 overs minimum.

Allowances eventually reduced the overall match fine for England to six overs, £720 per man.

That article underlines clearly that I was far less interested at the time in the fact that Atherton had looked at the edge of his bat when walking off than I was at the appalling attitude of the teams and the over-rates which cheat the paying public.

An interesting aspect of the affair came in an interview with Neil Fairbrother who is Atherton's county captain at Lancashire. The article gave a further insight into Atherton's determination. Fairbrother seemed in little doubt as to the effect the dramatic events had had on the England captain at the time, which in fact underlines what a steely character Atherton actually is.

Fairbrother, in a newspaper interview with Peter Hayter, said that when Atherton came back from Lord's he was in a terrible state. His main problem seemed to be that he hadn't placed all the facts of the matter before Peter Burge, the match referee, and that once he had seen the television sequence he knew how damning the whole thing looked. Fairbrother said he believed what made Atherton draw back from resignation was first of all stubbornness and secondly the support he received from Ray Illingworth. That certainly bears out my own assertion that the two best things I know Illingworth to have done are bringing back the Ashes for England in 1970–1 and saving Atherton's bacon during the Lord's affair.

One of the reasons cricket is such a character-building game is the way it changes from over to over, match to match, series to series. Lord's was a débâcle for Atherton but it led into England's great victory at The Oval over South Africa where Malcolm turned in one of the most blistering bowling spells it has been my pleasure to witness from 100 yards' distance. He was fired up to do well anyway but Fanie de Villiers made the mistake of crunching his first ball to Malcolm up against the batsman's helmet. Devon, like a lot of fast bowlers – not all, mind you – is a calm and gentle man until you place a five and a half ounce, or, as we insist in saying nowadays in Australia, a one hundred and fifty-six gram ball in his hand. Then he can be inaccurate, frustrating or a brilliant matchwinner. He was the latter at The Oval. He prefaced his nine-wickets-in-an-innings haul with a half smile to Fanie and the words, 'You guys are in real trouble.'

It reminded me a little of the day forty years earlier when Ray Lindwall, bowling to Frank Tyson at the SCG in Australia, dropped one short, hit Frank on the back of the head and he was carted off to hospital. Frank was gentle off the field but not so gentle the following day when he bowled England to victory with a devastating burst. Lindwall's head-cruncher was very much in his mind every time he ran in to bowl.

Malcolm was as good as his word at The Oval, and two men who made identical notes in their selection books were Atherton and Illingworth.

# 4

## Magnificent Michael Slater,
## the Australians devastate Atherton

On a scale of ten, it was Michael Atherton 9 and the Australians 1 before a ball was bowled in the opening Test of the Ashes series. With a superb blend of nonchalance and aggression at his opening press conference in Perth, Atherton concentrated so much attention on sledging and the Australian team, which was battling 5,000 miles away in Pakistan, that it appeared England were actually raging hot favourites to regain the Ashes. In fact, the situation was that in the last seventeen Test matches between the two countries Australia had won eleven, England one, and five were drawn.

Astonishingly, by the time England had been in Australia for two days, the general feeling was that not only were those statistics of little account but, somehow, the names of the countries might even have been transposed – and, that Steve Waugh's courage was suspect! The latter came about because Atherton was questioned over an article which had appeared in *Wisden Cricket Monthly* in England, where he expressed the view that Steve Waugh was 'wetting himself' when he played against England's fast bowlers. Michael evaded that one in similar fashion to a Merv Hughes bouncer, but the little interlude read strangely when one took into account the fact that on the last two occasions Waugh had played in England he had headed Australia's Test batting figures thus:

|      | M | I | NO | R   | HS   | 100 | Avge   |
|------|---|---|----|-----|------|-----|--------|
| 1989 | 6 | 8 | 4  | 506 | 177★ | 2   | 126.50 |
| 1993 | 6 | 9 | 4  | 416 | 157★ | 1   | 83.20  |

and, more recently against New Zealand in 1993–4, he had also been at the top of the Australian figures with:

| 1993–4 | 3 | 3 | 2 | 216 | 147* | 216.00 |

and then, against South Africa in Australia and in South Africa in the same Southern Hemisphere summer, his combined batting figures also had him at the top of the Australians' list with:

| 1993–4 | 4 | 6 | 1 | 360 | 164 | 72.00 |

They are figures of which even an England captain opening the innings might have been proud, particularly those achieved against England. Waugh then went on in this Ashes series to be one of six batsmen to make more than 300 runs, 99* and 80 of them in the two innings of the final Test in Perth on a hard, bouncy pitch favouring pace bowlers.

Atherton's comments about Waugh, and Devon Malcolm's subsequent claim that he could see fear in the Australians' eyes at The Oval in 1993, were not in what might be termed impeccable taste, but that is sometimes the way of the cricket world these days. It seemed to me it was an opportunity to murmur things about opponents when they were several thousand miles away, and it was clever. If you were looking to gain a psychological advantage before anyone bowled a ball in anger, this might have been the way to do it. One thing you do need in a situation of that kind is a team to back you up and, preferably, a bowling attack that will give the opposition something to think about.

No one had to wait long for the next stanza which, as it happened, concerned the bowling attacks. Still in Perth, and with pace bowling very much in mind, Keith Fletcher drew some comparisons between his 1995 bowling line-up and the one Australia had in 1974–5 when Dennis Lillee was returning from a back injury and Jeff Thomson was making his debut against England. 'Thommo' had played one Test against Pakistan at the MCG the previous season with a broken bone in his foot that he didn't bother to tell anyone about in case it meant having to drop out of the match. The next summer, in the First Test of that series between England and Australia, Thomson produced some of the fastest bowling I had seen in years, on a pitch where there was some uneven bounce.

Now in Perth, and twenty years on, Thomson and Lillee were to play at Lilac Hill for the Australian Cricket Board Chairman's XI against England and Fletcher was saying there was a comparison in pace to be made between his bowlers and the two great Australians. I studied his remarks for a time and then gave him top marks, not necessarily for accuracy, and certainly not for memory, but for ability to choose the words which would make the headline for the sub-editor. This was purely psychological skirmishing, because Fletcher's bowlers were the ones I had watched a few months ago in England and, unless in the past few months they had been on the same fruit juice as the Chinese swimmers, they were likely to be a yard or two short of the extreme pace of the vintage Lillee and Thomson of 1974–5.

Everyone has favourite stories about different players around the world. With Jeff Thomson there are a number, some of them to do with that tour of 1974–5 and concerning Colin Cowdrey, who introduced himself to Thomson at the non-striker's end with 'Good morning, my name's Cowdrey.' Cowdrey, after injuries to other batsmen, had been flown from the United Kingdom to play on the hard, bouncy Perth pitch and to face the great pair of fast bowlers. Thomson had just whizzed one past his nose.

But I fondly remember the Old Trafford press box in 1974, during the Test between England and India, where an English journalist friend of mine wanted some information about Lillee and 'this new bowler Thomson'. I told him the latest news I had about Lillee was that he was out of his plaster back-brace and his treatment, under Dr Frank Pyke, was said to be successful so far. As regards Thomson, I had seen him play in the NSW Colts side against Queensland in October, 1972, where he had taken 5/79 in an innings, and he was very fast. Then I saw him in the one Test in Melbourne where he was again fast but extremely inaccurate, and had the potential to be as fast as anyone I had ever seen. If I say this was met with scepticism, it would be to put it in its mildest form. As the conversation continued, I felt like apologising for having had the temerity to suggest such a thing – when, that is, I was able to get a word in edgeways. It did, however, turn out to be a reasonably accurate summing-up.

It was never easy to assess Thomson. Even Jeffrey Robert had some difficulty in describing his own bowling which, at his peak, I thought to be quite magnificent. He said once, in his slightly drawling Queensland voice, when searching for the answer to the question of how he generated such speed, 'Aw, I just sort of shuffle up . . . and go whang.'

In this current England side Devon Malcolm was the one who might go 'whang' and Darren Gough had plenty of potential at the start of the tour, but we needed to wait until the 'Gabba Test to see how 'Fletch's' predictions would stand up.

In all the years I have been playing, watching and commentating on Ashes cricket series, I have never quite known a build-up to match the one accorded the 1994–5 series with Mark Taylor and Michael Atherton as captains. There was an enormous amount of publicity and it was a wonderful example of the strong feeling aroused by contests between these two nations, and which started the Ashes battles in Test cricket. It was all the more remarkable because in the previous three meetings England had taken such a hammering that there was nationwide despair of the Ashes ever coming home, even though they actually stay under close guard at Lord's. With those defeats of 0−4 in 1989, 0–3 in 1990–1 and 1–3 in 1993, it required imagination on the part of Australia's cricket followers to see just how England would catch up, let alone go ahead of the Australians.

I confess happily though to being one of those to whom it did seem possible, and for what, at the time, I considered to be very good reasons. For a start, I knew England had some good cricketers. I had seen them in some of their lowest moments, though not in the West Indies where they made only 46 in an innings, but I knew if they used their brains as well as their skills, then they were definitely in with a chance. As is the case in any campaign, England needed some luck. You might have a splendid team, but if you have no luck you will be pushing uphill to defeat the opposition.

In charge of the selection of the team were two men of character. Michael Atherton from the Red Rose county, Lancashire, had plenty on his plate after the Lord's incidents involving dirt in his pocket being transferred to the ball, a confrontation with the match referee and a fining from the second man of character, England Chairman of Selectors, Mr Raymond Illingworth, former Test captain from the White Rose county, Yorkshire. No tougher cricketers play the game than from those two counties, and they play it well. I have seen some outstanding captains in Test and limited-overs cricket and Illingworth is one of them. Others are Keith Miller, who never captained Australia, but should have and was a brilliant skipper of NSW and the best captain I ever played under in any kind of cricket; Ian Chappell, who skippered his country and did a magnificent job in the 1970s; and Mike Brearley, captain of England.

When eventually the 1994–5 side was named to tour Australia it was based on pace bowling, with two spinners in the side: Phil Tufnell, who would certainly play in Sydney and might play in other Tests, and Shaun Udal, who was on a learning tour, and it was said would play in the limited-overs Internationals and might force his way into the Test at the SCG. I wouldn't have included Udal but, once he was picked, I thought this comment about his expectations of playing in a Test was one of the more unfeeling I had heard in a long time. What would happen if he bowled well? The other spinner, who would bat at number three, was Graeme Hick, a more than useful bowler, brilliant slip fielder and a rapidly improving international batsman. In the event only Tufnell remained fit enough to see out the Ashes tour.

The key to the selection lay in the pace bowlers, and if they managed to 'hit their straps', the Australians were in for a tough time. This was the millionaire fast bowling club, the select group who were about to do as Illingworth had done in 1971 and take home the Ashes.

When I first saw them play the Australian XI in Hobart, however, they were far from millionaires. You wouldn't have given 'two bob' for them in Australia's pre-decimal coinage. Manager Keith Fletcher described his team's batting there as pathetic, and one or two other things not destined to see the light of day in a family book, and thought their bowling was worse! He let them off lightly.

When the selection of the England touring party was imminent, I had written a plea for the inclusion of Angus Fraser. As it happened, it fell on deaf ears, but I had suggested it because of the emphasis I knew would be placed on pace bowling and the fact that with Malcolm and Gough certainties for the team and variable in length, the great need would be someone at the other end keeping things tight.

Hindsight is always a valuable commodity but Fraser, Salisbury and Bicknell might have been quite handy on the tour. The article said:

England have a wonderful chance of regaining the Ashes this summer *if* they choose the right team and include fast bowler Angus Fraser. The attack I have nominated will stretch the Australians to the limit and, despite the attitudes of the pampered batsmen of this world, it is bowlers who win Test series.

The selection framework I use for a sixteen-man party touring Australia is seven batsmen, an allrounder, one wicket-keeper, two spinners and five pace bowlers, and they line up this way:

| | |
|---|---|
| Batsmen: | Michael Atherton, Graham Gooch, Darren Bicknell, Graeme Hick, Graham Thorpe, Alec Stewart, John Crawley |
| Allrounder: | Craig White |
| Wicket-keeper: | Steve Rhodes |
| Spinners: | Phil Tufnell, Ian Salisbury |
| Pacemen: | Devon Malcolm, Darren Gough, Angus Fraser, Phil DeFreitas, Joey Benjamin |

I have included every player in England's sensational victory over South Africa at The Oval. And I have found places for Tufnell, the best of the spinners, and Salisbury, who could play a part in the Tests. But I am unable to find a spot in a sixteen-man squad for Mike Gatting, nor for Shaun Udal, good prospect though he is. He will be better served on the 'A' tour of India where he can have a lot of bowling rather than in Australia where Hick will bar his way to a Test spot as the second spinner.

I wrote the above despite the rumours that had been floating about Fraser and the fact there was a likelihood of him missing the tour, and that he hadn't been at all popular when he arrived back in England from the tour of the West Indies, very much out of sorts about Chairman Ray Illingworth's comments on his fitness.

Illingworth had been quoted as saying, 'I'm a bit worried about Gus's fitness. You wonder whether he can keep doing it.'

But Fraser hit back. 'I bowled 45 overs in the Antigua Test on a flat pitch and felt just as strong at the end as at the beginning. I didn't feel shattered. In the last two Tests I have bowled 90 overs in a period of ten days, more than anyone else. It's much harder bowling over there in the heat than it is here and I thought I got through it well. If he wants to talk to me about it he can. I don't know what else he wants me to do. It's going to be a tough time coming up with a lot of cricket but I'm ready for it.'

There was even a very strange rumour Fraser was heavily fined for replying to the allegation that he might not be fully fit, but that one was a little difficult to track down with English cricket officials.

Now he was in Australia, but not as part of the team, though the Fraser family had their say in a letter to the newspapers when he was left out of the touring party. Fraser was playing grade cricket in Sydney for Western Suburbs, something he had done in 1989–90. It was in that summer he had his first taste of watching limited-overs Internationals played at night. When I met Fraser at the SCG back then, with the lights on and a capacity crowd present, he said, 'I must be part of this, the atmosphere is marvellous. I just want to come back with the team next year [1990–1] and be out in the centre of the ground rather than watching.' He made it too and then I watched him bowl magnificently in the Melbourne Test after England's batsmen had fallen apart against Bruce Reid.

No Fraser then in Perth for the start of the tour, and no Fraser in

Hobart for the first match against the Australian XI. It all added a touch of spice to proceedings as we prepared for Damien Martyn and Michael Atherton to lead their teams into battle at Bellerive Oval.

The Australian selectors always have things going for them in an Australian XI versus the touring side game, and this match allowed them to play a number of young batsmen and three pace bowlers, each of whom was fighting for a place in the line-up for the 'Gabba. Merv Hughes bowled well, so too Paul Reiffel and Jo Angel, and England's batting was unable to come to terms with them. Hughes was never at full pace but showed he was just about fully fit after his enforced rest, and Reiffel continued the excellent form he had shown in the opening matches of the season. Jo Angel was in a different category, having been to Sri Lanka and Pakistan with the Australian team where he had bowled well. He is tall, able to gain lift from the pitch and looks a definite prospect if only he is able to add some speed to his bowling. He is lively enough and accurate but must gain at least another yard of pace for Test cricket, particularly if he is playing on pitches with less bounce than Perth. On that ground in the final Test of this Ashes series he bowled adequately but still lacked the extra pace. What he did produce though was a number of brilliantly bowled inswinging yorkers.

On the question of the England bowlers being too short in length in Hobart, the biggest surprise to me at first was that Atherton and the senior players were unable to persuade Darren Gough, Martin Mc-Cague, Joey Benjamin and Craig White that the ball had to be kept up. Not at half-volley length but just shorter than that. What I didn't realise at the time, in Tasmania, was that the English bowlers may have been told, may even have realised they were actually bowling badly, but were unable to co-ordinate their brains with their hands and arms and legs or, for that matter, any other parts of their bodies. I was to be shown later, on the first day of the 'Gabba Test, that those problems didn't disappear overnight but, if anything, magnified.

The Hobart match provided England with a mixture of weather conditions: sunshine, strong to gale force winds, rain, icy conditions blowing up from the Antarctic, and what seemed like snow at one stage but possibly wasn't; Alec Stewart made a very good second-innings century, despite all this. He had started off in the first innings by hitting Paul Reiffel for several delightful boundaries and his strokeplay in the second innings was magnificent. Atherton made runs and, out of a match badly marred by the conditions, England found some positive aspects.

Not for long though. I flew back to Sydney on the Monday night of

that game and on the Tuesday it was announced that Devon Malcolm
had chicken-pox and would miss the Test in Brisbane. For a couple of
days it was feared there may have been others in the England side who
had also been infected, but fortunately that didn't happen, though Joey
Benjamin certainly fell ill with symptoms said to be similar to shingles.
Fraser was called to Brisbane by the team management when it looked as
though they could have been a bowler short. In the end he flew back to
Sydney when the others were cleared, and if he watched it all happening
on television in the southern city, he would have had some very mixed
feelings.

There were worries about two of the Australian players as well but it
was found before the Test to be a throat virus and nothing to do with
chicken-pox.

On the Thursday both teams were able to settle down to full-scale
preparations for the First Test and there was a huge amount of publicity.
Much of it revolved around Shane Warne and what he might do to the
England batsmen. There was also a great deal of conjecture about how
the England batsmen would play him. If Warne took most of the
headlines, Craig McDermott had his share of publicity as well, but it was
in a different vein. The general theme about him was that Australia had
been struggling to break through the top of opposition batting orders
and the innuendo was that it was McDermott's fault. At the time, when I
read the first little offering along these lines, it surprised me. When I read
the second and the third I reckoned McDermott would be far from
pleased, particularly as, since making his debut in Test cricket, he has
shown a great deal of courage and skill in his bowling.

There is always something special about the start of a Test series
between Australia and England. There is certainly something very
special about an England–Australia Test at Lord's where the atmosphere
is electric. It would be hard to generate a similar atmosphere in tropical
Queensland, where the five-match Test series always begins in
Australia, and the feeling is very relaxed at the 'Gabba. I walked out
on to the ground a little more than an hour before the start of play to
have a glance at the pitch. It looked magnificent. There was some grass
on the surface, it was as hard as a block of concrete, and there were
some tiny cracks in it which didn't look as though they would extend,
something confirmed before the start of play by the curator, Kevin
Mitchell Jnr. He said, 'There is a great root growth under the surface
and that will hold the pitch together, no worries.' He was right. When
I walked out to have a look at it on the fourth morning, you could

have *started* a Test match on the same bone-hard surface, always excepting the bowlers' footmarks. It was one of the best Test match pitches in years.

One of the finest Test innings I have seen came on the first morning and was played by Michael Slater, the young Australian opening batsman who went in with skipper Mark Taylor. This is a very good combination and the left-hand, right-hand aspect of it has been present in Australian cricket since the beginning of the Ashes series in England in 1989. In that series it was a selection battle between Geoff Marsh, David Boon and Mark Taylor, who was a newcomer to the team, to see which pairing would be used for the opening skirmish. Australia were lucky that the manager of the Australian team was also the Chairman of the Australian Selection Committee, Laurie Sawle, and in the end it was his persuasive arguments which carried the day. Taylor and Marsh provided the left-hand, right-hand combination, Boon batted at three and then, when the team went back to England in 1993, it was Taylor and Slater who became the openers in the Test series.

After Taylor won the toss at the 'Gabba, he and Slater thrashed the England bowlers. It was one of the best and most calculated attacking ploys in recent years of Test cricket and it turned England's bowling and general out-cricket on the opening day into a shambles. The batting onslaught produced indifferent fielding, and nervous bowling set the pattern for one of the most devastating playing days Michael Atherton had ever gone through on a cricket field.

It may also have been that the other ten players went through a similarly devastating six hours in the tropical sunshine at the 'Gabba, but there is no confirmation of that. They looked a little tired at the end of play because Slater had slaughtered them in the first part of the day and then Mark Waugh had caressed 82 delightful runs up to the close. The key to Australia's cricket though was the speed with which they scored their runs on the opening day. It wasn't the first time I had seen this pattern – they had done the same thing against England in 1989 and 1993, as well as in Australia in 1990–1.

Slater started by slamming the first ball of the day from DeFreitas to the point boundary, a prophetic beginning and a real downer for England. One run short of the century partnership Mark Taylor was run out when he pushed a ball just wide of Tufnell towards mid-off and Slater hesitated to make certain the ball cleared Tufnell's desperate dive. Darren Gough at mid-off moved swiftly to his right, gathered in the ball and, throwing off balance to Rhodes, ran out Taylor by the length of the

pitch. Taylor looked at his younger partner from under a slightly
furrowed brow and is said to have murmured something along the
lines of, 'Better make it a big one.' Slater did just that.

I have seen few better innings, perfect defence and a delightful and
exuberant mixture of strokes all around the ground, and this in front of
the best Test match crowd seen at the 'Gabba in thirteen summers.
David Boon lasted only twenty-four balls before he played on to Darren
Gough and the partnership between Slater and Mark Waugh then
controlled much of the remainder of the day, with Slater out thirty-
five minutes before the close of play at 5 p.m. Queensland doesn't have
daylight saving so Test matches at the 'Gabba must start at 10 a.m. and
finish at 5 p.m. There's no point in trying to go through to 6 p.m. as
tropical Brisbane has a very fast twilight. One moment the light is quite
good, a minute or two later you are struggling to see the bowler, let
alone a cricket ball hurtling towards you at 90mph, or 145kph. Also
dismissed that evening was Michael Bevan, a very good young left-
hander who plays with NSW and was now playing in his first Test in his
own country. He had been included in the Australian team to tour Sri
Lanka and Pakistan and had been slotted into the batting order at
number five to take the place of Allan Border.

He did a great job in Pakistan against a top-class bowling attack and,
despite the amount of competition for batting places in Australia, Bevan
had at that time a real chance of becoming a permanent number five. His
career in Sheffield Shield cricket had been remarkable up to this time
and, in the season prior to England touring Australia, he hit five centuries
and eight half-centuries, making 1,312 runs in the summer. Later in the
Australian season he was to suffer a reverse in fortune. He was left out of
the Adelaide Test for South Australian Greg Blewett and the latter was
an instant success. Bevan went back to Sheffield Shield, broke a finger
and missed the short tour of New Zealand and the longer tour to the
Caribbean to play the West Indies. It is a very tough game, and careers
can easily be built or destroyed.

There was no doubt, before the Ashes battle began, that Australia had
some excellent back-up batting to the Test side and Bevan was one of
those players; another was Matthew Hayden of Queensland who had
found it equally difficult continually to catch the selectors' eyes. Hayden,
just as Bevan was batting so well for NSW, had walked out and hit six
centuries in the Sheffield Shield competition the previous summer for
Queensland. He was chosen to tour South Africa and some of his
problems encountered there are noted elsewhere in this book.

Bevan didn't have much chance to show a great deal in this First Test though. He was dismissed, caught by Graeme Hick at gully off Gough's bowling – two wickets for the Yorkshire bowler and thoroughly deserved too, in a day that will not go down in English cricket history as one of the more memorable. Only a few minutes earlier Slater had fallen victim to Graham Gooch, bowling his medium-pacers from the Vulture Street end – excellent captaincy from Atherton who was prepared to try many things in the face of such problems with his bowlers. To complete the gentle irony of the brilliant young batsman being dismissed by the oldest man in the opposition, it was the second oldest, Mike Gatting, who took the catch at extra cover. Slater and Mark Waugh had added 182 for the third wicket, and a measure of Slater's brilliance had been that Mark had to take a back seat. The significant fact there was that Waugh was perfectly happy to allow Slater full rein and himself to concentrate on being there the following morning, which was something England certainly didn't want.

The opening day definitely belonged to the Australian batsmen, and confirmation of the brilliance and scoring speed came in the fact that England somehow managed to bowl exactly 90 overs in the day, underlining that if they want to do it and if they consider it to their advantage, the players will always manage to play just within the playing conditions. Had the playing conditions said 96 overs, or 102 overs in the day, I'm equally certain the last over would have started a minute before time. We were to have plenty of evidence of this as the series progressed.

There could have been no greater contrast on the second day of the match when Australia, having started at 329/4, struggled through to lunch to be 420/8 with Waugh 137★ and May yet to score. It was a great opening session for England with the second new ball, and a quarter of an hour after lunch the Australians were out for 426, having lost 6/97. A good score, but well short of what they might have hoped for and a real credit to Atherton and the manner in which he drove his men and the way in which they came back. Phil DeFreitas, very ordinary on the opening day, was magnificent on the second. Mind you, he didn't have a great deal to show for it at the end of the innings, and a classic case of statistics not quite being the definitive aspect of cricket careers is that his figures of 2/102 were worse than Martin McCague's 2/96. DeFreitas had bowled very badly on the opening day but McCague hadn't even been as impressive as that, looked nervous when he started, more nervous when his first spell ended, and he couldn't come back at the end of the first day. Nor was he able to do anything on the second morning with the new ball, but towards the end of the innings, he collected the wickets of McDermott and McGrath. 'Take what you can get in this game' is worth remembering, because for every easy wicket which may come your way, there are many canings around the corner from the same quality batsmen who gave McCague a bit of stick on the first day and the second morning.

DeFreitas showed great character to fight back for Atherton and he and Gough ensured the Australians wouldn't get away from England.

There had been shades of 1990–1 in the opening exchanges of the tour when Atherton's side played their practice matches in Perth and Alec Stewart broke a finger. Four years earlier Graham Gooch had badly broken a finger in a similar practice match and was out of the playing side until the Second Test in Melbourne. Allan Lamb captained the team in the 'Gabba Test, Australia won in a canter and England never recovered. Stewart's absence from Perth to Hobart wasn't as serious, other than to Stewart himself, but it was a nuisance. It meant that Atherton opened the batting with Rhodes in Newcastle and upset Illingworth who wanted Craig White to go in first, and the proposed Atherton–Stewart opening partnership had just one outing in the Australian XI game before the Brisbane Test. Atherton and Stewart are professionals and could handle that, but it certainly wasn't the way they would have wanted it to happen.

The first four overs bowled by the Australians were roughly along the lines of those bowled by England on the first morning: too short, too wide and with very little need for Stewart and Atherton to play at many of the deliveries. Taylor wasted little time in trying spin, bringing on Tim May in the tenth over, and there was some turn for the offspinner out of the roughened footmarks, but not a great deal when the ball landed on the rolled portion of the pitch. May's degree of spin had no real relevance to how much turn Shane Warne would extract from the same pitch because I reckon he could turn the ball on glass. Almost immediately Craig McDermott broke through for Mark Taylor, having Stewart caught behind playing defensively and Graeme Hick caught by Ian Healy trying to hook. It was early days but I thought then I might not see any better thinking from a bowler during the series. Stewart's wicket was a little classic on its own. The batsman played a splendid pull shot off a short-pitched delivery and then did it again – wonderful shots and they brought justifiable applause from around the ground. McDermott then produced a superb outswinger, the perfect ball in a sequence like that, and Stewart's correct, defensive push only provided an edge to Healy. It was great bowling, and when he out-thought Hick with another short-pitched delivery with an extra yard of pace, the break-through was complete.

Shane Warne came on in the twentieth over of the innings, just before the tea interval, but there was no further breakthrough. Atherton was still there, having watched from the other end while those two wickets had gone, and he was 19 at tea after an hour and a half during which 22 overs had been bowled. For England it looked like a long haul.

It looked even more grim when, after tea, Craig McDermott, Shane Warne and Tim May bowled magnificently to take four more wickets, though not the one they prized so much, Michael Atherton. Atherton went through the session for another 30 and was still hanging on grimly at the end when Martin McCague was lbw to McDermott from the final ball of the day. The Australian fast bowler might have been a little lucky to dismiss Gatting but there was no doubt about McCague. With his last delivery McDermott slipped a very fast yorker under his bat to give him his fourth wicket of the innings and Australia a great opportunity to send England in again if they wished. Warne bowled very well, spinning the ball sharply off the rolled part of the pitch and turning it a prodigious amount out of the footmarks. He had only the one wicket but he was a great foil for McDermott whose rhythm was improving all the time in his impressive bowling spells.

With Atherton caught by Healy attempting to hook McDermott the next morning, and Warne proving too much for DeFreitas and Tufnell, it needed Gough's cheerful batting to improve England's score to 167, though that was 60 short of avoiding the follow-on and gave Australia a lead of 259. Warne, who has only been in the game a short time but is already rewriting the record books, took his 50th Test wicket in Australia.

McDermott's bowling figures of 6/53 had only been bettered four times by an Australian against England on this ground. It was his tenth five-wicket haul in Tests, the fifth time against England. It was also a little more than seventeen months since he needed an emergency operation in London after he collapsed at Lord's with awful pains which involved a twisted bowel. He was resourceful enough to grab a taxi and race to University College Hospital, but it was a close thing. He played no more on that tour of England, flew back to Australia for an operation but was back into Test and limited-overs Internationals against South Africa in 1993–4. The fact that he had made such a great comeback from a nodding acquaintanceship with death only emphasised the worth of his bowling. He had also moved to 244 wickets in the Australian Test table, a fine achievement and one which meant that possibly he would go past my 248 and set sail for Dennis Lillee's 355 in the next Test in Melbourne. There is also a youngster named Warne who will be setting out after him. Warne has already taken more than 150 Test wickets and in this series went ahead of Bill O'Reilly who is classed by Sir Donald Bradman as the greatest bowler of all time.

Both McDermott and Warne were given a short rest by Mark Taylor, who didn't enforce the follow-on but still won the match, though not before there had been a stirring fightback from England and some startling bowling from Warne. I was quite happy at the time with Taylor's decision to bat again, though it wouldn't have worried me if he had enforced the follow-on. The purpose of batting a second time, as I saw it, was to blot England out of the game completely and ensure that the only two possible results could be an Australian victory or, at worst, a draw.

It was perfectly reasonable for Taylor to want to make certain Australia didn't have to bat last, trying to make something like 120–150 on a wearing pitch and with Tufnell bowling into the footmarks.

With eleven hours to play, and something like 164 overs remaining in the game to the scheduled close of play, there was no earthly chance of England winning by making over 500. Had anything like that suddenly loomed as the scenario, Warne would simply have come around the wicket and bowled into the footmarks and no one would have made a run against him bowling in such a manner. That is something Australian captains will always bear in mind for as long as he plays; there is now a new dimension in declaring an innings closed – that Warne might bowl you to victory as an attacking bowler, or save you from defeat as a defensive one if the footmarks are there. Taylor, with all this in mind, batted until 10.50 a.m. on the fourth day, at which point England had reduced them to 248/8 and, when the closure came, Healy had 45* and May 9*. England needed 508 to win, and they had 74 overs to the close of play on the fourth day plus the full last day's ration of 90 overs. At 211/2, with 297 needed for victory and those 90 overs to be negotiated on the final day, they were still in with a chance of saving the game but, for the reasons advanced above, there was no possibility of them winning it.

Warne came on in the tenth over and in his twelfth he bowled Alec Stewart who had made a very brisk and attractive 33. He bowled him with one of the best 'flippers' I have seen; it was perfectly pitched, was just short enough to have Stewart thinking momentarily about the pull, then the cut, and then oblivion. The delivery with which Warne dismissed Gatting at Old Trafford in 1993 was a beauty and has been classed as the ball of the century. It may well have been, but this one, which first deceived Stewart and then dismissed him, wasn't much inferior, if at all.

Straight after lunch, in his next over, Warne had Atherton lbw with a ball which was meant to go straight on but turned just a little from the leg. Later Atherton was to say it was simply a leg-break which didn't turn as much as he thought it would. I have a feeling Michael will change his mind about that in later years because Warne has been working hard on a new topspinner which could, in my opinion, bring him more wickets than his 'flipper'.

This topspinner, which is allowed to slide between the second and third fingers, looks exactly like a leg-break and is extremely difficult to detect. Before the Brisbane Test began Warne held a press conference, or rather was asked by the English media to give one and to explain what deliveries he was using. Shane came out of that conference knowing more about the media than they ever learned about what he was bowling and, with all the advantageous publicity, it seemed only a matter of time before Warne would demoralise England.

In fact, he did it on the last day of this match, taking 8/71 from 50.2 overs to give Australia victory with two and a quarter hours to spare. He did it in spite of heroic resistance from Hick and Thorpe who had batted together from just after lunch on the fourth day to half an hour after the start of play on the fifth. Once that partnership was broken the floodgates opened and, despite some more dogged and fighting batting, England had no real answer to Warne and Tim May, who didn't take a wicket in the second innings but was a perfect bowler to have at the end opposite the legspinner. There were times during Graham Gooch and Mike Gatting's hour-long partnership when the saving of the game was still possible, but every time I thought that, Warne would bowl another brilliant over. Gooch is one who has always played Warne well and his 56 was the best confidence-boost England could have had. The problem for England though was that they had already started to try to outwit Warne, if that is not a contradiction in terms, by blocking him out of the attack. No one was interested in belting him out of the attack; the emphasis seemed as much on playing him with the pad and not the bat, potentially a fatal method.

This defensive ploy is the one the South Africans tried in 1993–4 and it didn't work then either. In that scenario, Warne will still be wheeling away 25 overs after the defensive measures begin, with very few runs taken off him, and he only needs a wicket to start his mesmerising effect once again. McCague, after his early bowling problems, had missed a day of the Test with a stomach complaint, then Warne trapped him lbw in the second innings with a great flipper, and Tufnell was the last to go after some comical exploits. This was to be the last we would see of McCague who was diagnosed as having a stress fracture of the shin and flown back to England for rest, recreation and recuperation. The replacement player was Angus Fraser!

As a start to the Test series it could hardly have been better for Australia that Warne had taken eleven wickets in the game, was Man of the Match, received an enormous amount of publicity, including from that beautifully orchestrated press conference the day before the match, and gave a magnificent exhibition of over-the-wrist slow bowling. When asked about the result, Atherton said he was devastated. He had every right to be.

# 5

## *England go slow and pay dearly, captains and selectors*

One down after Brisbane, the captain devastated, the team seemingly demoralised, injuries and illness bringing gloom to the touring party, it was not a pretty picture when, in the Second Test in Melbourne, Atherton took one of the greatest gambles of his career and sent Australia in to bat.

Giving the opposition first use of the MCG pitch is fraught with danger. I did it twice, once against England in 1959 and once against the West Indies in the final match of the Tied Test series in 1961. There was a very good reason for doing so on both occasions. There had been rain in Melbourne in the week before each Test began, the outfield was sodden the day before the toss, the pitch had been covered for much of the week and almost certainly would have been sweating under those covers. It was inconceivable there would not be plenty of life for the pace bowlers for much of the opening day. In the first match, in 1959, the selectors obviously thought along the same lines, though I had no prior knowledge of this when I was preparing to go out to toss, as the Chairman of Selectors, then Sir Donald Bradman, would only tell me who was to be twelfth man at that late stage, or perhaps when I was having a look at the pitch an hour before the start. The selectors told me on this occasion that Les Favell would be the drinks waiter and my reaction was, 'That means four fast bowlers, I'll have to send them in now.'

The reaction I got back from the Chairman of Selectors was, 'That's for you to decide, Richie. Our job is to give you the team, yours is to captain it.'

The Australian captain is not only excluded from selection meetings choosing the twelve players for a Test in Australia, but he doesn't have a say in who will be twelfth man. Or perhaps it would be closer to say he *didn't* have a say: things have changed a little in recent years and Mark Taylor these days would almost certainly have some input in the choice or nomination of the twelfth man. That doesn't alter my own view that it is much better for a captain to have no input at all in nomination of either the eleven players or the twelfth man – I always read the team in the newspaper or heard it on the radio.

Australians want their captain to be independent, he wants to be independent and, generally, it works. There are some occasions where it might not but that usually is the fault of the captain, not of the selectors. I can't recall a poor Australian selection committee over the years, although one of them was responsible for axing Bill Lawry as skipper in 1970–1 when Ian Chappell was promoted to that post. That was a matter of human relations rather than any lack of selection knowledge.

There was a very good reason I was pleased to be part of that system so decried in the past by English cricket authorities, players and critics, and then again obliquely criticised by Michael Atherton during the 1994–5 Ashes tour. My independent spirit wanted to be totally in charge of the team. If I had sat in on proceedings at the selection committee, and had pressed for a player or players to be either included or left out, I have no doubt that would have been reflected at some stage in my captaincy on the field. What I wanted was to be given the eleven players and then no one was able to influence what I did on the field. I was prepared to take the blame for anything that went wrong without whingeing about having been outvoted at the selection table. I could use players on the field as I wished, not as we might have all decided had I been part of the selection committee. In addition to taking the blame for any stuff-up, I was prepared to take the credit if it went right, but the crucial part was that I wanted to take the blame for *my* mistakes, not someone else's! The one thing I didn't want was to be part of a group of cricketers and selectors, and officials and others, all peering in learned fashion at the pitch an hour before the start of play and eventually deciding which team would bat and who would be carrying the drinks.

The difference in selection methods between the two countries is one of independence, and I prefer to be independent.

The second time I put a team in to bat in Melbourne was against the

West Indies, in similar weather and pitch square conditions, and, once again, it was a question of trying to make the most of those conditions. In 1959 we bowled England out before stumps for 205; the West Indies two years later made 292. There was no doubt in 1961, when Australia began batting on the second day in front of the world-record Test crowd of 90,800, that the pitch and the general conditions were more in favour of batting than on the opening day. We didn't make the most of it and only achieved a lead of 64, then had to make 258 in the fourth innings of the game to win. It was a tense time, I can assure you.

That's why I knew what Mike Atherton would be feeling in Melbourne because, although there have been Test match totals of more than 1,000 runs at the MCG, low-scoring matches are more the norm and it is tempting fate if you are required to make more than 225 on the final day.

I had difficulty coming to terms with Atherton's decision, although a prediction based on the results achieved at lunch-time after a team is put in to bat is likely to be well wide of the mark. The only time to look at the success or otherwise of the move is at stumps on the first day and, by then, the Australians had, if not quite got themselves out of trouble, then at least done reasonably well in the face of having been sent in.

At the close of play they were 220/7, with Steve Waugh on 61 and Warne out to what was the last ball bowled in the day's play. It was the last-wicket partnership which, as occasionally happens, gave Mark Taylor and his team the chance to claw their way back into the game. Thirty-nine runs between Steve Waugh and Damien Fleming, the latter playing his first Test in Australia, took the Australians to 279, which if not sensational was certainly a more than reasonable reply to being asked to take first strike. Steve Waugh was left six short of his century which was a pity.

In the light of the initial press conference in Perth, when questions were asked of Atherton concerning his doubts about Waugh's courage against pace bowling, there was a little extra bite in the on-the-field exchanges between Waugh and the English pace bowlers. Waugh saw them off on this occasion but England's bowlers fought back very well as the series progressed, particularly in Sydney and Adelaide, but then Waugh came back at them again with his excellent performances in the final Test in Perth.

It has always intrigued me that a player with a style which strays from the beautifully orthodox should instantly be criticised by those who consider themselves to be the purists of the technical side of the game.

There was a time when Waugh was so side-on in his stance, and in his playing of the ball lifting at his chest, that he was vulnerable to the fielders close in on the legside. He has worked hard at this particular technical problem, has got himself around more front-on in playing the short ball and now does it more effectively. I have seen few batsmen play the short ball well when they remain side-on to the bowler in the execution of the stroke. The ones who best play the short delivery are those who are more front-on, have a clearer sight of the ball and can play it down on the ground without needing to make their little jump at the moment bat meets ball. As noted elsewhere, two advocates of being front-on to the short ball in playing the pull or hook, and in keeping the rib-high ball down in defence, are Sir Donald Bradman and Sir Garfield Sobers. Neither had a purely orthodox technique, something for which we should all be grateful.

Steve Waugh at the MCG had once again held together the middle of the order for Australia and it was enough to provide a great confidence-boost for Taylor's side as they prepared to walk on to the field.

Luck's a fortune in this game. Skill is extremely important, but if you have no luck to go with it, then you can finish up in a lot of trouble. Atherton and Stewart saw England through to the luncheon interval on the second day with ten on the board, no wickets down and no great alarms. Then, McDermott's first ball after lunch to Stewart jumped at him from a good length and struck him, not on any old finger but right on the spot where he had suffered a broken finger in Perth. That was awful luck for it was an across-the-bone break, not the more simple one down the bone, and would take a considerable time to heal. Stewart had to retire hurt and came in later in the innings, but it was a cruel blow for England, just another in the line of problems with injuries and illness.

It also exposed Graeme Hick to McDermott, and after he was caught at the wicket by Healy it was left to Atherton and Graham Thorpe to provide a 79-run partnership which took them to within three quarters of an hour of stumps with only two wickets down. Both were out within five runs of one another, then Mike Gatting was dismissed sweeping at Warne and the tail was very exposed as the players trooped off at the close of play with England 148/4 and Gooch and Gough the not out batsmen. It wasn't disastrous yet but, with Shane Warne in top form, England desperately needed Graham Gooch to take over on the third morning, score quickly and reduce the deficit. England would have been looking at a first-innings lead of some kind, which is definitely the requirement when you bat second after putting in the opposition on a pitch where there is a history of low-scoring matches.

Sometimes just one ball can change the course of a Test match and it happened with the first ball of the third day. Gooch was facing McDermott and, although the cynical version was that it was just a loosen-up delivery, in fact it was meant to be a yorker but turned out to be a full toss. That in itself wasn't dangerous; it was what Gooch did with it that posed the problem. He hit it straight back to McDermott who took the catch, and Australia then accepted the further presents handed out by the England batsmen. It was one of the most extraordinary sessions of the year.

Gooch caught off a full toss. Rhodes caught at silly-point off a leg-break which hit the angled bat full on and was brilliantly caught by Mark Waugh. Stewart, batting again despite his badly broken finger, caught and bowled by Warne from a massive skier. Gough caught at the wicket off McDermott. DeFreitas stumped – well, that's the way we will read about it as the years roll on: stumped Healy bowled Warne. It doesn't actually convey the total beauty of the dismissal, the footwork and the shimmy by the batsman.

Warne bowled the ball; DeFreitas, a fraction of a second before the ball left Warne's hand, started down the pitch. Warne sensed he was coming and bowled a beautiful leg-break which swerved sharply in the breeze, starting on off stump and finishing outside leg stump. Seeing this DeFreitas realised he was in trouble and tried to jump in front of the ball, unfortunately without making contact. It looked something of a cross between the sport of curling, where the competitor pushes a stone down the ice, allied to the Canadian three-step dance we used to do at the co-educational Parramatta High School under the eagle eye of headmistress Miss Mackaness. We were no more successful at it, incidentally, than DeFreitas in his bid to sashay down the pitch at the MCG. DeFreitas was to have his revenge in the Adelaide Test on the final morning when his dazzling array of strokes set up a magnificent victory for England and gave them the chance, if they played well enough, to square the series.

If DeFreitas's Melbourne dismissal were to be classed as slightly bizarre, then Philip Tufnell surpassed it by running himself out with only five runs added. When he was facing his fourth ball he played a defensive shot at Shane Warne and the ball ran off the pad down to fine leg. Devon Malcolm was the non-striker and he called for a single. Tufnell was very slow getting off the mark. In fact, a couple of seconds went by before he started to run and then turned for a second. There were actually something like two and a half runs there but, somehow, Tufnell turned them into one and three quarters and was easily run out by a great chase, pick-up and throw from Mark Taylor. It was ludicrous. England had lost 6/64 in the morning or, rather, in an hour and twelve minutes of the morning, all beginning with Gooch's moment of mental aberration.

With a low-scoring game, particularly if it is to be played on a pitch like the MCG, where at times the run-rate can be curtailed by bowling short of a length, it is important to have at least one batsman in the batting side who makes a good score. Ideally that would be a hundred, preferably many more, but certainly it would be more than a half-century. In the England side the top score was 51. In the Australian first innings Steve Waugh had made 94 not out and Mark Waugh 71, and that was the difference. The Australian lead was 67 and it came about because the Australians recognised what they had to do, how important it was to make their way towards 300 in the first innings after they had been sent in to bat, and how necessary it was that at least two batsmen should do well.

Facing a 67-run deficit is one thing, and how you go about combating that in the field is quite another, but what is paramount is that you must maintain some form of attack against the opposition. Unfortunately England's answer was very half-hearted. Michael Atherton had said before the start of the match how important it was that England should not be beaten in the Second Test. Admirable thoughts, sensible too. But it would have been better had he kept them to himself, or at least phrased them without mentioning the possibility of being beaten, because once you talk like that your thinking is always more likely to be defensive. It certainly proved to be so when England went on to the field for the start of the Australian second innings.

For a start, Darren Gough couldn't get an early bowl. He had been England's best and most enthusiastic bowler throughout the series to date and suddenly he was on second change. Very mysterious and very theoretical. When eventually he came on in the nineteenth over he got a good one through Mark Taylor's defence to make even more of a nonsense of the theory of not bowling him with the new ball.

Once again Devon Malcolm had bowled well but without luck, and at the close of play on the third evening the Australians had stretched that first-innings lead of 67 by another 170, England had fallen back on defensive field-settings and time-wasting, and some of their heads were starting to go down. That is not what a captain wants to see with two days to go, nor for even one moment does he wish to see a batsman of quality and determination like David Boon unbeaten at the close of play on 64.

The Australians were in no hurry on the fourth day. The weather forecast was good, that first-innings lead of 67 had become a total lead of 313 by lunch and England were going slower and slower. This always has an effect on the game of the fielding side. I don't like seeing time wasted, but if you are going to do it, then at least try to be clever about the matter. The slow walk up to the bowler, the long-winded discussion with him about field-setting and the slow walk back to your own fielding position are guaranteed to do two things.

First, it puts the spectators offside, and they are quite likely to let you know about it, which is something that happened here. To the captain in the field, that may not be a problem because all spectators are entitled to voice their disapproval after paying their hard-earned cash at the turnstiles, and it is something he can live with. Len Hutton, in 1954–5, never had a problem with it. However, the effect on the team is more marked. They are the subject or subjects of the hooting, they become silently antagonistic to the crowd, and it does then affect their attitude. Their shoulders slope even more and that happened this day in Melbourne. They knew the declaration would be delayed to the Australians' convenience and they were gearing themselves for that. Their cricket fell away.

The Australians, with Boon making his twentieth Test century, played it quietly, as if they knew what was going to happen, although not even the best of mystery writers could have come up with the final denouement. There was one curious aspect of the Australian second innings – or at least it seemed curious to me. I had read about Michael Atherton's refusal to clap an opposition batsman when he reaches 50 or 100 because he considers such an attitude to be soft. I had forgotten about this, but then noticed during Australia's second knock that he had developed into a great clapper of every ball bowled by his own bowlers. This is a modern-day fetish, and a strange one to my way of thinking, because the clapping appears to go on no matter what kind of ball has been bowled. It could be a straight one, it could be a wide one or a nothing ball, but still the clapping goes on. When my eye was caught by this at the start of the Australian second innings, I watched for a time and saw it was happening every ball. To a pattern. Four times each ball. I reckoned that by the time the innings finished Atherton had clapped his bowlers approximately 2,500 times. What's curious about that? He didn't clap David Boon once when he reached his century!

When England began their second innings there were approximately 120 overs to be bowled and something like eight hours of play remaining. When that fourth day concluded England were 79/4, with Gooch, Atherton, Hick and Thorpe despatched, Gatting unbeaten on 23 and Rhodes on 13. It was a wonderful session for Australia. The crowd loved it because Victoria's opening bowler and home-town lad, Damien Fleming, had taken the first two wickets, McDermott had the other two and it was an exciting final two hours. England still needed 309 to win the match, which was out of the question, and it was merely a matter of whether or not they might be able to see it through on the fifth day. That in itself was against all the odds but it needed to be kept in mind in case Gatting set himself to play a long innings. In fact, he lasted just two balls, the whole thing disintegrated, and the team was out for 92 with Australia winning by 295 runs. England were condemned to finding some way of appeasing their supporters, and even those who were not actually supporting them. Craig McDermott took 5/42, Shane Warne, who had been on 0/16, finished with 3/16 for the ninth Test hat-trick by an Australian. England lost 6/13 in the 56 minutes of play and it was one of the most comprehensive wins by an Australian team in years and a real credit to Mark Taylor and his men.

There were various matters raised after England's defeat in this game and they ranged from bitter editorials in the English newspapers to condemnation from supporters who had come out from England to watch the Test series. Among others I was asked if I felt any sympathy for England and there appeared to be some surprise when, after thinking about it, I said, 'No, not much.' I had a great deal of sympathy for them on the score of illness and injury – I had never known anything like it and unfortunately the situation was to become much worse within the next month. Sympathy for that certainly, but not for being outplayed in an Ashes battle.

If this seems a tough stance, bear in mind that I had made my debut in first-class cricket on New Year's Day, 1949, and it was ten years and thirty-five days before I played in an Australian team which won a series against England. Anyone who has gone through that is most unlikely to shed a tear for the opposition in an Ashes battle. I'm very happy to see England play well against every country, and I'm delighted to watch and be enthralled by those series. It would be a little strange though if an Australian, not having won over a ten-year playing span, should suddenly start shedding crocodile tears. Nor do I have any English friends who would want that to happen.

During those ten years and thirty-five days I played in one series when Alec Bedser kept bowling us out, another when Frank Tyson and Brian Statham knocked us over and a third where we couldn't lay a bat on Jim Laker and Tony Lock after we had actually won the Second Test at Lord's on a green-top pitch! In 1954–5, we were bowled out for 184 in the second innings in Sydney to lose the Second Test, 111 in Melbourne in the next Test to lose the match and 111 in the following game to lose the Test series in Adelaide and allow England to retain the Ashes. I closely studied what the opposition had done to us, and how they had done it, and it was to serve me well after I became captain of the Australian team.

At the time, unsurprisingly, there was a great deal of conjecture about the composition of the Australian team. The general feeling was that players like Benaud and others might not be up to Test match standard and there were replacements around who might do a better job. Hence my lack of sympathy for any opposition players who might be having a tough trot. So, feeling sorry about beating England? Ten years and thirty-five days? Steady!

What I am happy to do though is make constructive suggestions in this book and elsewhere which might be of assistance to English cricket because I want to see it brought up to date and to be better and more competitive. Even taking into account the stirring win in the Adelaide Test in 1995, there is no doubt in my mind that the question of the structure of cricket in England needs addressing. The biggest problem is that it will require the counties, all eighteen of them, to make a commitment to the same goal rather than look at the situation through a narrow lens. There needs to be a degree of both selfishness and unselfishness attached to the whole resurgence of English cricket, improving it and at the same time keeping up with modern trends. *The needs of world cricket also have to be addressed but, until England's administrators get it right, world events should take second place.* England's players and administrators need tunnel vision about their own cricket and need to do what is best for it, rather than worry about what might be best for the rest of the world.

Whether England in Australia in 1994–5 deserved the rubbishing they received from their own media is another matter. Times certainly have changed when a newspaper publishes an editorial saying a cricket team should not be allowed back into England because they have been beaten.

Not even in 1954–5 and 1956 did Australia's players receive treatment remotely approaching that!

Reflecting on the Ashes tour after Melbourne, one of the more intriguing aspects of the first two Tests was that Craig McDermott had almost as many wickets as Shane Warne but received only half the publicity. By the time the Third Test was played McDermott had caught up with Warne and then passed him, but not before there was another little backhander for him. It was suggested, in the context of a discussion about McDermott and the Tests already played, that some players needed occasionally to be reminded of their responsibilities to Australian cricket. McDermott is not only a fine fast bowler but he must have a more even temperament than some other fast bowlers I have known over the years if he allowed that one to pass through to the wicket-keeper.

I have seen McDermott in action over the past eleven years in all the Test cricket he has played in Australia and England, plus the tour of the Caribbean in 1991 and South Africa in 1994. His form has not always been top class but then neither was mine when I played. There has not been one occasion where I have thought it necessary to write or say he may have needed a reminder of his responsibilities as an opening bowler for Australia or as an Australian cricketer.

He made his debut in the match against the West Indies in Melbourne on December 22nd, 1984. He took 3/118 and 3/65, made a duck and was launched on what was to be a very good Test career. In that series against the West Indies in 1984, he took ten wickets and it should be borne in mind that this was a very poor series for the Australian players and for Australia as a cricketing country. Then, in that 1994 Melbourne Test, he moved into second place on the all-time wicket-taking list for Australia. Only Dennis Lillee was ahead of him then and his interview with Ian Chappell on Channel Nine Television made it clear that, having just claimed mine, he was after Dennis's scalp as well.

McDermott played in that Melbourne Test because Terry Alderman was omitted and, it turned out later, intending to be on his way to South Africa with an Australian team which was to be captained by Kim Hughes. McDermott suddenly was thrust into the job of opening the bowling in England and he made a very good fist of it, taking four wickets at Headingley in 1985 in his debut against England, and then six in the first innings at Lord's and two in the second, in a match the Australians won by four wickets to take a 1–0 lead in the series. He took four at Trent Bridge, eight in the England innings at Old Trafford, two at Edgbaston and four at The Oval, by which time he was, I should think, close to exhaustion. His first tour had been a busy affair and had indicated to him just how important physical fitness would be in future years. He was fit on that 1985 tour but from then on he worked even harder, sometimes training with and learning from Australian Iron Man, Trevor Hendy, and then using his own scaled-down version of those training techniques as his career unfolded. In that series against England his figures in the six Tests were: 1,406 balls; 21 maidens; 901 runs; 30 wickets; 30.03 average.

That is a lot of work for a young fast bowler making his debut tour and I have always been of the opinion that initially it set back his career, particularly as Australia, after winning at Lord's, then lost the series and the Ashes and went down to an innings defeat in the last of the Tests at The Oval. It was a low point for the players, and for Australian cricket. It wasn't until the 1987–8 summer that McDermott started to recover his bowling poise and really it took until England played in Australia in 1990–1 for him to start into the second phase of his career, which continued against the West Indies in the Caribbean and went through to the day he moved into second place in the Australian wicket-taking table behind Dennis Lillee. His performance in Melbourne was brilliant, one of the best I had seen in years from an opening bowler, and he thoroughly deserved success, as did the Australian team.

For English cricket followers it was a sad week, made worse by the news that Peter May passed away aged sixty-four.

May was the finest batsman produced by England in the fifty years since the end of the Second World War. There have been some other very good ones like Ted Dexter, Ken Barrington, David Gower, Colin Cowdrey, Geoff Boycott, Graham Gooch and Tom Graveney, but May had the edge on all of them.

He was also one of the finest players of legspin bowling in my time in the game. His footwork was excellent, going right back or down the pitch; he was predominantly an onside player but very strong on the offside as well and no more determined batsman ever walked on to a cricket field.

I had my first glimpse of Peter at The Oval when Australia played Surrey in 1953, and Lindsay Hassett told us the youngster clearly was an outstanding batsman. Ray Lindwall was given the job of unsettling him. Five marvellous outswingers and an inswinger failed to make contact with either edge of the bat in Lindwall's first over, and Peter made 0 and 1. He played in the First Test at Trent Bridge but then not again until the Fifth at The Oval when the Ashes were regained for the first time since the Bodyline series.

He was an outstanding captain, overburdened in 1958–9 by incessant media claims that the England side was so strong it could beat the world, let alone puny Australia, and then by media pressure of a different kind which sadly brought premature retirement from the playing side of the game.

No one I ever played against had more determination for England. Ken Barrington always looked as though he was draped with a Union Jack when he walked on to the field; Peter, shy and self-effacing, had no such adornment but he gave a hundred per cent for England every match he played.

He was a great batsman, a wonderful competitor and a credit to the game.

# 6

# Darren Gough, Tufnell's catch of the summer and May and Warne save the Ashes

1994 finished well for Australia and 1995 could not have started in better fashion, with a wonderful game of Test cricket at the Sydney Cricket Ground. Perhaps it was a good omen because 1994 had started with a Test between Australia and South Africa at the SCG, to be followed by two great Tests, one in Johannesburg, the other in Cape Town.

The pitch for the 1995 Test between England and Australia looked a beauty on the opening morning, quite different from that Australia–South Africa match, and the hope was that it would play well. It had the appearance of an SCG pitch of many years ago, certainly not of the one just twelve months earlier. From that point of view it was an important toss for Michael Atherton and Mark Taylor. Atherton won it and, having put Australia in in Melbourne, decided to bat, thereby taking the commonsense course, despite the fact there is always something in the SCG pitch for the bowlers in a New Year Test. In the latter part of December and in January there is a heavy morning cloud cover in the eastern suburbs of Sydney which front the Pacific Ocean, the atmosphere is sticky and humid and the general conditions two miles away at the SCG often make it difficult for the early batsmen in the opening Test match session. Then it will settle down and the spin bowlers often come into their own late in the match.

The Australian selectors have been seeking a new swing bowler to join the opening attack since the retirement of Terry Alderman after the 1993 tour of England. Alderman was an outstanding swing bowler, particularly in English conditions where not only did he bowl excellent outswingers to the right-handers but he had perfected the ball which cut back off the seam into those same right-handers. In 1989 he destroyed Graham Gooch's batting, to the extent that for the Test at Trent Bridge the great England opener let it be known that he wouldn't be averse to having a rest. The selectors gave him one.

Apart from Alderman's excellent bowling, there was also the matter of the special field-placing which Alderman came up with, in conjunction with Australian skipper Allan Border, where the short forward square-leg was moved back a yard and then just past his left shoulder, and in a short mid-wicket position was another fielder, not quite hidden by the first man close in to the bat but it must have been disconcerting to Gooch who was the only batsman it was used against. It all came about because Gooch has a habit, when his feet are not working perfectly, of falling away to the offside in playing his strokes through mid-wicket. The placing of those two men in such positions meant Gooch had to be very careful of the manner in which he played that stroke and it definitely inhibited him. As soon as he stopped playing it, he was then vulnerable to the ball that Alderman brought back off the seam from outside off stump and, with Alderman's hand delivering the ball almost on a line drawn between the umpire's eyes and the stumps at the batsman's end, there were a lot of lbw appeals and successes.

The Australian selectors have had a tough time in trying to find his successor but, in the end, after he rediscovered his outswinger, they went for Damien Fleming. Fleming wasn't in the first flush of youth, and it is true that to find his lost awayswinger he had to go to England to play a couple of seasons of league cricket. It worked and the selectors thought enough of him to send him as a replacement to South Africa at the end of the 1994 tour when Craig McDermott had to return to Australia for a knee operation. Then he went to Sharjah, Sri Lanka and Pakistan and, having had his great success in the Melbourne Test, he was ready to sample the delights of the swinging ball in Sydney after Atherton had made his decision to bat in front of an excellent crowd which later was to grow to 31,317.

Both Fleming and McDermott beat the outside edge several times in the first few overs. Fleming beat Gooch twice and then, with one starting at middle and leg, he turned him around front-on, found the edge and Healy took a good diving catch. There was one run on the board at the time and, with Hick and Thorpe going to McDermott, after 13 overs England were 20/3 and the alarm bells were ringing.

There are some Test match days which will live in the memory for a long time and this was one. Three wickets down for 20 in the first hour, four wickets fell for three runs in the thirty-two-minute session just before stumps were drawn and, in between times, Michael Atherton and John Crawley shared a great partnership. England finished at 198/7. The dressing-room would have been a gloomy place because at one point they must have had high hopes of being 200/3 at the close, and then suddenly it had all gone wrong.

Any thoughts the Australians may have had of bowling England out the next day for the addition of only a few runs disappeared in a blaze of strokeplay from Darren Gough. It was a good combination: Gough, who had already made a great impression on everyone, and Angus Fraser, brought into the Test in place of the injured DeFreitas. Fraser is very tall. When he plays for England he looks taller and broader and gives the impression that he is clad in a Union Jack or the flag of St George. On the first evening he had been involved in a farcical run-out of Steve Rhodes, Fraser playing the ball to the offside, not responding to Rhodes' indication that he was coming for one after Steve Waugh misfielded, then both batsmen, to considerable mirth, were charging towards the same end. Fleming took the return from Waugh, threw to Healy and the run-out was completed. It was comic-strip stuff! It didn't make Fraser feel happy that evening but he set himself to stick around on the second morning and did so.

At the other end Gough hit brilliantly, striking 51 from 56 balls faced. There were one or two odd strokes but his fighting spirit was widely applauded around Australia. It was, I can assure you, widely applauded in England as well. Devon Malcolm made his highest Test match score, 29 from just 18 balls, and Phil Tufnell stayed there while 14 were added for the last wicket. It was stirring stuff and it had another big crowd roaring right from the start of the day. They cheered Fraser off the field, recognising not only a courageous performance of batting from the big man but an intelligent one as well, where he made 27 in two hours and 20 minutes and, in the face of the rain delays, played a passive role when that was just what was wanted. It was 2.05 p.m. before play could get under way after the end of the England innings. Mark Taylor and Michael Slater put four on the board and then the light but very persistent rain didn't stop all day. Play was abandoned at 5.30 p.m., with 224 minutes lost, and we had to wait for the third day for the real sensations of the match.

These took the form of the Australians struggling right from the start: Slater played on to Devon Malcolm; David Boon was bowled not offering a shot; Mark Waugh was well caught by Rhodes off Malcolm.

Michael Bevan was badly out of touch, and with the first ball Fraser bowled around the wicket at him he was caught at slip by Thorpe. Steve Waugh failed to play a shot and was bowled by Gough, and Ian Healy was caught at slip from what was effectively the final ball before lunch. Through all this, Taylor took 62 minutes to get off the mark, was 19 not out and the Australians were 57/6 at the interval.

When Australia had gone down so narrowly against South Africa on the same ground in 1994, Craig McDermott had almost pulled off an extraordinary victory with some very unorthodox batting. Now he did it again after Shane Warne had been dismissed for another duck and Tim May had failed to improve on that score. McDermott strode to the crease with the score at 65/8, and the Australians needed another 45 runs to avoid the follow-on. This was a crucial moment because of the way the weather was behaving, and the weather forecasts indicated there would be something there for the bowlers during the rest of this third day. McDermott stopped all that conjecture in the next hour and the 30 balls he faced. He only made 21* but I doubt if he will ever play a more valuable innings for Australia because a follow-on might have been disastrous. When Mark Taylor was brilliantly out-thought by Darren Gough and caught and bowled off his leg-break, and Damien Fleming lasted only one ball, Australia had saved the follow-on by six runs, and in the final analysis this was to be conclusive, even though there were other matters which were important.

There were some good statistics from the England first innings; some were not so good. Mike Gatting's failure to score was his fourteenth Test match duck, and Mike Atherton's 88 was his eighth score between 80 and 99. He is a batsman who sells his wicket dearly, which is just as it should be, and there are very few more determined openers in the world. In recent times, since becoming captain, he has come up against some of the finest opening bowlers the cricket world has seen in many years and the runs he has made have been of very high value to the team. In 1994 he made more Test match runs, 1,136, than any other player. Devon Malcolm, with his 29, made his highest Test score. Darren Gough was in a losing side which was being pilloried from Bunbury to Breakfast Creek, but had still taken 19 wickets in the series with 6/49 his best return in a Test innings. I hope he is still in the game ten years from now because he is wonderfully refreshing. Very few cricketers are good enough to make a half-century and take five wickets in an innings in a Test match and Gough joined them. In addition, when the Australian second innings began he was on a hat-trick, having dismissed Mark

Taylor and Damien Fleming in successive balls at the end of the first.

For the Australians, Craig McDermott took his twenty-first wicket in the Ashes series, even though we were only in the middle of the Third Test. He also had his twelfth haul of five wickets in an innings, an outstanding effort. It was a performance which put in clear perspective the manner in which Test matches and series are won. You must have a balanced bowling attack and you need to have them firing on all cylinders if you are to come out on top. Australia had McDermott, fast and bowling outswingers; Fleming, medium fast and bowling outswingers; and Warne, spinning away from the right-handers, who took his 300th first-class wicket, which is pretty good for an Australian playing in only his third season of first-class cricket. Tim May was there as well, bowling offspin as a good foil to Warne. Mark Waugh was a very useful fifth bowler. They were performances from men playing in a winning side, or at any rate a winning side up to this third Test match.

On the fourth day it now became urgent for England to finish their innings quickly or declare, to give them enough time to press for victory. Perhaps I'd better rephrase that. *It seemed to me a very urgent matter!* At stumps on day three the England lead was 283 and eventually, next day, the closure came with Graeme Hick on 98 and Graham Thorpe 47. It was a controversial declaration because no batsman has ever before been so close to a century in a Test when the captain has called a halt. Atherton took a lot of criticism for making the decision to deprive Hick of a century.

*None of the criticism came from me.*

On the contrary, I said at the time the batsmen should have allowed Atherton to declare, setting a target of 475 and doing so twenty minutes earlier. In the event the batsmen went too slowly, almost as though they were playing in a county match with a declaration which might have been pre-determined. It seemed a case of okay, let's set them 450 and we'll declare some time before ten past three, to take into account various playing conditions pertaining to intervals. A great lack of imagination was shown and, although no one knew exactly what effect this would have, with weather forecasts as they were, it was essential England have as much time as possible to get through the Australian batting. I have no doubt Atherton was frustrated in the end by Hick's inability to score fast enough to reach his century, but I believe he would have been even more frustrated by Hick's inability to read the game.

It was no coincidence that Alec Stewart was the man deputed to carry out drinks, batting gloves and messages to the batsmen concerning the urgency of the situation. The batsmen didn't completely ignore the instructions, or I assume that to be so, they just didn't realise there was any real urgency attached to them. It becomes much more understandable if you think of the arranged matches which go on in English county cricket and the number of times batsmen are allowed to go on to make a hundred, or even to receive joke bowling to allow them to make a hundred, after which the closure is applied. The facts were that England closed their innings at 2.58 p.m. with the score at 255 for *two* wickets. What they should have been doing was to be quite satisfied with 280 for *eight* wickets, or even all out, and close their innings at 2.38 p.m. Losing another six or eight wickets was of no consequence at all.

The Australians began their innings at 3.08 p.m. on the fourth afternoon, they needed 449 to win and a minimum of 128 overs had been set by the umpires. By the time the day's play was concluded, Australia had wiped off 139 of those runs with a scintillating display of batsmanship from Taylor and Slater. They were batting on what was the equivalent of a third-day SCG pitch which was still good and was likely to be in quite reasonable shape on the final day as well. The light rain which had fallen at different times during the match, the early morning rolling, and a lack of wear and tear on the surface had meant there was very little deterioration, though, as always at the SCG, much depends on how the ball swings; that has little to do with the pitch, other than relating to wear and tear on the ball. On this occasion swing was non-existent. Malcolm, Gough and Fraser were gun-barrel straight from the first ball and Taylor and Slater quickly picked up this little piece of information. They hit straight through the ball when it was pitched up and pulled and forced it away when the bowlers dropped a little short. Once again Gough bowled very well, so too did Tufnell, but Malcolm suffered a little from over-eagerness and wasn't quite able to pitch it as he wanted.

England must have come off the field very disappointed at not having taken a wicket and they might have even felt a little nervous at the thought of Australia on the final day needing only 310 to win. They shouldn't have done. No team with any kind of a half-decent bowling attack and a captain with intelligence at Test level is going to allow the opposition to make 449 to win. Bradman's side in 1948 made 404/3 in less than a day, England having batted on into the last morning before declaring and, even then, in the face of brilliant batting from Bradman and Morris, the delayed declaration didn't work.

Atherton's problem throughout the final day was going to be keeping his tactics up with the play. He needed, in fact, to be a couple of overs ahead of the play, judging what the opposition would be thinking, particularly the moment when Australia would call off the run chase, because from that point it would be all bluff from Mark Taylor's side. There were provisions for extended play, up to one hour of it, if the weather intervened again and certainly the radar screen didn't look good. We have access to radar weather in the commentary box and this day it looked as though there could easily be showers. By the time lunch came along on the final day England had done very well in the saving of the game, not well towards winning it because they hadn't yet taken a wicket. What they had done was restrict Australia to 67 in the full two hours of the first session and that was the absolute end of a victory chase for the Australians.

I have seen many games where the fourth innings has gone well for a time, very few where that impetus is maintained right through the innings for victory. It all comes down to fear. Not physical fear, but fear of losing and fear of the fourth-innings syndrome in a cricket match. It's all right being 448 behind when you start your own first innings, you have a second chance, but to be that many in arrears when you start your second innings is another matter. You have no second chance. It is this psychological block which poses the problems as soon as a wicket falls. Two quick wickets and suddenly there is a mist across your brain as batting captain and you are becoming very nervous.

Michael Slater was the first dismissal of the innings. The man who took the catch was Philip Tufnell; he was fielding at deep square-leg and it was one of the best outfield catches I have seen in years. Tufnell is known as 'the Cat', which could be construed as a contradiction in terms, but it was equally true that he had tried hard and had tightened up his fielding in the four years since Australian audiences last saw him. In 1990–1 there were signs around the ground inviting applications to Phil Tufnell's Fielding Academy but there were none in 1995. When Slater pulled Fraser hard and flat, Tufnell sighted the ball instantly, which is not always easy with a red ball and the background of the Ladies Stand and the Brewongle Stand at the SCG. He then ran twenty yards away from the pitch and slightly to his left but there came an instant when you knew, watching him, that unless he did something out of the ordinary, the ball would elude him.

In fact he did a 'Campese'. David Campese and his 'goose-step' have confused Rugby Union defenders the world over, the only difference here being that Tufnell didn't have time to make that deliberate little hesitation. Hesitation would be fatal. Tufnell took a great leap, propelling himself in part by what looked like a goose-step, and clung on to the ball. Suddenly, this was England's chance.

As soon as David Boon instead of Mark Waugh came through the gate at first wicket down, there was no question the Australians had shut up shop. Would England realise that? Would Atherton get himself two overs ahead of the play? The answer was no but the Australians did con Atherton with their mid-wicket conferences every over, their obvious interest in the electronic scoreboard, and body language which signalled they were still on a chase for runs. The only thing they didn't do was pull out a calculator and start doing their sums. Taylor's only interest was in being there for the second new ball because he had a good idea of the pressure that would be on his team if wickets started to fall. In fact, the Australian captain was the second to go, playing no stroke at Devon Malcolm and having his off stump cartwheeled back near the wicket-keeper. Now there was a problem, accentuated by David Boon's dismissal, followed swiftly by those of Michael Bevan, Steve Waugh and Mark Waugh. The Australians lost 4/24 in 41 balls, 5/27 in 53 balls, and when Ian Healy was caught at the wicket by Rhodes off Fraser, Australia still had to survive another eighteen overs with only three wickets in hand, two of whom were on a pair and the other, Fleming, had lasted one ball in the first innings.

The rain delays, the subsequent calculation of overs, and the ability of the umpires to take the game past 6 p.m. and then have fifteen overs as a minimum from the start of the final hour all added to the tension, as did the decision by umpire Darrell Hair not to call for a television replay for the third umpire to adjudicate on the possible run-out of Mark Taylor. It happened off a ball Taylor smashed away off Fraser on the onside and Devon Malcolm chased. He picked up and threw well, Fraser moved away from the stumps to allow Gooch to take the ball, which he did, and then broke the stumps. I was watching on the monitor in the Channel Nine studio, part of the commentary box, and I said at the time, 'Taylor's in trouble.' It was hardly the kind of prediction which made Old Moore a household name because, unlike Oliver Twist, Umpire Hair didn't bother to ask. There was no call for adjudication and Taylor stayed. This followed a similar happening in an England versus Zimbabwe match in Sydney a few weeks earlier, so it was no wonder the Englishmen were less than pleased. On that occasion Grant Flower was run out but no adjudication was called for. Atherton and England didn't realise at the time what a close shave Taylor had had, but they found out when they went back to the dressing-room. Ray Illingworth had been in the Channel Nine box looking at the replays and, even for a phlegmatic Yorkshireman, he seemed a trifle upset.

I wasn't surprised! There are many aspects of the third-umpire television replay system which require close examination, one of which is when an umpire will call for the adjudication. My fear, which I had expressed earlier, was that the umpires would end up not being needed at all, other than for the most mundane aspects of the play. They would become robots, lose their skills and instincts, so fearful of being shown in error that they would be calling for run-out replays even when the batsman was in by a good two feet. It was a justifiable fear and it merely involved taking the easy way out and making the sign of the television set whenever there was anything remotely possible as a dismissal. It would produce a lower standard of umpiring because umpires would become lazy.

The other extreme was the one we saw in that England–Zimbabwe match mentioned above where England were beaten. The scores were Zimbabwe 205, England 192. There were four double-figure scores in the Zimbabwe innings: Andy Flower 12, Alistair Campbell 23, David Houghton 57 and Grant Flower was 84 not out. He batted right through the innings. He was also run out for 26 in the incident mentioned above. It wasn't surprising the Englishmen were bitter about losing that match, and no television adjudication with the Taylor incident, because, under instructions from the ICC and the match referee, players are not entitled to ask for the television umpire to be used in a close call. On the one hand the television is the deciding factor, on the other it is no factor and the umpire has the last word even if he is wrong. It needs looking at. Ironically, the Zimbabwe–Flower run-out was effected by a throw from DeFreitas to Gooch; the latter was also the player in the Taylor run-out on the final day of the Test.

There was a further touch of irony immediately after the Test in the ninth Benson & Hedges World Series match between England and Zimbabwe, played at the 'Gabba as the first game in a double-header weekend. In that match the umpires called for television on two close run-outs, both of which were given out, then a close stumping which went the same way when Andy Flower produced a magnificent piece of work. One of the run-outs, that of Neil Fairbrother, was a brilliant exhibition of modern-day television umpiring because Fairbrother was only ambling and, to all intents, had easily made his ground when Heath Streak's throw arrived. Fairbrother, in fact, was out by an inch.

If we are going to have to use electronic aids, then they should be used all the time and, although every situation should be equal in a matter of this kind, there are times when it is even more important that every possible precaution should be taken to ensure both teams have the benefit of the technology. Notably at a crucial moment where one team is striving to stay in the battle for the Ashes. Not to ask for an adjudication in the Taylor instance merely took us to where we were before the technology took over. It was a matter of an appeal being made to the umpire, he said not out and declined to produce the evidence that could have shown the batsman to be out. Taylor batted on for another thirty-five runs, important from the viewpoint of the time used up.

As it happened, a few days later came news of some South African expertise in this area involving the use of new camera equipment and the third umpire with television replays. Ten out of ten to South Africa. To the ACB who have refused to bring in a similar system in Australia, nought out of ten!

It took Atherton far too long to sense that the Australians had called off the chase and to get his players into catching positions. When he did, they put so much pressure on the home side that it needed Shane Warne and Tim May to bat together for 1 hour and 26 minutes, one of the more unlikely scenarios of our time. Atherton tried everything he was allowed but there was not the slightest doubt that the late finish and the poor light cost England a major chance. It meant Devon Malcolm could not be used in the latter part of the day and the early evening, that Darren Gough had to be taken off, so too Angus Fraser, and in the end the overs were bowled by Phil Tufnell, Graeme Hick and Graham Gooch. It's not possible to say that Warne, May, McDermott and Fleming would have been bowled out by the faster men but I believe there was a good chance of that happening. All part of the game though and it underlined what a sensible Playing Condition is in operation in Australia these days in connection with the light. It is, in fact, originally an English Playing Condition with which I was very, very impressed when I was working with the BBC in England and first saw it in operation. Whereas the umpires used to have no scope for common sense, only an arbitrary decision to make, now provision is made for the type of bowler operating at the time.

The Playing Condition is related to Law 3.8 and it says, as an addition to the Law:

The umpires will only suspend or continue to suspend play for bad light when they consider there is *a risk of serious physical injury to the batsman*. Among the facts to be considered are background, sight-screens and type of bowling. Before deciding to suspend play, or not to resume play after an interval on account of bad light (but for no other reason), the umpires shall establish whether the captain of the batting team (the batsmen at the wicket may deputise for their captain) wishes to continue in unfit conditions; if so, his wishes shall be met.

Former New South Wales Cricket Association Chief Executive, Bob Radford, was the one to whom I first mentioned it and he pressed hard for this to become an Australian Playing Condition. Eventually it was adopted.

It allowed 26,000 spectators to stay to the end of the match, or the two ends of the match to be more precise, and millions of television viewers to watch. It is a great Playing Condition, and should be made a Law of the game as soon as possible, and on this occasion it was very sensibly administered by the umpires. It must have been very frustrating for England not to be able to use their pacemen, but had they originally been able to put a more balanced bowling attack into the field in this Test, they would have had more of a chance of winning in the prevailing circumstances.

For two lower-order batsmen to bat as long as May and Warne did was remarkable. To do this when each of them was on a 'pair' was quite a feat. Just getting off the mark was the first requirement! Warne and May batted extremely well and, when the final over of the fifteen was bowled, they were overjoyed at having batted together and been successful in retaining the Ashes for Australia. Warne faced 59 balls and batted 86 minutes, May had 64 balls and went through 64 minutes, and they worked out their own plan to keep England at bay. They knew the faster men couldn't come back until the light improved so the bowlers they would be up against would be any combination of Tufnell, Hick, Gooch, Atherton, who can bowl legspin but has had a bad back, and Gatting who bowls medium pace.

They decided, as far as possible, to stay at their own end, May at the Southern or Randwick end and Warne at the Paddington or Members' end. It worked perfectly and one of the reasons it worked was that England didn't use their heads to break it up. Once again, slow thinking. They bowled Tufnell from the Members' end all the time, May kept thrusting his pad forward and the umpire kept saying not out. What should have been done was to switch Tufnell to the Southern end as an experiment to have a go at Warne and to test out what Umpire Bucknor thought about the provisions of the lbw Law as it related to batsmen not playing a stroke. After all, the Law was brought in so that batsmen could be and would be penalised if they played the ball with their pad instead of the bit of wood they had been given as an implement with which to defend their stumps. I'd have thought Atherton's memory-bank would have produced his own dismissal in Melbourne, and one or two others which indicated different umpires might easily have different interpretations of that aspect of the lbw Law.

Some of the players were shaking hands on their way off the field and for some reason the tractors and ground staff were on when Michael Atherton, I suspect slightly wearily, and with rightful annoyance, called the umpires' attention to the fact that there was still one over to go. The fifteen overs minimum had certainly been bowled but had been bowled in 59 minutes, so there was still one over to go, which assumed even more importance because the last ball of the previous over had been a perfectly straightforward catch from Warne to Malcolm at mid-off. Malcolm dropped it and at the time it didn't seem to matter because the match was over, or so the umpires said. They were wrong and, had Malcolm held the ball, then McDermott, Fleming and May had to survive the proper last over. What would have happened had Malcolm and everyone else not thought the game was effectively finished with the final ball of that so-called last over? I don't know, nor does anyone else, but it is not because of the glorious uncertainty of cricket that we are unable to answer.

There shouldn't be uncertainty of the kind we had there with the incorrect drawing of stumps and, as well, what on earth were those tractors doing on the arena and out at the pitch square before the players had left the field? It totally detracted from the enjoyment of 26,000 spectators providing a standing ovation and paying homage to the England team, and to the Australian batsmen, for a wonderful cricket match. When Tim May was asked about it after the game he was quoted as saying the advice he had been given about the overs could have been very costly. Too right it could.

Ruminating on it later, if I had told anyone that a thrilling Test match would be turned by a stunning catch by Phil Tufnell, they would have considered I had, at the very least, been affected by the sun. There was, in fact, no better catch taken all summer, certainly no pair of clutching fingers will take a more important one than Tufnell's effort which broke the double-century stand between Mark Taylor and Michael Slater. This was a classic Test match. It is difficult to recall many games where a team, 65/8 at one point and then just avoiding the follow-on, found themselves in with a very rough chance of an historic victory and finally managed to retain the Ashes only through a partnership of more than an hour between a pair of late-order spin bowlers. It was a match where there were little stories inside the main story all the way through, none better than the fact that it was Angus Fraser who bowled England close to a sensational win, a great tale because he wasn't in the original touring party, his call to arms being brought about through the shin soreness sustained by Martin McCague.

It took a long time for the penny to drop with Michael Atherton that the Australian batsmen had decided not to continue the chase for runs after the rain. In fact, Taylor and Boon did something of a con-job on the England captain but he should have been far more alive to the situation. Atherton's main memory of the game might well be that the light deteriorated to the extent where he had to take off Darren Gough and couldn't bowl Devon Malcolm at all in the final hour. This was exactly the same situation which cost New Zealand a Test against England at Lord's in July 1994, when New Zealand captain Ken Rutherford had to take off his brilliant potential matchwinner, Dion Nash, who was scything through the England batting.

Darren Gough had a great game in Sydney and, deservedly, was named Man of the Match, but there were many heroes in this SCG game. Not least were the spectators, particularly the 26,000 who attended on the last day and braved the rain and the delays.

A total attendance of 127,000 was excellent and the cricket matched the enthusiasm of the spectators. Australia deserved to retain the Ashes because they had played the best cricket in the first three Tests; England could only rue their uneven performances. The fielding on the final day, apart from Tufnell's sensational catch, was very ordinary indeed. Fumbles, stopping the ball with the foot instead of the hand, missed chances and general sloppiness all served to highlight the athletic difference between the teams. And the ICC have a job to do with their third umpire and the calling of television replays for adjudication – among the oddest things I saw in the 1994–5 season in Australia involved the failure of Darrell Hair to call for replays for those Taylor and Flower run-outs.

John Reid may already have solved that but we shall have to wait and see. After the Test the match referee said he had spoken with Atherton and entirely agreed with him that if there is any doubt then the television should be called upon. 'It removes all the doubt and it takes the heat off everyone, not least of all the umpires themselves. If it's close then go to the replay. That will be spelt out in very clear terms every game from now on.' A separate issue to be reported to the ICC would be the premature calling-off of the Test.

No one should cavil at Reid's opinion that Atherton's response was justified, least of all the umpires. Players are under strict rulings from the ICC these days, so there is no reason why the umpires controlling them should not be in the same position. There should definitely be some method introduced by the ICC to ensure that if the third umpire can see an error has been made, he is able to be in communication with the umpire on the field. Otherwise, why have the technology?

# 7

## England attack at last and win

If Michael Atherton thought life and luck were about to change after the dramatic events at the SCG, he was in for a rude shock when he arrived in Adelaide for the fourth of the Ashes battles of the summer. The one thing he needed was a full squad from which to choose; what he got was a restricted choice with Graeme Hick left out of the match on the first morning with a back problem. Hick was diagnosed as having a prolapsed disc and he went home to England before the tour was completed, yet another addition to the injuries and illnesses which had beset Atherton and the England side. The following list highlights the degree of misfortune which the team suffered:

Michael Atherton (back spasm, missed a World Series match)
Alec Stewart (right index finger broken three times)
Graeme Hick (prolapsed disc)★
Graham Thorpe
Mike Gatting
Graham Gooch
Steve Rhodes
Phillip DeFreitas
Darren Gough (stress fracture left foot)★
Martin McCague (stress fracture shin)★
Phil Tufnell
Shaun Udal (side strain)★
John Crawley (calf injury, missed a Test and World Series match)
Craig White (rib cartilage damage)★
Devon Malcolm (chicken-pox, missed First Test)

Joey Benjamin (shingles, missed World Series matches)
Neil Fairbrother (shoulder dislocation)★★
Angus Fraser (played in Tests)★★
Chris Lewis (played in Tests)★★
Jack Russell★★
Mark Ramprakash (played in Test)★★
Mark Ilott★★

★ Went home to England.
★★ Replacement player.

That is a remarkable list and I have never before seen anything like it
happen to a touring team in Australia. When researching this book
though I came across some information concerning Gubby Allen's tour
of Australia in 1936–7 which indicates that most things which happen
in cricket have, to some extent, happened previously. This was the tour
where England won the opening two Tests of the five-match series and
then lost the next three, the only time this has occurred in the history
of Tests, and it is unlikely ever to happen again now pitches are
covered.

There were seventeen players on that tour of Australia which began
in Perth and their catalogue of injury and illness problems looked like
this:

Gubby Allen (muscle strain)
Walter Robins (badly broken finger in Perth, first match)
Bob Wyatt (broken arm in Adelaide, third match)
Ken Farnes
Walter Hammond
Hedley Verity
Maurice Leyland
Les Ames (back trouble first match in Perth, then illness)
Bill Voce (strained chest muscle, Melbourne, later fit for all Tests)
Charlie Barnett
Joe Hardstaff
Stan Worthington
Bill Copson (hamstring problems)
Jim Sims
Arthur Fagg (rheumatic fever, returned to England)
Laurie Fishlock (broken bone in hand in Adelaide, January)

George Duckworth (fractured finger in Perth, then broke a finger
again in Sydney)
Tommy Wade (replacement player-wicket-keeper)
Rupert Howard (team manager who played in Geelong because so
many players were injured or ill)

It doesn't look as imposing a list as Atherton's litany of woe, but I
can imagine the problems, particularly as travel in those days was by
ship and it was impossible to send replacement players. Wade, the
Essex wicket-keeper, was already in Australia on private business
when he was called up to solve the problems caused by Ames's
illness.

For Atherton, in 1994–5, it wasn't quite a question of whichever of
his team could stand up would make it on to the Test match field, but
once or twice it wasn't far short of that. In the end Adelaide was a
reprieve for Mike Gatting who had gone through a short horror stretch
with the bat and was resigned to sitting out the Adelaide game. When
Hick had to pull out Gatting immediately volunteered to bat at number
three in his place, although in the earlier Tests he had been going in in
the middle of the batting order. Gatting is one of the great competitors in
the game and, even when the team were struggling in Australia, he and
Graham Gooch, the two oldest players in the side, were also two of the
most enthusiastic and hardest working. They both announced their
retirement from Test cricket in Perth. The reward for Gatting in
Adelaide was to make the 200th century for England in Ashes battles.
It was also ten years between Test centuries for him against Australia, his
previous three-figure score in an Ashes match being at Edgbaston in
1985.

The first thing for Atherton was to win the toss, which he did, the
second was to make a good start with Graham Gooch, and they did that
as well with an opening stand of 93. Gooch underlined the fact that
when luck is running with you, you have a chance of getting the benefit
of any umpiring decisions. His luck had been out and was so again when
Fleming had him caught at second slip by Mark Waugh. Atherton and
Gatting played with great determination until a fierce storm hit the
fringes of the ground and 93 minutes of play were lost. The winds were
so strong that the covers, when they were brought out to protect the
square, could only be held down by the ground staff throwing
themselves on top of the plastic sheets.

Gooch batted well for his 47 and Atherton once again was very determined, getting right behind every ball and concentrating on making sure the Australian bowlers were unable to break through. There are two matters he will need to address as a batsman: firstly that he has now been dismissed nine times between scores of 80 and 99, a clear indication that something goes wrong as he nears a century. There is nothing at all wrong with his application; he is an old-style opener and a very good one and, as a side issue, there could hardly be a more vivid contrast with the Australian opener, Michael Slater, who goes at the bowling right from the start of the innings.

The second point Atherton might do well to consider is his inability to keep the ball down when playing the hook shot and the leg-glance, the latter against the ball bouncing around hip height. It is a fair point to make that it is difficult to keep the ball down when hooking; it is the pull shot where the ball is able to be smashed into the ground and hit in front of square-leg. The hook provides problems of a different kind, depending on the height of the ball when it reaches the batsman. If it is above his head then any upward swing of the bat must hit the ball in the direction of the man at deep fine-leg or, these days, either of the two men positioned behind square-leg and just in from the boundary edge. Against the faster bowlers Atherton is definitely a candidate for being caught in that area. He has great difficulty in controlling the stroke and he will need either to learn how to control it or cut it out altogether. He might even be a compulsive happy hooker, as has been the case with quite a few of us over the years. However, unless he is to continue to light up the eyes of pace bowlers the world over, he needs to make a decision on this. When McDermott bowled some short-pitched stuff at him in Brisbane he couldn't control the stroke, sometimes miscueing it near Healy and then eventually into Healy's gloves. Twice in Perth he was caught down the legside, glancing. In Adelaide he miscued some short balls from McDermott but got away with it. Then, after he had made his 80, Fleming put a second man back on the boundary and bowled a couple of short balls to Atherton, the second of which he hit straight to David Boon, placed quite obviously and deliberately in the squarer of those two positions.

When in 1991 David Gower was under the hammer on the same ground for throwing away his wicket by being caught by a man specially positioned for the stroke, he was heavily criticised. Atherton wasn't four years later. In fact, sympathy came his way for being unlucky enough to be out again in the eighties. I doubt if he will have had much sympathy for himself. He will have known he fell for the three-card trick and, unfortunately, it was one where the cards had been turned up for all, including Atherton, to see. It was no less culpable than Gower's rush of blood four years earlier.

Mike Gatting's tenth Test match hundred was a hard-fought affair. The batsman needed to battle with himself and his form and footwork as much as with the Australian bowlers for the early part of his innings. Later he played some very good shots and showed great temperament for 77 minutes when the Australians tied him down in the nineties. It was agonising when he was stuck on 99 for 29 minutes and eventually, when the run did come, he was very close to running out his partner, Phillip DeFreitas. It was a thick edge down into the gully area where Steve Waugh threw himself to the left, brilliantly gathered in the ball, rolled over and threw at the stumps, missing by a matter of an inch or two with the batsmen having only just crossed.

That would have been a ludicrous run-out but no more so than when Gatting 'did' Angus Fraser a little later in one of the more comical efforts of this or any other season. Peter McIntyre was hit through mid-off and Glenn McGrath chased the ball. Fraser got a good start on Gatting who waited to see if the fielder would get across to the ball and then found himself valiantly trying to make up five yards. McGrath chased and picked up the ball then threw a magnificent return to the bowler, McIntyre, and then stood watching, hands on hips, as the ball zoomed on its way. Gatting's problem was that when he turned and looked up, McGrath was still standing, hands on hips, down at long-off. Gatting, in that fraction of a second, reasoned that something must have happened to McGrath and he had been unable to throw – the other explanation, that McGrath had already thrown, hardly seemed a possibility – so Gatting set out to beat the throw from that long part of the ground. The ball was half way to the bowler's end by the time Gatting and Fraser were beginning negotiations in mid-pitch; he then tried to send Fraser back but it was all too late and Fraser sacrificed his wicket for his county captain and the senior batsman of the pair. It was chaotic! Gatting's innings ended when he sliced McIntyre to Steve Waugh behind point; it was his tenth Test century, his fourth against Australia, his second at the Adelaide Oval and his first Test century since August 11th, 1987, when he made 150* against Pakistan at The Oval. England had again collapsed in disastrous fashion, losing 3/3 in 11 balls and, in all, their last seven wickets went for 67 runs.

Michael Slater and Mark Taylor again got Australia away to a great start and were 81/0 at the close of play on the second evening, looking very confident and comfortable. This pairing has been one of the real strengths of Australian cricket in the past two years and in this innings they once again shared a century partnership. It does wonders for the team when the openers play in this fashion and, since they have been together, this is the list of half-century partnerships they have registered for Australia.

| *1993 v. England* | | *1993–4 v. New Zealand* | |
|---|---|---|---|
| Old Trafford | 128 | WACA | 198 |
| Lord's | 260 | Bellerive | 65 |
| Trent Bridge | 55 | 'Gabba | 80 |
| Headingley | 86 | | |

| *1993–4 v. South Africa* | | *1994–5 v. Pakistan* | |
|---|---|---|---|
| MCG | 57 | Rawalpindi | 176 |
| Adelaide | 83 | Lahore | 97 |
| Durban | 55 | | |

| *1994–5 v. England* | |
|---|---|
| 'Gabba | 99 and 109 |
| MCG | 61 |
| SCG | 208 |
| Adelaide | 128 |
| Perth | 75 |

At the end of the Ashes series they had nineteen other partnerships as well and it is interesting to note their efforts in both the first and second innings of matches. Generally there will be more life in the pitch for the bowlers on the first morning of a Test and the openers' job will be correspondingly more difficult. Against that is the possibility, if they bat second, that the pitch could be better than on the opening day. Their average first innings partnership was just under 71 runs, and second innings 57, both very good, and overall they stood at 65 per partnership. In this game in Adelaide they put on 128 before Slater was well caught by Atherton at second slip trying to play a back cut off DeFreitas. Almost straight away England had David Boon for a duck from a good outswinger from DeFreitas and the Australian surge was halted.

Test cricket is a matter of exciting fluctuation though it can also be a matter of dull and predictable play, but there was nothing of the latter on this third day. From the time Boon was dismissed the Australians gradually took control. Taylor continued to bat very well, so too Mark

The Benauds raising a glass to, and having a laugh with, Sir Garfield; Gary himself raising a laugh with Brian Lara after the young batsman made his 375 in Antigua, and no laughs at all for the Durham bowlers on the receiving end of the 501* made by Lara in June 1994 at Edgbaston. 501* out of 810, what a performance!

Monty Noble (*above left*) shows the remarkable grip he invented for the ball which swerved, 'with a drop in it' as well. This was along the lines of the baseballer's outcurve drop. He wrote about it as far back as 1926, then Clarrie Grimmett advanced his own theories on swerve and Shane Warne is the latest to add to the problems of the batsmen in this way. Grimmett was the greatest of all legspinners, but Warne is the best young one I have seen.

Alan Davidson (*above right*), the bowler I was very happy to have at the other end. Batsmen were not quite so happy. They were always pleased to get away from 'Davo's' dangerous swing and movement off the seam. Legspin at the other end seemed like a holiday.

Clarrie Grimmett (*left*) in the Australian touring side in 1934. In the first game I ever saw at the Sydney Cricket Ground he took 6/118 and I was one of 30,400 spectators. Bill O'Reilly said that if Grimmett had been in the Australian team on tour in England in 1938, then Australia would have won. Grimmett seems to have been many years before his time with his analytical approach to swerve and spin.

Imran Khan (*above, both arms raised*) was one of the finest all-round cricketers the world has seen and an inspiring leader. This late inswinger accounted for Bill Athey during the Headingley Test of 1987, won so brilliantly by Pakistan.

Rod Marsh (*below left*) is a great and most beneficial influence at the Adelaide Commonwealth Bank Cricket Academy. When England's cricketers were going through their darkest moments in Australia in 1994–95, there were incessant calls for an Academy, or two or three, to be started up in the United Kingdom. England's Adelaide victory put that on hold for a time.

Sir Richard Hadlee (*below right*) was eventually overtaken by Kapil Dev as the greatest wicket-taker in Test history. Kapil remains the only player to make 5,000 Test runs and take 400 Test wickets. Hadlee's performance in the New Zealand side over the years was outstanding and it was difficult to understand why he never captained the national team. He was the first ever to reach 400 wickets when an outside edge from this outswinger was caught by Andrew Jones in Christchurch. The batsman was Sanjay Manjrekar.

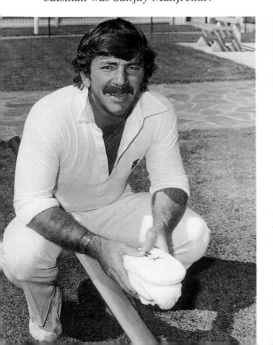

This is the first scoring stroke of Sachin Tendulkar during his remarkable 119* for India against England at Old Trafford in 1990. An unusual position for his right hand, almost on the blade. He is one of the most gifted young batsmen the cricket world has seen in many years and bowlers will have much to ponder when they come up against him or Brian Lara.

Eddie Hemmings was the bowler, Kapil Dev the batsman. Narendra Hirwani, the non-striker, was known as a genuine number 11 and there were 24 runs needed for India to save the follow-on at Lord's in 1990. Kapil Dev did it with four successive blows over the boundary at the Nursery End.

Wasim Akram (*right*) is one of my favourite cricketers. He is a great allrounder, a wonderful opening bowler with the ability to cut through the top half of the opposition batting, a fine fieldsman and one of the best ball-strikers in the game. When he concentrates more on his batting he will set new records.

Although Shane Warne has taken many of the headlines in the past few years, two other legspinners, Mushtaq Ahmed of Pakistan and Anil Kumble of India, have performed very well. Mushtaq is a fine bowler whose wrong'un bewildered English batsmen in the World Cup Final in Melbourne, Kumble is tall and is very accurate. Here (*below*) he bowls John Morris for 13 in the Old Trafford Test of 1990.

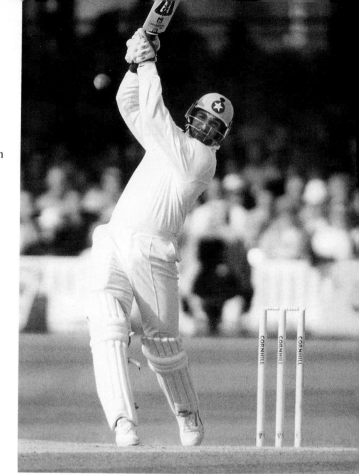

Cause and Effect. The **cause** (*above*) was the first ball Fanie de Villiers bowled at number eleven Devon Malcolm at The Oval in 1994. It smashed against Malcolm's helmet and broke off the piece of metal seen hitting the ground between the two players. The **effect** (*below*) was devastating, Malcolm taking nine wickets in the following South African innings, one of whom was Hansie Cronje who did most things right, but was very late with the almost perfect stroke.

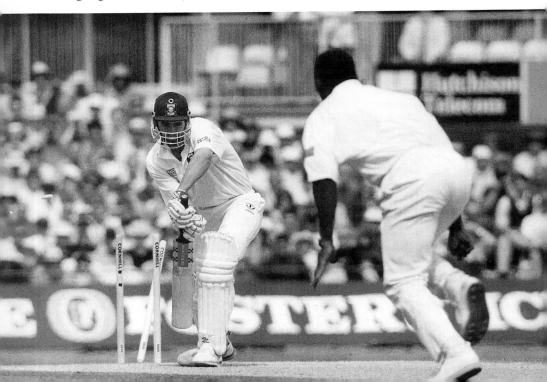

I love this shot of Richie Richardson batting in the Caribbean. He is inches off the ground in playing it, his tongue is tucked in his cheek, his eyes are following the ball to the cover point boundary, and although the ball was hit with tremendous power there is not one ounce of brute force in the stroke.

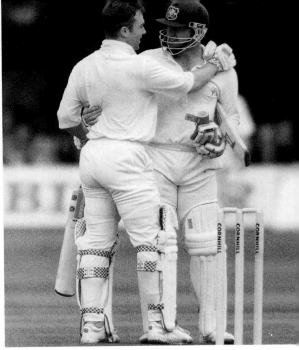

Michael Slater's greatest moment (*above left*), a century on his first appearance in a Test at Lord's. He is pictured seconds after he had acknowledged the standing ovation and kissed the Australian coat of arms on his helmet. It was one of his best innings, but no better than his brilliant performance at the 'Gabba where he tore into the England bowlers on the opening day of the First Test of the 1994–95 Ashes series.

The Australians have tried, as often as possible, to use a right-hand–left-hand opening batting partnership. The first thing you need is quality and there is an abundance of that with Mark Taylor and Michael Slater (*above right*), whose differing styles have confused many opposition new ball bowling attacks.

Steve Waugh has been an outstanding cricketer for Australia in recent years. Alec Stewart keeps on eye on him at Headingley in 1993 (*below*) in the course of his 157* which helped Australia win the match and retain the Ashes.

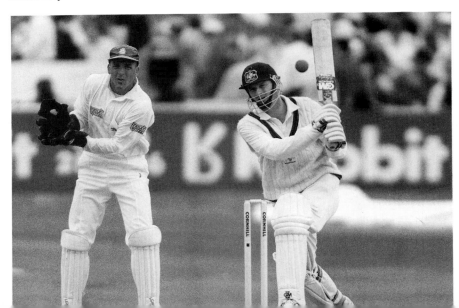

Waugh, but then suddenly three wickets fell for 30, the last of them, the fifth, twenty minutes before tea. Now there was a problem for Australia. At the tea interval Greg Blewett, making his debut in Test cricket, was 8★ and Ian Healy, that stalwart of so many tough Test match situations, was 1★ and neither had looked at all comfortable although they had faced only four overs to that point. The pressure was on.

No one enjoys a situation of that kind more than Healy and no one takes better advantage of any frailties the opposition might show. It was one of the best sessions I have seen from an Australian team in years and one of the worst of the tour from England – two hours of cricket where they completely lost the plot. Once again it was to do with an inherent defensive line of thinking where England, far too often, believe that by slowing down a game they will be able to win. We saw it from Atherton in Melbourne, then in Sydney and then again in Adelaide. It did nothing at all to help them, and was only a hindrance.

It all began in the fourth over after tea when Blewett and Healy each took three runs off DeFreitas, and in the next they made eleven. From that point something seemed to happen to England's thinking and they went slower and slower in the field, becoming correspondingly sloppy, and by the time drinks were taken after 14 overs, 61 runs had been made. Not an insurmountable problem, but then, in the next period of play, England slowed it down even more. Their 22 overs, which they had to bowl to catch up on the ridiculously slow rate earlier in the day, cost 98 and in the final session Australia had made 159. When the players walked from the field after almost half an hour of extra time, Australia were 394/5, Blewett was 91★ and Healy 72★, the lead was 41 and Australia still had five wickets in hand.

Blewett batted magnificently. He had impressed me in the Australian XI game at Bellerive in Hobart earlier in the summer and it was a plus mark for the Australian selectors that they had pulled him from Sheffield Shield to play in that match. That's why it is of such importance for the Australian XI matches to be encouraged in Australia, despite the fact that the programme is so crowded these days. Blewett also played in the Benson & Hedges World Series competition in Australia in 1994–5, though only in one of the Australian teams, and looked an interesting prospect, even to the extent of bowling well, using an inswinging yorker to advantage. In the Tests, however, his bowling was more exposed because there was no restriction applying that he had a maximum of ten overs to bowl; in the Tests the batsmen didn't have to be on the attack every ball. He was put under pressure to bowl accurately and it didn't work out. That is understandable. He's not regarded as a bowler although he is a very good young batsman and, in a sense, it is unfair to expect him to do the job done for so long by Steve Waugh, desperate though the Australian selectors may be.

Everything was put into clearer perspective the following morning by Devon Malcolm and Angus Fraser who ripped through the Australians, taking the last five wickets for just 25 runs. Malcolm took 3/8 in 29 balls and Fraser 2/17, also from 29 balls. It was a sensational collapse. It brought England back into the game and, with a deficit of 66 and with the Australians condemned to bat last, though on what was still a good pitch, it looked as if we could still be in for an excellent contest.

Graham Thorpe was the man who made that a certainty with a little gem of an innings after England had lost their first three wickets for 83 which gave them an overall lead of only 17. Thorpe came in at the fall of Mike Gatting's wicket for a duck, a sense of *déjà vu* for Gatting after his first innings century, and exactly what happened to him in 1987 when he last played at the Adelaide Oval: a century in the first innings and a duck in the second. Thorpe started to play his strokes right from the start and as usual he was very strong square of the wicket on either side. He is a fine player and I have been very impressed with his cricket since I saw him make a century on his debut against Australia at Trent Bridge in 1993. This was a good innings: he carried the attack to the Australian bowlers, forced Taylor to make swift bowling changes and generally took the game away from Australia with excellent commonsense batting. It was also the type of batting England had needed throughout the series, having fallen somewhere between attack and defence. He handled Shane Warne well and, with his runs coming from only 117 balls, suddenly opened up a whole new perspective for England.

His partnership with Graham Gooch was worth 53, that with John Crawley 71, and it was something of an anti-climax when Thorpe played a perfectly solid-looking cover-drive to McDermott and was caught at cover-point by Warne. He didn't quite get over the ball in playing the drive but he hit it well enough that, had Warne not been in the way, it would certainly have gone to the boundary. Thorpe's was the fourth wicket to fall and a very welcome one it was for Australia because now the soft middle order was exposed. Steve Rhodes, who can bat well but hadn't done so far, lasted only 8 balls, Chris Lewis made 19 and they fell to Warne and Fleming respectively, Rhodes playing a stroke we would all like to forget and Lewis unluckily playing on. This brought in DeFreitas, who I think is a very good cricketer but one whose batting at times puts him in the category of an under-achiever – plenty of ability but not always the common sense to go with it, though I had seen him play beautifully in a partnership with Darren Gough against South Africa at The Oval only a few months previously. On this fourth evening he stayed around with Crawley and they had added 39 by the close of play, not in any startling fashion but with good strokeplay and some sensible running between the wickets.

That gave England a lead of 154 and they still had four wickets in hand and, in the preamble to the Channel Nine telecast on the final morning, I said if they could put together another 70, with the time taken up in doing that, they would set a good target for Australia, something like 225 from 65–70 overs.

DeFreitas soon made a nonsense of that by playing one of the best innings imaginable in the circumstances of the match, a brilliant 88 in all, and he added 68 in the morning session before being dismissed after an hour and a quarter. It wasn't even the runs he made but the manner in which he struck the ball which so captivated the crowd and the millions of television viewers around the world. England added not the 70 runs I had been talking about but 108 in the morning session, more importantly taking only 82 minutes to do it. This was perfect as regards the timing of the end of the innings and it meant they had a minimum of 67 overs to bowl at Australia which gave them a chance of victory, though it is unusual for a team to be bowled out in that number of overs unless they have decided to make a real bid for a victory of their own. The surprise packet for Australia had been Mark Waugh who took 5/40 from 14 overs; Shane Warne and Craig McDermott had two wickets each and Damien Fleming one. The latter also had problems with a hamstring and was later to be left out of the Australian team for the final Test in Perth, though there was no doubt about his selection for the tour of the West Indies, providing he was fully fit. Australia began their run chase 28 minutes before lunch and they moved along smoothly enough up to the interval with 16 from the seven overs bowled, nothing too ambitious about it but enough to set the scene for an exciting run chase in the afternoon.

Already more spectators were pouring through the turnstiles at the Adelaide Oval, rightly sensing a great afternoon's entertainment, but perhaps not quite in the manner they anticipated. In the space of three overs after the luncheon interval Devon Malcolm bowled England into a winning position, taking the wickets of Mark Taylor, Michael Slater and Steve Waugh, and any thoughts the Australians might have harboured of winning disappeared very quickly. Malcolm bowled very fast and with great hostility and no one was at all comfortable against him.

It is a source of wonder to many Australians that he should not be an automatic selection for England teams when he is fully fit. I suppose it is fair to say it is Australians who have seen him at his best in recent years though perhaps not in his debut Test against Australia, at Trent Bridge in 1989, when Mark Taylor and Geoff Marsh shared a 329-run partnership for the first wicket and he finished with 1/166. When he came to Australia in 1990–1 he took most wickets in the Test series and then he bowled well against Allan Border's team in the final Test at The Oval in 1993 where England won. In between times the England selectors have left him out of teams, questioned his ability, got his name wrong and generally treated him like a bowler who is useless to them unless the moon is in the right quarter. I would have thought a better plan would have been to say he is a potential matchwinner and that every possible move should be made to bring him to a peak of form and keep him there.

When I once mentioned that line of thinking to an English administrator he didn't think it to be such a good idea because, in a sense, it would be treating Malcolm as a special case and it might create problems with other players who could be seen not to be receiving the same preferential treatment. I pointed out that the reason I would do it was that I didn't care if anyone else's nose was out of joint, my main aim was to win a Test match. He looked at me for a time and said, rather sorrowfully I think, 'Yes, I know that,' and I was instantly aware that we were unlikely to be on the same wavelength regarding the tunnel vision required to come out on top in Ashes battles. Even after Malcolm's success in this Adelaide game and after he bowled well without any luck in Perth, English cricket followers were saying to me that yes, Malcolm had done well but you couldn't really rely on him all the time. I just went away shaking my head because I would have wanted Malcolm regularly bowling at that pace in my Test team. I reckon I would soon have had him doing what I wanted: I would programme him so that he bowled very fast just outside off stump which, on his angle, would have him hitting middle and off, and generally keeping the ball on an awkward length for the batsman. 'Bowl fast' would be the first instruction. The England selectors will be confident they have given Malcolm every chance but I have a much higher regard for his ability than they do.

Later in the afternoon he came back for a final spell when the Australians were threatening to save the game, and trapped Peter

McIntyre lbw at the Cathedral end with just 35 balls remaining. It was fitting he should have taken the last wicket as his extra pace and hostility had turned the match for England. In fact, Malcolm had by the end of the match taken 7/14 in 57 balls in three phases – at the conclusion of the Australian first innings, at the start of the second and with the last ball of the match. It was a great effort from the fast bowler.

The final day of this Test was wonderful to watch. It had the brilliant batting from DeFreitas in the morning session, then the breakthrough from Malcolm and later from Chris Lewis and a wicket each to Fraser and Tufnell. Tufnell's wicket, that of Mark Waugh, was a curious affair: the batsman played the ball down towards Gatting at short-leg, the ball bounced up, Gatting caught it and held it in the air to a chorus of appeals. It was said that the ball had hit Gatting's foot and bounced straight up in the air, but it was a very brave decision by the umpire at the bowler's end. The ball was struck quite firmly, didn't appear to hurt Gatting at all and on none of the replays did it show that it had bounced directly off the foot. Nor did it show how the umpire at the bowler's end could have seen what happened. At 83/8 the Australians were just about gone and forgotten, still with 34 overs minimum to be bowled, and Ian Healy, who came out to bat after Mark Waugh had been given out, only had Damien Fleming and Peter McIntyre to stay with him. Fleming did a very good job, lasting for 66 balls and almost two hours, by the end of which time England just had an edge of panic in their cricket. Fleming had been playing the pull or hook shot with a lot of luck and a little skill, but there always looked to be a chance of trapping him with that stroke. In the end Lewis dismissed him with a short ball which didn't bounce much and would have hit middle stump six inches from the top. Then Peter McIntyre looked absolutely 'plumb' lbw to Malcolm in the final dismissal, although there seemed to be some dismay from McIntyre and Healy when the umpire's finger went up; it may only have been that this signalled the end of the Test and meant a brilliant win for England.

This was a triumph for Michael Atherton and his will to win, and also for the fact that he was able to transmit that to his team. He had called them together on the final morning and said he wanted to go for a win and that sensible attack was the way to do it. He was right, although it is equally true to say there had been several occasions during the series when he and his team went on the defensive rather than on the attack, but no matter. This was a moment to savour, a great performance, and it was very much a case of England having won the match rather than Australia having lost it. There were long and delightful celebrations and

Atherton was quite clear about the fact that now England had a real chance of squaring the series.

There were several little matters to come out of the Test, the first of which was the announcement of the Australian team for the Perth Test. Jo Angel and Brendon Julian were included on their home territory, Damien Fleming was rested because of his hamstring problem and Peter McIntyre was dropped.

Then there was the matter of match referee, John Reid, fining Chris Lewis $A1,600 for pointing Craig McDermott to the pavilion after dismissing him, and issuing warnings to other players about their behaviour.

Michael Atherton was reprimanded for not ensuring his team observed the spirit and the Laws of the game, and he was quoted first of all as saying that John Reid had reprimanded him for not preventing Chris Lewis from pointing Craig McDermott to the pavilion, which Atherton believed would have been quite a remarkable effort as he was fifty yards away from Lewis. Atherton promised he would again impress on his bowlers not to point a dismissed batsman towards the dressing-room in the Fifth Test but he could offer no guarantee that it would not happen:

When you get a situation where you have dismissed a batsman, I don't think you are in such a cool, calculating mood to think about what you're doing. It's an instinctive reaction, a rush of blood, if you like. We knew as soon as 'Lewie' waved McDermott on the way to the pavilion that he would be fined. He was, and that's fair enough. We have no complaints. You are always going to have the odd moment in a game. These things happen on the spur of the moment. It's inevitable.

John Reid is a strong referee and all the players know he's not here for a holiday. But you can't play cricket worrying about the referee. He's been told by the ICC the game needs cleaning up and all the players understand and accept that. I think the England team's discipline over the past few years has been exemplary and the series has been a really well-behaved contest.

The Australians always play their cricket hard and fair and it has been a pleasure to play them and I'd like to think we've tried to play the same way.

Atherton said the threat of further fines, following the $A1,600 penalty imposed on Lewis, hopefully would not prove counter-productive and dilute England's new-found aggression. 'I want England to play aggressive, hard and fair cricket,' he said.

That was straightforward enough and is precisely the way the game should be played. The curious bit came in another conversation to do with over-rates where Atherton was quoted as having deliberately set out to achieve a slow over-rate in the Melbourne Test.

'We slowed it down deliberately in Melbourne and got absolutely hammered for it in the press. And the Australians did the same thing in Sydney but I didn't see too much written about that,' Atherton said. 'It's always used. You're going to get sides taking every advantage they can get.' (The Australians, in fact, were not admonished by the match referee for their over-rates in Sydney.)

It seemed to me to be courting disaster to make it so clear to a match referee that he had been the victim of something like a con-trick. Match referees, like umpires, have long memories.

It's not as though the ICC's match referees have shown themselves to be reticent in handing out various penalties and they see their job as being helpful in ridding the game of bad behaviour. The list of fines for players and teams on the behaviour question is interesting, so too the list of fines that have been handed out to teams for slow over-rates.

John Reid had some good points to make when I talked with him before the Brisbane Test and then again in an interview with Mike Coward in *The Australian* newspaper.

Reid told me he was against the 'sledging' that had been going on in Test cricket. 'I think the spirit of the game has taken a big knock over the last few years,' Reid said. His strongest point was that Test and limited-overs International cricketers are heroes for millions of children and they are copied by youngsters around the world, and bad behaviour was something to which he strongly objected.

He repeated the gist of that in his interview with Coward and added that cricket's act needed to be cleaned up. 'Some parts of the cricket world are worse than others but I think it is coming under control. I'm sorry there is a need for a referee's role but I am happy in it. And I think I can offer something for the betterment of cricket.

'If I'm responsible enough to fine people and perhaps take them out of the game for up to three matches, I'm responsible enough to tell you why,' Reid said. 'I think the public would be more interested in Test cricket if they knew there are people trying to bring out the spirit of the game and bring traditions back into the game.'

I've already said it is my belief that umpires can do the same job as the

referees but to do that successfully they would need the backing of the
ICC and all its individual member countries. Until that happens we will
have referees and it is disturbing that instead of there being fewer
breaches, there seem to be more. A list of these, to the end of the
Australia versus England Perth Test in 1995, can be found in Appendix I
on p. 255. It is quite a list, and it would certainly be better if players and
teams were prepared not to add to it in the immediate future.

In the aftermath of the Adelaide victory for England, it was interesting
to observe how England's cricket followers, administrators, politicians
and media reacted to the idea of a cricket academy. England's cricket,
prior to the Adelaide victory, was said by their own supporters and
media to be limp, insipid, lacklustre, without fight and, even at the best
of times, thoughtless. The answer clearly was to produce an Adelaide
Academy-style organisation in England, or possibly several of them, and
it would be a case of hey presto, all would be well, something like the
short movie serials we used to watch at the Roxy Theatre in Parramatta
where the episode would end with the heroine and Jack tied to the
railway lines with the steam train bearing down on them. The next
episode always began, 'With one bound Jack was free . . .'

With one bound in Adelaide, English cricket seemed to be free
because not a word was written immediately after that victory about the
necessity of having a cricket academy in England. It's marvellous what a
win can do for a country and how it can divert criticism.

One of the best things about Australian cricket is the wide variety of
pitches on which Test matches are played. Brisbane is a very hard and
solid surface with some help for the pacemen early on, after which the
spinners come into their own. A good cricket pitch. Melbourne varies
but is certainly better now than in the 1980s; Sydney has had one or two
odd strips in recent years, but basically hasn't changed a great deal and
still favours spin under most circumstances; Adelaide has produced
results in past years and did so in this series, and is a good batting
pitch. Perth, hard as a rock, is generally in favour of the pace bowlers,
though in Sheffield Shield matches years ago I always found it a good
pitch on which to bowl legspin, with the Fremantle Doctor blowing in
around lunch-time each day to assist in swerving the ball in the air. Shane
Warne was to find this in the Perth Test where he was back on track
with his bowling action and stock leg-break.

Weather and pitch conditions for the start of the fifth and final Ashes
match in Perth were close to ideal and it was a very good toss for Mark
Taylor to win. The Australians made Brendon Julian twelfth man;

England, worried about their batting, left out Phil Tufnell and decided to play Mark Ramprakash who had been flown out from the England 'A' team tour in India.

The pattern of the first day was set with the fourth ball of the opening over, Devon Malcolm bowling to Michael Slater. Slater got a thick edge, and the ball flew at knee height to the right of Graham Gooch at third slip, who dived and failed to hold the catch. Malcolm looked distraught, and probably was, but then he was later to drop two catches of the five which went down on this opening day. It was a fielding catastrophe, compounded when another two catches were dropped on the second day, ten in all in the match.

It doesn't do to allow an Australian batsman one life in an Ashes battle; when you allow several lives then the odds are that you will be putting yourselves out of the game. That is exactly what happened to England on that opening day of the Perth Test and Atherton, despite his phlegmatic appearance, must have found it agonising after the great effort in Adelaide which had given England the opportunity of squaring the series. Their sloppy fielding dissolved that opportunity on the first day in Perth where the Australians cruised calmly to 283/4 with Steve Waugh on 23 and Greg Blewett 17 at the close of play. More awful fielding on the second day allowed the Australians to make further progress, even though they lost Blewett at 287, Healy at 320 and Warne at 328. England then weren't able to press home the advantage, and what should have been an Australian total of something around 340 was boosted by a 58-run partnership between Steve Waugh and Jo Angel. It hardly needs adding that during this phase of play the England fielding did not improve. When Craig McDermott, troubled by back spasms, came out to bat with Mark Waugh as a runner, the interest was in whether or not Steve Waugh could reach his century but he remained unbeaten on 99 when a smart throw found Mark Waugh short of the crease at the bowler's end after the twins had a slight difference of opinion over a quick single.

The whole innings was typical of the manner in which the Australian team had managed to turn potential problems into constructive cricket during the series. There were times on the opening day when England must have felt, even with the fielding problems, that they had a real chance of bowling Australia out for something like 240–250, and then suddenly England were looking at needing 203 to avoid the follow-on, a much more difficult scenario.

With a start of 5/1, 5/2, 77/3 and 77/4 England were not looking good; the men back in the pavilion were Atherton, caught down the legside by Healy off McGrath, Gatting, bowled first ball by the same bowler, Gooch, lbw for the fiftieth time in Tests, and Crawley, caught at second slip for a duck by Warne off Mark Waugh, whose bowling, following the Adelaide Test, was again imaginative. What came next was one of the best happenings for the future produced by England on the whole of the tour. Graham Thorpe and Mark Ramprakash, two of the younger players in the side, shared a resourceful 158-run partnership and, even more important, Thorpe went on to make a century.

He was 54* on the third evening when I attended a cocktail party hosted by former England cricketer Paul Allott, now with ITC Sports. Mike Atherton was also present, and I expressed the view to him then that if Thorpe could only go on to make a big hundred the next day it could be the making of him as a Test batsman. Atherton too was of the opinion that his left-hander was on the verge of playing some very good cricket and, when Thorpe reached his century, Atherton's applause would have been the most heartfelt in the dressing-room.

I have no doubts about Thorpe. I believe he has the ability to become one of England's good post-war batsmen, it's just a matter of him being convinced he can do it. The usual England batting collapse was triggered by Thorpe's dismissal at 235, brilliantly stumped by Healy off Warne's wrong 'un or topspinner. If I seem unsure of the delivery, it is only that my eye impression was topspinner but the replay showed that the ball definitely moved away from the bat after pitching. Ian Chappell was certain it was the wrong 'un and I'm happy to stay with his verdict. The one thing we both knew was that Thorpe picked it as a legspinner and, when he found himself short of the ball in his attempt to drive, he then tried unsuccessfully to hit over the top. The ball bounced steeply, Healy made a magnificent take at about shoulder level and Thorpe's full swing of the bat didn't allow him the chance to regain his ground. Warne then spun one from outside Ramprakash's leg stump to flick the pad and hit middle, Ramprakash not playing a stroke but trying to kick the ball away.

I know theories abound in cricket these days, but I can still find no better way in which to play the ball than to hit it with the bat. Gary Sobers's stricture about Brian Lara not playing with his pads but with his bat came instantly to mind when watching Ramprakash's dismissal. I like Ramprakash's style of batting and it has been disappointing that he hasn't done better in Test cricket, though it is impossible to be critical of the England selectors for not playing him more often. He went for a long time without making a score of over 30 in a Test, while others were outscoring him and deserved to be chosen ahead of him. There is no doubt though that he has ability and he is a brilliant fielder as well. He also tends to become a little uptight with his cricket and already has run into a problem or two in that regard with the Middlesex side. I just hope that final Test match in Perth will be the making of him because he could be a good player for England. When you think that at the conclusion of that game his last three innings against Australia had been 64, 72 and 42, it underlines his considerable ability.

Chris Lewis hit 40 from 62 balls towards the end of the innings but, in fact, England lost 4/12 in 58 balls and despite the 46-run partnership between Lewis and Fraser, they still faced a deficit of 107. It was one of those rare innings in the summer where McDermott failed to take a wicket, although he bowled only 13 overs firstly because of his back problem, then the considerable time that he was off the field had to be made up before he could bowl again. The wickets were shared between Jo Angel, Glenn McGrath, Mark Waugh and Shane Warne, the latter looking as though he had sorted out the minor problems with his bowling action which worried him in Adelaide.

England's inability to take charge of a situation, having done the hard work, was again underlined in the Australian second innings where half the side were dismissed for 123 and there was a good chance, if England had played well, that they would be chasing fewer than 300 for victory instead of their eventual target of trying to survive for a minimum of 104 overs facing a target of 453.

It wasn't so much that England couldn't bowl out Australia or that they again couldn't hold their catches, it was simply that the Australians were too good for them. Devon Malcolm broke Michael Slater's thumb with a 'flyer'; Jo Angel the night-watchman was brilliantly run out by Graham Gooch; on the fourth morning David Boon, right out of batting form, was caught at the wicket, a fate that also befell Mark Waugh. Then, with the first ball Angus Fraser bowled around the wicket to Mark Taylor, the Australian captain played the ball down and it brushed the off stump and removed the bail. It was also quite clearly a no-ball, with Fraser's back foot plonked on the return crease as he delivered the ball from very wide on the bowling crease. Not even something one can blame on the front foot Law, only on the umpire!

At 123/5, and Taylor on his way back to the dressing-room, England had high hopes of making a real challenge, but this was dashed in three quarters of an hour up to lunch when Steve Waugh and Greg Blewett counter-attacked to such effect that at the interval, in only ten overs, they had added 63. It was brilliant to watch, even more so after lunch when the pair added 126 in 29 overs and again tore the game away from England. Blewett became only the fifth batsman in the history of Test cricket to make centuries in each of his first two Test matches and, by the time Steve Waugh was out, brilliantly caught by Ramprakash at gully, the partnership was worth 203. It was highly entertaining and, when Taylor eventually called a halt to the slaughter, the Australians had a lead of 452 and England still had the problem of trying to survive for 14 overs on the fourth evening. It was all too much for them. Gooch went, brilliantly caught and bowled by McDermott in the fourth over, then 4 more wickets fell for 10 runs and at the close the score was 27/5. Atherton was still there in body, but I suspect not in mind after watching that carnage, and with him was Ramprakash. Thorpe went first ball to McGrath and Crawley bagged a pair, and when Atherton said after the game that he felt he had hit a brick wall in Perth, that certainly was the way he looked walking off the field at the close of play on the fourth evening. The following day was predictable, Ramprakash and Lewis making some sort of a stand, the wickets eventually falling before lunch and the presentations extolling the virtues of the manner in which the Australians had played and both praising England and at the same time lamenting that they had not been good enough.

Steve Waugh when he was named Man of the Match made a very good speech, particularly as the award might have come as something of a surprise to him. Greg Blewett was the other contender for the honour. Craig McDermott was Player of the Series and also the Benson & Hedges International Cricketer of the Year, the most sought-after material prize in cricket for which he received two motor cars. He bowled magnificently throughout the series and I have already noted elsewhere why I was so pleased to see him do well, being the subject of behind-the-hand questioning of his commitment at the start of the series.

McGrath, although taking only six wickets, was an improver for Australia as the series went on, and the fact that Mark Waugh was able to bowl well was a distinct bonus for the Australian selectors as they continued their desperate search for a bowling allrounder to replace Steve Waugh whose injured shoulder no longer allowed him to bowl.

For Mark Taylor the series was a triumph. It is not at all easy to take over from a captain like Allan Border and for Taylor it was his first experience of skippering an Australian team in his own country, other than when Border was injured. Taylor was always ahead of the game; his two decisions, in Brisbane to bat on instead of enforcing the follow-on, and in Perth to bat on and make England face three quarters of an hour of hostile bowling on the fourth evening, were sensible at the time, not just in hindsight.

Greg Blewett was the batting find of the summer and Michael Slater batted magnificently all the way through the series, a young player of rare brilliance going in at the top of the order facing the fastest bowlers. He is one of the most entertaining and yet technically correct batsmen I have seen in many years. Taylor played very solidly all the way through and at times he was brilliant, even outscoring Slater; Steve and Mark Waugh did a great job in the middle of the batting order and Ian Healy's all-round abilities were again highlighted. The Australian bowling attack wasn't quite restricted to two men but McDermott, with 32 wickets (strike-rate 43), and Warne, with 27 (strike-rate 57), did the bulk of the wicket-taking and consistently none of the England batsmen had much idea of what to do with them. It was further confirmation that when Australia have quality fast and legspin bowlers in the same side they will always be difficult to beat.

England had two players, Atherton and Thorpe, who made more than 400 runs in the series but it was the team's regular batting collapses which posed so many problems. If the Australians made a break, they were almost guaranteed another, and another, and sometimes even total collapse. It was cruel luck for Atherton to lose Gough and Hick for the last two Tests and, as mentioned elsewhere, I have never seen such ill luck as regards injuries and illnesses with any team touring Australia.

The biggest problem though was in the fielding and, at times, in the captaincy. The latter first. I thought Atherton grew in stature on this tour, that he showed great resilience and character throughout the Australian summer, and that he was able to stay with the fight for as long as he did was remarkable. It is necessary to divorce the ill luck from the actual performance, while accepting the connection between the two. Atherton took steps to rectify this in the Adelaide Test where he had a quiet dinner with Ian Chappell, the former Australian captain, just so he could have a chat about captaincy. He could not have gone to a better man. 'Chappelli' is one of the four best on-field captains I have ever seen; he can't stand humbug, is as honest as they come and, if asked, is happy to help young cricketers from any country. No one has a better cricket brain than Chappell.

Atherton is an inexperienced captain and I have already said that he needs to keep up with the game, not only in making his decisions but, more important, in implementing them, rather than agonising over possible problems for a couple of overs, by which time the game has again caught up with him. He is keen to learn and will do so quickly and the few hours with Chappell over dinner will be some of the most profitable time spent during the whole of his captaincy career. I am confident he will turn out to be an excellent captain in the future, if he is given the right well-balanced team.

Atherton's touring side, in the end, was a disappointment. Their batting collapses were one thing, their fielding lapses quite another and there were times when I found myself relating it all back to the type of cricket played at county level where there is less of an accent on playing hard cricket and more on making sure something is set up to achieve major points for one of the teams taking part in a Championship match. There are times in county cricket, when the outcome is being arranged, where brilliant or sloppy fielding is immaterial.

The Perth Test, with its ten dropped chances, provided the classic example but there were two instances in that last Test which even more perfectly underlined what I mean. The first was when wicket-keeper Steve Rhodes chased a ball to the boundary when two other players couldn't be bothered, the second when Thorpe dropped a catch at slip and then booted the ball away and the Australians were able to take a second run. Mediocrity *is* contagious! There is no reason why young English cricketers should not be able to field as well as young Australians. Atherton at the end of the tour was nonplussed over his team's astonishing inconsistency in batting, bowling and fielding and also by the difference in athleticism between the two sides. Those four aspects were fact not fancy and it requires hard work to redress that balance, though, as was seen in Adelaide, a victory can do wonders for the morale of the captain, the players, supporters and even politicians 12,000 miles away.

Atherton will pick up the pieces and he will come out of the tour of Australia a harder, tougher and better cricketer and captain for it. He started the tour still with the aftermath of Lord's hanging over him, handled that well, played his own part in the good things England did and, as well, showed that not only is he a good cricketer but a young man of character. He is a fine batsman, the only Test player in 1994 to make 1,000 runs, is gutsy and skilful, and he will become a good captain when he is prepared to back his hunches and not ponder over the awful possibilities of a decision going wrong. He faces a stiff task against the

West Indies in 1995 in England, but then so too did Mark Taylor when the Australians went to the Caribbean after having retained the Ashes.

It was on that tour Taylor found himself in a similar position to Atherton in Australia, when first Damien Fleming and then Craig McDermott broke down and were forced, because of their injuries, to return to Australia. It was an awful setback for the Australian captain and his team.

# 8

# *A new ball game for television and Percy Sledge makes his name*

Over the past forty-seven years I have had a great deal of fun, travelled to many countries, played what in the first fifteen years was comparatively a lot of cricket, and, as a media man, have seen a lot of stories unfold. Having started as a journalist, I have always had a love of the written word; now, as a writer and television commentator, the job is even more interesting, combining the written and spoken word.

Television is the reason behind many major changes in the game of cricket, but no one should confuse those changes at Test match and international level with changes to the grass roots of the game. Cricket itself doesn't change as a game, even though the most publicised version of the game certainly does.

A club match in London, a game between Tillingfold and Ravely, or between Jugiong and Harden, will still be played in the same fashion as sixty years ago. Afternoon tea will be between innings and, in their own fashion, the games will be as hard and tough as in the Test arena under the scrutiny of the television cameras. A cold beer under the giant eucalyptus tree by the river or the spreading oak on the village green mirrors the end-of-match drinks at a Test match on a ground holding 30,000 spectators.

In Australia, Test cricket is still drawing reasonable crowds in some areas, not so good in others. Limited-overs Internationals draw very big crowds in Australia; domestic limited-overs games also do relatively well. Administrators need to gear their television thoughts to those facts.

In India and Pakistan Test attendances are often quite ordinary, but occasionally there will be good days. Attendances at limited-overs

Internationals are excellent, so there is some different planning to be done there. Certainly that applies also to South Africa, where no Test cricket was played for more than twenty years and, although the Currie Cup competition between the provinces kept going through all that time before becoming the Castle Cup in 1991–2, limited-overs matches took over as spectator spectaculars.

People simply became unused to attending Test cricket in South Africa because it didn't exist. Instead, they saw some first-class matches, some matches between local sides and Invitation XIs, which were termed rebel matches and, in one of the more ridiculous decisions ever made, were later decreed to be not of first-class status. Fortunately this purely political gambit seems for the moment to have been given short shrift by most statistical authorities, including *Wisden*.

The limited-overs game flourished in South Africa and the matches I watched in early 1994 were very entertaining, on smallish grounds with excellent facilities where, for day-night matches, the lights were sometimes good, sometimes very ordinary indeed.

Sri Lanka and New Zealand have followed the same pattern – good crowds for limited-overs games, not so good for Tests – and we don't know about Zimbabwe at the moment, although I would be very surprised if spectators in Zimbabwe were holding their breath waiting for the Test matches to come along. Far more likely that they will be queuing up for the one-dayers for their education in international cricket.

England is a different matter because its small grounds can be filled on the first three days of Test matches and for all limited-overs Internationals, and there is no need to worry about attendances, with a vast cricket-watching audience and high-priced tickets which sell out months in advance. The West Indies is different again. There too the grounds are small.

It is worth noting the ticket prices at grounds compared with England. Around the world the cost of tickets rightly reflects economic circumstances and sponsorship benefits, and the West Indies could never attempt to charge the same as England. Nor could Australia for that matter.

It was good to see Alan Crompton, the Chairman of the Australian Cricket Board, in print after the end of the Benson & Hedges World Series in 1994–5 saying with conviction that Test matches are standing on their own feet in Australia now as financial propositions. His theme was that limited-overs Internationals have always been said to be the financial lifeblood of the game because Test match attendances are dropping in some countries, and this has now been shown to be incorrect. I'm actually one who has said that, and I still believe it to be correct. Mr Crompton though wouldn't have a bar of that so far as Australia is concerned, and good on him – *if* he is right.

Administrators need to bear in mind that there are other matters to be considered, including the cost of running a domestic competition such as the Sheffield Shield these days. The loss on that is prohibitive. What might have been more to the point would be to underline that the Australian team under Allan Border, and now under Mark Taylor, have some great players going around and that they are winners. I would hope Australian audiences go to watch them when they are playing well, but it doesn't do to get too carried away with numbers of spectators going through the turnstiles.

When New Zealand and South Africa toured Australia in 1993–4, attendance figures were something of a mixed bag and the comparison looked like this:

| | Tests | LOIs | Total |
|---|---|---|---|
| | 293,487 | 458,396 | 751,883 |
| (v. NZ | 60,285) | | |
| (v. SA | 233,202) | | |

The attendance for the 1982–3 Test series against England was 556,601. Compare this with the 1994–5 England tour of Australia:

| Tests | LOIs | Total |
|---|---|---|
| 474,302 | 362,346 | 836,648 |

The Test match attendance for this series breaks down as follows:

| | Best Day | Total Crowd |
|---|---|---|
| 1 Brisbane Nov. 25–9 | Day 1: 15,097 | 43,764 |
| 2 Melbourne Dec. 24–9 | Day 2: 51,620 | 144,492 |
| 3 Sydney Jan. 1–5 | Day 1: 31,317 | 126,485 |
| 4 Adelaide Jan. 26–30 | Day 1: 24,190 | 89,448 |
| 5 Perth Feb. 3–7 | Day 3: 21,192 | 70,113 |
| | Total | 474,302 |

# 1994–5 World Series Attendances

| | | | |
|---|---|---|---:|
| Aus. v. Zim. | Perth | Dec. 2 | 8,293 |
| Aus. A v Zim. | Perth | Dec. 4 | 7,287 |
| Aus. v. Eng. | Sydney | Dec. 6 | 38,602 |
| Aus. v. Zim. | Hobart | Dec. 8 | 7,472 |
| Aus. A v. Zim. | Adelaide | Dec. 10 | 6,368 |
| Aus. v. Aus. A | Adelaide | Dec. 11 | 20,470 |
| Aus. A v. Eng. | Melbourne | Dec. 13 | 39,837 |
| Eng. v. Zim. | Sydney | Dec. 15 | 6,337 |
| Eng. v. Zim. | Brisbane | Jan. 7 | 9,589 |
| Aus. v. Aus. A | Brisbane | Jan. 8 | 17,002 |
| Aus. v. Eng. | Melbourne | Jan. 10 | 73,282 |
| Aus. A v. Eng. | Sydney | Jan. 12 | 38,152 |
| *Finals* | | | |
| Aus. v. Aus. A | Sydney | Jan. 15 | 35,890 |
| Aus. v. Aus. A | Melbourne | Jan. 17 | 53,765 |

*Total 362,346*

During the 1994–5 summer in Australia we were constantly being told that the Test attendances were the best since 1982–3 when Bob Willis captained England to Australia, the year constantly produced for comparison. That was great news because it provided an indication that sports followers were retaining an interest in Test cricket, and perhaps more significant was the fact that the attendances held up even in the face of England having lost the first two Tests in Brisbane and Melbourne. One reason for this is that the ACB and the states have been persuaded over the years that setting up a pre-match booking system is the way to go.

At the same time, it is still a worry to me that over a five-match Ashes series the number of spectators going through the gate was down by more than 80,000 and the limited-overs crowds down by more than 150,000 when compared with 1982–3.

I would have thought administrators might expect to draw more people through the gates for Test matches in a season when Australia and England are head-to-head and there are four teams playing in a limited-overs competition, rather than when the competition comes from New Zealand and South Africa; and it should be a cause for alarm if that were not so. We haven't yet seen the figures for the gate-takings for all the games and they could be quite significant when they are published, as I assume they will be, particularly with various price fluctuations organised by the ACB and the State Associations to boost Test match attendances, which means many pay less than normal at the turnstiles.

If Test cricket is perceived as being primarily a good contest, and good entertainment as well, then there is a chance people will go to the matches. Much of the responsibility for that lies with the administrators who need seriously to address matters such as over-rates and the recalculation of overs at the end of an innings.

Not least of the strange things to happen at the ICC meeting at Lord's in July 1994 was that two proposals in connection with over-rates were defeated. The first urged that the minimum number of overs in the day be increased from 90 to 96. In effect, with all the allowances taken into account, this would have increased the true figure from around 85 overs to 90 overs. The ICC delegates knocked it back. Then the second proposal, to stop the present method of recalculation of overs when an innings ends, was also defeated. Politics came into these decisions; sometimes politicians and cricket administrators are just like a lot of little kids.

Crowds deserve the utmost consideration, particularly if they are going along to Test cricket. There is every chance you will be able to fill your stadium for a limited-overs International, but filling it for Tests these days is not as easy, despite what Mr Crompton said. When England toured India in 1992–3 administrators were doubtful if spectators would come along to the Tests though the limited-overs Internationals were booked out well in advance. Then India dominated the First Test and 25,000 spectators came into the ground on the last day to see their team make just 43 to win. They then turned up for the other Tests as well, which was great for Test cricket in India. It hardly needs stressing that success will always do more than smart marketing to pull Test crowds through the gates.

There are many factors which go into assessing Test match and limited-overs match attendances, indeed into the whole question of whether Test cricket will be able to keep pace with the ever-changing lifestyles of young people. One of the great difficulties lies in the increasing variety of choice for people trying to decide which sport to play or to follow. They have had that problem in the West Indies in recent years where basketball has made inroads into the numbers of youngsters who might in previous years have laughed at anyone suggesting they would not be devoted to cricket.

One of the problems for the administrators is to balance the needs of the game against the wishes of those who sit in their living-rooms. The latter would be very happy if all sports events were to be televised in their entirety. That would mean cricket could be on from the start of play at 11 a.m. through until 6 p.m. There are many who consider that to be their right, whether or not all tickets for the match have been sold for that day. So far as they are concerned, they pay their television licence fee, or at least they should do so, and everything should be on air.

This feeling has been accentuated in recent times by the advent of Pay TV in England and Australia and the same feeling exists in other countries. Pay TV's aim is to bring programmes to the watching and subscribing public, who then want the programmes, initially, to be exclusive to them. There's no point at all in putting on a programme and charging for it if the same programme can be seen at the same time on network television. Administrators have realised, in the aftermath of succeeding Olympic Games and other special events, that the television rights fees can make a great difference to their financial forecasts and final balance sheets. We had a good example of the way modern cricket administrators think about television during the 1994 cricket season in England. It was the year the Test and County Cricket Board and the various television organisations were to negotiate a new scale of rights fees for a four-year period and the administrators, as is their duty to the game, set out to make the most of it. To enable them to balance their own cricket accounts, they wanted a substantial increase in fees.

For many years there had been only BBC Television with whom they needed to negotiate, but then BSkyB became a player and began to televise the Sunday League. Now, in 1994, BSkyB were players again and it was not only a matter of negotiation but of savvy and each player trying to outguess the opposition.

The counties received what was meant to be a confidential message early in the season intimating they shouldn't be surprised by any publicity appearing which might indicate Test cricket had a good chance of being taken from the BBC. The message suggested that this was merely a smokescreen and they should pay no attention to it, and that in fact the idea was in line with making sure the game received the best possible price for the television rights which were likely to be split between the BBC and some commercial organisations, with the commercials handling limited-overs competitions. A commendable object.

When it came to the final phase of the negotiations, the cricket authorities claimed they had got what they wanted. This was excellent because it was a considerable increase on the figures from the previous contract with the BBC, who also said they were very happy with the new contract, with good reason: they were well aware of the original letter sent to the counties, and they knew they were likely to get the Test cricket anyway plus the NatWest competition, and that the various publicity splurges were a screen with smoke but no fire. However, they also knew they would be paying considerably more for it and were happy to do so, providing they were able to have a four-year contract instead of three. This is what happened: Test cricket remained with the BBC but this time for four years; they paid more money and they were very satisfied with the result. So too were BSkyB who got what they wanted and will provide tough competition and excellent coverage as they have done previously from outside England.

Where the senses of humour of the BBC's negotiators' might have been tested a little though was in the story which appeared later in the summer suggesting they had been outsmarted, outplayed and well stuffed into the bargain. It was a noteworthy exercise in PR and is unlikely to be forgotten in 1998 when again everyone sits around the bargaining table to negotiate the next round of TV rights.

One of the real problems faced by television in years to come will be what liaison there is between the cricket countries of the world, the cricket administrators negotiating the television rights, the local television networks in each country, and the ICC.

ICC? Do I hear you wondering what the ICC might have to do with all that? Well, I believe that in future years the ICC, for so long a milk-and-water organisation, could be playing a far greater role in world cricket than has been the case in the past fifty years. They have been keeping an eye on the television rights as they have applied to the Olympic Games and, from the time the Los Angeles Games made a profit, other sports administrators certainly took a keen interest. The very good reason for this is that the LA Olympic head, Peter Euberoth, made certain his organisation retained the television rights for LA and then he charged a 'motza' for them. It will never happen again because the Olympic Committee suddenly saw the large pot of gold available and now all countries who win the rights to stage the Games have only a share of the TV rights, not the lot.

Cricket administrators have watched this closely and it is for this reason Mark Mascarenhas and his organisation won the rights to the 1996 World Cup. At the time of writing they were doing well with the selling of them to individual countries and I hope they continue to do so because they have shown great courage and excellent business ability.

But, there could be a problem looming for the ICC because of what happened in India in the Hero Cup, a five-nation limited-overs event which was played in November 1993.

The events, as reported, consisted of the following:

Trans World International (TWI) bought the rights to televise the Hero Cup. Doordarshan, the Indian television station/network objected to TWI being allowed to purchase the rights because they, Doordarshan, had never paid for televising cricket in India, indeed Doordarshan charge a fee for televising the matches. Very strange.

TWI had gained all the proper government approvals for the coverage, and they had paid in advance for their satellite links. Two days before the first match was to be televised, VSNL, the satellite licensors, withdrew the permission granted to TWI, citing technical reasons and an instruction from the Indian Ministry of Information for the cancellation.

The Indian Telegraph Act, an archaic relic of the time of the British Raj, was then brought into the battle, following which the High Court in Delhi issued an order instructing the government to cease all attempts to interfere with TWI's coverage and in future to provide full co-operation.

It was then claimed that TWI had entered the country illegally and the next step was that all their equipment was seized. The High Court of India reversed this and ordered that TWI be given all co-operation and were not to be impeded.

It was an extraordinary happening, more so when TWI refused to be cowed and still somehow managed to have their pictures shown on Prime Sports.

Bill Sinrich, the livewire head of TWI's cricket coverage around the world, was detained by police as part of the harassment, serious enough in itself, but the whole question is even more complicated for cricket around the world. The ICC need to keep abreast of the situation and, if there are problems, then they will have to act with courage and skill, not something that has always characterised their efforts in years past. They have a new administration nowadays however and it could be the making of them, so long as they do not allow themselves to be cowed as was clearly the intention against TWI and Sinrich. It looms as a real problem.

Television, as we move towards the twenty-first century, will play a much greater part in cricket and one of the problems is that both the game and television are continually changing so fast. The added complication is that they will change in a different fashion in each country.

One thing the excellent and well-deserved increase in income from TV and the general revolution in television will do is allow administrators the opportunity, if they are able to grasp it, of having all kinds of cricket shown to viewers. In Australia, for example, the Australian Cricket Board have the opportunity to sell the television rights to Sheffield Shield instead of having to give them away.

One of the reasons it is not always possible for television companies to show cricket at less than international standard is that it costs so much to provide a television production. It needs cameras, cameramen or women, tape operators and a cast of, if not thousands, then certainly scores of people. Although administrators ideally would like to see cricket on television most of the day and night, the truth is that it has to battle these days against a multitude of other sports, all of which also would like air time, and are livid that it is not happening, and they have quite a good argument which cricket has to combat.

Television is constantly being wooed by those sports, some of which are occupying prime time in countries other than England and Australia. Basketball, football and baseball, for example, are top sports in America and, more important for the television companies themselves, top-*rating* sports. With 255 million people in the United States, vast amounts of money are paid for the television rights, since those same ratings bring in a great deal of advertising and sponsorship money.

In Australia, the equivalent top television sports are cricket, Rugby League, Rugby Union and, for the moment, Australian Rules, although the latter is by no means guaranteed as a long-term project. In England it is football and cricket. Britain has 58 million people, Australia only 17 million. More than one Pay TV organisation seems to me unlikely in Australia if, that is, they wish to run at a profit.

It will be a real challenge for administrators in Australia to see what they are able to make of future television negotiations. It will also be a challenge for the Australian Minister for Communications, who at the time of writing is Michael Lee.

In both England and Australia there is a list of television programmes which must be available for free-to-air television. In Australia it is known as an anti-siphoning list and, at the moment, is a matter of great argument.

What the English counties do with their deserved increase in TV rights money is one very important aspect of the windfall. There appears to be some thought that the money will be given to the counties but they will also be instructed on how they are to spend it. I would be extremely unhappy about that last note if I were in the position of running a county. Give them the money and make sure they account for what they do with it on paper, and by December 31st each year. But the counties, not the TCCB, are the ones who know best where they are faced by a shortfall in income. Perhaps it might be in facilities for spectators, attention to cricket in schools and to the balance of male and female sports teachers, maybe in not sending county players to schools to coach but finding some way to bring the schoolchildren to the county.

Preparation of good pitches is an area where attention could be paid. There has been considerable publicity in recent times over pitches which are said to have been prepared to provide an exciting finish but, in fact, have seen the game finish a day ahead of the scheduled time. The inspector of pitches is always likely to be a very important part of this aspect but I shall continue to believe that pitch preparation for a four-day match should be undertaken with the very basic idea that the first session of play is for the batsmen and the pace bowlers, the next seven sessions for the batsmen and the spin bowlers and the final four sessions for the spin bowlers, pace bowlers and the batsmen. That cannot always work out but it is a sensible starting point. The TCCB each year produce a county pitches table of merit where the umpires give points out of six in a marking system. I would have thought the aim of each county would be to have their average over the whole summer in excess of five, it just seems common sense. Instead, no one seems even to average five. Very strange.

I won't say the only thing which matters in television is ratings but, for commercial stations, they must play a very big part in programming. In Australia there is a rating period when viewers are measured quite accurately by machines which are activated whenever selected sets around the country are switched on to various programmes. Then there is a non-rating period from late in the year until early in the new year and it is for much of that time the cricket is on. It has been said that television was partly the reason World Series Cricket came into being, but the initial reason was the universal dissatisfaction of the Test players with the administrators. Then the ensuing conversations between John Cornell, Kerry Packer, Paul Hogan, Austin Robertson, Dennis Lillee and others embraced first of all the dissatisfaction angle and then tied it in with televised cricket where it was decided, if the Australian Cricket Board would not allow exclusive television on cricket, that a different style of cricket would be organised.

One of the curiosities of television to my way of thinking is that although much of the advertising is geared to ratings and to capturing the eyes, minds and certainly the attention of children, most of the television watching is done by adults. Something like twice as much in fact. Sport these days occupies a great part of television viewing in Australia; news and current affairs is very popular, as are good films and even mediocre films, also documentaries. Sport though – good sport, that is – captures the attention of the watching public and in Australia cricket is right up there with excellent figures, particularly considering it is summer and there are many outdoor activities in which to participate or to watch.

Showing a film like *Crocodile Dundee* will produce an estimated two and a half million viewers, which is very good in a country with a population of only seventeen million. The Rugby League State of Origin games pull in an audience of between two and a half and three million, sometimes more, and the Winter Olympics drew well over two million viewers.

Not everyone likes all aspects of the televised cricket in Australia or overseas but I have always been keen to pay attention to any criticisms of our television production and presentation on Channel Nine. At the time much was made of David Boon's extensive criticism in the *Launceston Examiner* of Channel Nine's coverage of the incidents between Merv Hughes, Shane Warne, Andrew Hudson, the umpires and the match referee in Johannesburg. The theme of David's criticisms was that television was intrusive, far too intrusive, and the cricket authorities needed to do something about it because it was unfair to the players.

In the article, Boon said that Channel Nine had to take much of the responsibility for the furore over the recent sledging incidents by Australian cricketers in South Africa. Really! The Australian batsman claimed the incidents involving Shane Warne and Merv Hughes had been blown out of all proportion and had only been allowed to become public because of the Nine Network's unfettered intrusion on to the field of play.

I'm not condoning what my team-mates have been captured saying to opponents on replay, but when the Australian media starts calling for players to be sent home in disgrace, it's gone too far. The producers and camera people know Merv Hughes and Shane Warne's willingness to give the opposition advice between deliveries – so Nine focuses in, full close-up. Again, I'm not condoning outright swearing or overt sledging – other than to acknowledge that it's been part of the game since W. G. Grace strapped on his pads – but there is too much emphasis placed on this aspect of the game. When Nine covers Rugby League the broadcast contract specifies what can and cannot be shown, much as Seven's charter with Australian football limits films of reportable incidents.

I'm always keen to see people express an opinion and I was interested to read David's ideas which, taken to their logical conclusion, could have all cricket covered with a long lens.

Well, the Australian Cricket Board don't often leap into the breach but they did here. They instituted a course in public relations and media acceptance for all the players in a bid to teach them what they should be saying in public, what they should be doing, and that television and the media are in fact the best friends cricket could possibly have. The latter dictum was the case when I last wrote about it in *On Reflection;* in fact it is even more so now. There are so many other sports and claimants for a share of the spectator's dollar, or pound or rupee or rand, that every possible aspect should be explored in a bid to cultivate the media. There was a time when it was simply common sense, now it is absolutely essential because time on television is vital, space in newspapers is precious and a share of radio hours is high on everyone's agenda.

What the ACB did was engage a firm of consultants to advise the players and, most important of all, brief them on how best to come to terms with the fact that they are public figures and entertainers, responsible to the media, and how to be clear-headed in their approach to it. Their privacy should be respected, something not always done, but they were told that there are various methods available to rebut any medium which doesn't respect their privacy as allowed by law. In those cases, as on the field, they need to use their common sense and to bear in mind that the media can be used to project a great public relations image.

One of the prime points at issue is that cricketers should always believe whatever they do on the cricket field is being recorded for posterity. To believe otherwise is simply to be naive.

There have always been long lenses on the cameras of newspaper photographers; now the television cameras take every incident, big or small, into every living-room in the cricketing world. I believe the players need to understand this and accommodate it, but above all the captain needs to understand that he is totally responsible for the conduct of his team. Common sense also needs to be used. When Michael

Atherton gave a couple of plastic chairs a 'bunt' in Perth at the end of the Test series in Australia as he walked back through the tunnel to the dressing-room, match referee John Reid didn't bother taking any action. Nor should he have. The WACA might have taken some had they been pieces of furniture carved by Mr Chippendale, but it was not a case for the match referee. Australian players though, now they have been through the ACB's charm school, should be aware of all the problems television might bring. At the same time television producers need to have a good idea of what constitutes a player's privacy in the dressing-room itself.

For example, if the players' balcony is to be shown at the moment a team-mate reaches a century and everyone is doing the mandatory standing and clapping and waving flags, then any players in the background need to take care and should understand they too could be shown on television doing whatever they might be doing at that moment. I believe though that if a producer or director show a players' balcony shot at another time, then it should be just that, the balcony, and players should be able to feel safe. The shot would be whatever spectators are able to see through binoculars. Otherwise we will reach the stage where players will need a black stage curtain to separate the dressing-room from the television cameras.

I am able to claim a reasonable knowledge of this conflict between cricket and the media, having been a journalist for the past forty years and having worked in television for the past thirty-five. More important than that though is that I was able to break the mould of cricketers and the media which had existed in Australian cricket from the time it started until 1958. Up to that point the administrators had been at war with the media, which in turn had taken every opportunity to have a dash at the administrators, and there was a deep distrust by the players of the media. This had not happened overnight, but in his excellent book *Cricket Crisis* Jack Fingleton alludes to the players clamming up whenever pressmen approached. There was no communication. This attitude was fuelled by the administrators and their insistence that there should be a player-writer rule where transgressions would be the subject of financial penalties.

When you think of the matters which had to come to pass before the Australian Board of Control, as it was in 1958, finished up with me, a media man, captaining Australia, then it's no wonder they had an edge of panic at first. Ian Craig had been made captain of NSW over me after our return from England, Pakistan and India in 1956. He was then made

captain of the Australian team to New Zealand and South Africa and we
had beaten the Springboks, as they then were, 3–0 in the series in South
Africa. When we came back to Australia Neil Harvey, who was more
senior than me, moved from Victoria to NSW for business reasons and
was going to play under Craig's captaincy for that state. I was vice-
captain to Craig in NSW, but instead of being relegated to third selector
in the state side with Harvey's arrival, I suddenly found myself captain of
Australia, after Ian Craig contracted hepatitis and had to pull out of
selection. This placed the Australian selectors in a very awkward
position. I had captained NSW, in the absence of Craig, against
Queensland in the opening Sheffield Shield match of the season and
we had gone well, in a bid for an outright win. The other contender,
Neil Harvey, had captained the moderately credentialled but unfortu-
nate Australian XI team against England in Sydney on a pitch where
Fred Trueman had been allowed to scuff up the surface to an
extraordinary degree. Tony Lock, bowling into the footmarks, dismissed the Australian XI for a meagre second-innings score, and when
the Australian captaincy was announced, I was named.

I have managed to get all of this into three hundred words, but it must
have seemed more like a lifetime to the Australian Board of Control.
From having a settled side, with a captain who had just come back with
glowing tributes after a 3–0 win over South Africa, they were suddenly
faced with having a captain who was only third in line a month
previously, who was also a journalist actually writing for newspapers
and who, only two years earlier, had undertaken a television course with
the BBC in London.

It only took the first six hours of the Test in Brisbane to let them know
their misgivings might not have been misplaced. I asked the cricket
writers covering the tour if they would like to come into the dressing-
room to say hello to the players, with, of course, the sensible note that
everything was off the record.

Nowadays all that has changed and the players are able to be
interviewed and quoted. Cricket is under siege, trying to hold its
own against other sports and pastimes and, belatedly, the cricket
administrators have realised that the media in fact can be the greatest
ally of the game. The biggest change has been that move to have the
players made aware of their responsibilities on the field as regards being
part of an entertainment, because you can be quite certain television
producers, directors and commentators are constantly being made aware
of *their* own responsibilities to the game.

Television has been responsible for changing many aspects of cricket including the fact that newspapers have been forced to alter their type of coverage. Television shows it all and cricket rates very highly on television. It follows that viewers, who are also newspaper readers, have already seen the happenings and made up their own minds, so that newspaper writers need to be far more geared towards writing features than news stories.

Television has changed the face of reporting and it has brought about a change in the players' line of thinking. When Shane Warne and Merv Hughes were involved in those incidents at the Wanderers in March 1994, there was the reported unease from the match referee, the Australian Cricket Board and many millions who watched it on television. So far as the players were concerned, there was worry that it had happened, that suddenly they were under the hammer from not only the media but from cricket fans as well, but the real problem seemed to be that television had actually had the temerity to show it to the world.

This indicated, at best, an unsophisticated attitude to modern-day life, a lack of knowledge of how television works in relation to the cricketing public and, at worst, an ignorance of the fact that nothing is shown on television that doesn't actually happen. No player will be shown shouting at another player, brandishing a fist, running around the ground, charging an umpire or appealing for lbw from square-leg if it hasn't taken place. The mood in the Australian camp, after those Johannesburg incidents, was along the lines of being hard done by.

On the question of players' behaviour, Percy Sledge is the one given the dubious credit for the introduction of the term sledging in cricket; the definition is doing something or saying something which might upset the opposition. It came about in Adelaide many years ago when a New South Wales player, after making a remark at a barbecue, was said to be 'subtle as a sledge-hammer'. Percy Sledge, the singer, had a song in the hit parade at the time, 'When a Man Loves a Woman', and it was a natural progression from sledge-hammer to sledge to 'sledging'.

There was plenty of it in first-class cricket in Australia when I played, but the method does seem to have changed a little over the years. I always liked Fred Trueman's 'Ay, but wasted on thee!' reply to the young batsman who, in upper-class tones, congratulated him on the ball which had just uprooted off stump.

These days, with the close-up camera and the batsman's head jerking around, Fred would be said to have given his opponent a 'send-off' and would certainly be carpeted by the match referee. All quite harmless but, as we approach the twenty-first century, it is something the public and the media watch very carefully.

We used to have some wonderful 'sledging' matches when NSW played Victoria in the Sheffield Shield. P. Sledge hadn't been heard of in those days and we called it good, hard cricket and no one thought twice about it. At the close of play we would be in the opposition dressing-room, or they would be in ours, and we would be discussing the day's play.

Jack 'Snarler' Hill from Victoria was a legend in his own time and no one escaped. These days Jack, who was a fine cricketer, would never have kept any of his match money, though the match referee would have a hard time making ends meet with players who were paid $20 a game.

Ian Chappell and Rodney Marsh swear it's an apocryphal story but at Lord's, in 1975, David Steele is reputed to have done well in the repartee department. Tony Greig, who had just replaced Mike Denness as England captain after the fiasco of Edgbaston, had been instrumental in bringing Steele into the team. Steele was the grey-haired right-handed batsman from Northamptonshire who was thirty-three years of age but looked older. When he made his way to the centre after Barry Wood's dismissal it is said someone chided Lillee that he had failed to notify them his father was playing in the match. The reply from Steele was unexpected but definitely in character, as later events showed: 'Marshie, you see this arse of mine, take a good look because you'll be seeing a lot of it this summer.' Steele made 50 and 45 on his debut, then 73 and 92 and 39 and 66, topping England's averages for the series. He also hit a century against Australia at Northampton later in the summer and Rodney was keeping wicket then as well.

It might be apocryphal, as the Australians are so quick to claim, but I like it. What a match referee would have done with it, I've no idea. The astonishing thing about Steele was that although he made 44 and 42 in the final Test against the West Indies in 1976, he never again played for England. Selectors do some strange things at times, particularly in England.

# 9

## Nicklaus and Seve
## and chaos in the commentary box

Television takes us to some strange places, to some wonderful ones as well, and there is always the chance to meet interesting people whether they be strangers who are viewers, strangers who know nothing about cricket or television, or sportsmen and women who make their names in other jobs, pastimes or professions.

One of the more interesting aspects of those lives of international sports people is what they do away from the playing arena. In cricket it used to be that every Australian cricketer had a profession. I was a journalist, having started on police rounds in the mid–1950s and worked through various other areas until lack of time, and being constantly on the move with cricket, meant I became a full-time sports journalist, something I had been doing part-time since 1956 along with the police rounds job. Starting off as a journalist of the print variety, with the need to write 250 words to fill a space, has been of great value to me in television. No point in writing 400 words if the space only takes 250. It was a great lesson in putting as much as possible into the shortest time, or smallest space. Others in the cricket team worked as salesmen or clerks, and some had interesting hobbies as well, like Bill Lawry who took up pigeon racing at a very early age.

Tastes in the arts were varied. Neil Harvey took me to watch Dame Margot Fonteyn dance at Covent Garden the first week we were in London, in 1953, and it was one of the greatest things I had ever seen. Classical music was as popular with me as whatever might have been the equivalent of the Top 20 of the day. Opera? Well, not quite as popular, though I did make the effort to listen. It was a bit much for me then but listening to great opera singers provides pleasure these days, far more on CD though than on stage. So too does playing as much golf as possible, though time restraints, and a change of focus in business, mean there is never quite enough time available. My wife Daphne and I covered the Masters Tournament at Augusta over a fourteen-year period for news-papers, radio and, if needed, as a presenter for Channel Nine Television.

Sometimes though, because of the time difference, as the event was beamed back to Australia, our job was more likely to be a straightforward pick-up from CBS: 'And now we take you to the thirteenth fairway where your commentator is . . .' The Masters was always one of our hardest jobs, with the conclusion of the tournament, 5–6 p.m. in Augusta, coinciding with edition times of the *Melbourne Herald* and morning drive-time for Radio 2UE in Sydney.

After the daily work was done there was the chance to relax and each year during the tournament Mark McCormack put on a splendid party which started in the early evening and could go late. It was always delightful conjecture to see which of Mark's many clients and business associates outside golf would be there and it was nice to be able to talk with the golfers, if they wanted to talk about golf, and to catch up on any other things they might be doing. In 1992 I was chatting with Irishman David Feherty, each of us with a glass in hand, and he knew he probably needed to shoot no worse than a par seventy-two the following day to have a chance of making the cut. David was slightly on edge musing about the morrow, so thinking it might help a little, I asked about operas he had seen lately, knowing there is no keener opera buff in the golfing world, and few in the real world. He hadn't had much time to see anything because of practising for the Masters and other golfing events but he had spent many hours listening to CDs, some featuring Dame Kiri Te Kanawa. Kiri may have greater fans in the world than David Feherty but I doubt it. She and husband Desmond Park are also two of the keenest golfers you would find anywhere. I was just starting to say, 'Well, David, there's a chance at a McCormack party . . .' when his eyes widened and, although the rest of the room still buzzed, he didn't. He was looking past my left shoulder and had stopped talking. I turned around and Kiri was threading her way across the patio towards us.

'Richie,' she said.

'Hi, Kiri, how are you? Meet David Feherty.'

I chatted for a few moments and then left them to it, David asking about opera, Kiri wanting advice on the short chip from alongside the green when the putting surfaces are like lightning. I don't think I have ever seen a sportsman from one area more excited to meet a great performer from another.

Did David make the cut? He certainly did and shot his par seventy-two to make it by a shot, knowing he had to have a par four on the very difficult eighteenth to have a chance to play the last two days. It might, in the event, have had something to do with the refresher course on chipping he gave Kiri the previous evening!

It was at Augusta I had one of my best moments in sport. You know how it is to be able to say, 'I was there.' Well, I was there when Jack Nicklaus pulled off one of the greatest-ever sporting victories. I've seen many other wonderful happenings in various sports, and played in one of them in the tied Test in Brisbane in 1960. I've met 80,000 people who talk as though they were there at the 'Gabba that day although, in fact, the actual crowd was 4,100. I've been very grateful to have had the opportunity to be a part of those matters but, in golf, the Nicklaus one was special.

It was the usual wonderful finish to four great days at Augusta and, out on the course, I was mentally tearing up several intros for radio and newspapers back in Australia. Daphne and I had followed Greg Norman at the start of the final round and he was playing with Nick Price of Zimbabwe. We had already experienced all the thrills of Price's course- record sixty-three the previous day where, because of his first two rounds, he was off the first tee before mid-day and played in front of a remarkably small gallery and took only thirty shots on the back nine. Now here we were watching him again but the adrenalin wasn't quite flowing on the final day, nor was it for anyone else for that matter. Norman, leader by one stroke at the start of the day, quickened our heartbeats on the first, second and fourth holes by sinking putts to save par; Seve Ballesteros played the first nine well enough, but no one was really on fire.

One of the many great features of the Masters Tournament is the brilliant work done on the scoreboards around the course, and the clarity of the scoreboards themselves. They still showed Norman in the lead, then suddenly Ballesteros eagled the eighth and went one ahead of Norman. New intro! Up ahead Nicklaus sank a putt for birdie that started his charge. Four groups behind Nicklaus we were watching Norman and Price and, as the scoreboards changed, so did the intros; Nicklaus was just getting into gear for an eagle and other birdies.

Meanwhile, we watched Norman double-bogey the tenth, having seen him four-putt the same hole on the second day of the tournament. Now it was close to decision time for me for there were editions to be caught back in Australia and, as the enormous roar signalled Nicklaus's birdie on the sixteenth, we decided Daphne would continue with Norman and Price, who had just putted out on the fourteenth, and I would wait for Nicklaus to come up the seventeenth, the green of which is close by the fourteenth.

I wasn't the only one to leave the pair. One moment Norman and Price had hundreds clambering all over one another to get a glimpse of them, the next something like forty people remained, one of whom was Daphne, walking just behind them as hundreds raced for the Nicklaus–Ballesteros pairing. She got the quote and I missed it. It was a little like Merlin waving his magic wand and the crowd disappearing, and a moment later Greg said tersely to Price, 'Come on, Nicky, let's show these people we can bloody well play golf,' and they strode off to the fifteenth tee. Because Nicklaus was two holes ahead, I positioned myself at the back of the seventeenth green and purely by chance, when he putted, the hole was perfectly placed between him and me so I saw every inch of the twelve-foot putt which broke to my left and then to my right before going into the centre of the hole. I was there!

Relatively it brought one of the greatest sporting roars I have ever heard, bearing in mind you can only get so many people around a golf green even when there is a great spectator mound as well. We caught all our editions, the newspaper one by three minutes, and I used Daphne's exclusive Norman quote in my intro. When I phoned the subs' desk a little later to enquire if all was okay, the sub-editor told me everything had gone in as written, except the Norman quote.

He said he had changed it to: 'Forty-six-year-old Jack Nicklaus won the Masters Tournament at Augusta today, defeating Greg Norman by a stroke.' Never argue with a sub is a good rule but I did think Daphne's on-the-spot exclusive would have had just a little more oomph!

Television is a very interesting and challenging medium and the commentary box requires intense concentration. There is never a shortage of little glitches through the wires which transport the sound and pictures from the producer's van. It is astonishing though that there are so few of them in either Australia with Channel Nine or in the UK with the BBC. In England, the BBC's Keith Mackenzie is the Executive Producer, a man who learnt his cricket in Australia and knows many other sports as well. He produces the Grand National, used to produce the Cheltenham Gold Cup Festival until Channel 4 gained the rights, has handled the snooker production for a considerable time and is a highly regarded producer in the line of those who have handled cricket for the BBC over the years.

Alan Griffiths is Welsh, and would love to see Glamorgan win any of the cricket championships, cups or trophies, or all of them for that matter. He is a cricket and Rugby man and, like other BBC producers, can produce or direct anything. There are times when, sitting back in your living-rooms, you might think from the slight rise in tone in the commentator's voice that he is excited, or, without you knowing it, it could be that one of those little glitches has appeared. It might be that a camera has 'gone' just at a crucial moment, or a cameraman has been defeated by an on-drive that goes past point, something to do with sound, or someone may have pressed an unusual button somewhere in the world. It might be something to do with the commentator, it could be something to do with production at the ground, and on the rare occasion the latter might occur, I have been known to say softly into the 'lazy-mike', 'Everything all right down there . . . ?'

Just after the England versus New Zealand Test at Old Trafford in 1994 we went to Headingley to cover the NatWest match between Yorkshire and Somerset. Alan Griffiths was on his own as the main producer, though John Shrewsbury was also there to lend a hand on what turned out to be a rain-marred day.

Because of the rain, the commentators' roster turned into a dog's breakfast with additions, deletions and initials everywhere and Tony Lewis, as presenter, was doing another brilliant job of providing interviews, detail and all other things necessary when nothing at all is happening on the field. Coming up to what would have been tea-time, I knew that I, in the commentary box, needed to keep an eye on things for Jack Bannister who was on air in the studio with Tony and Geoff Boycott but, for some reason, I put my brain into Plan B mode and settled down at the small table in the even smaller commentary box, earpiece in my ear, and started on a sandwich and a cup of tea. I was able to hear the interesting discussion between Tony, Jack and Geoff and see it on the monitor at the side of the commentary box. Suddenly there was a frenzied shout from the van and in my ear because Tony had said, 'And now to Richie Benaud in the commentary box.' Plan B changed to Plan A in an instant. I moved at considerable speed and the following ensued.

I dropped the sandwich on the floor, and banged my right knee hard on the side of the chair. With the pain from that, I dropped my binoculars on the chair and my earpiece, which was connecting me with the shouts from the van, became tangled in the connecting wires.

When I joined it all together, I found the plug was out of, instead of in, the sound box.

Eventually, while everyone else in the commentary box was hysterically helpless, I was able to say in a suitably calm voice, with only a slight edge to it, 'Now that you've had time to study the scorecard at your leisure . . . !'

In my ear there came an equally calm Welsh voice, but with a definite hint of laughter about it: 'Everything all right up there . . . ?'

It was the ultimate Welsh '*touché*'.

The perils in being the senior commentator are those associated with the name itself, which might be an indication of being more aged and infirm than your colleagues. Occasionally, senior or junior, things go to air and you wish they had not, but it is difficult to pull them back as they are leaving your mouth. Sometimes though the position produces some interesting and amusing situations, one of which occurred at Brian Lara's home ground, Queen's Park Oval in Trinidad, during the Third Test of that 1991 Australia versus West Indies series. The first day was washed out at 2.50 p.m., and on the second morning I did the usual in-vision presentation in front of a grandstand in the outer.

Throughout the Caribbean this was the equivalent of making one's way from the Channel Nine commentary box in the Bradman Stand at the SCG to a spot five metres from the front row of a packed Hill. For Channel Nine in the Caribbean no luxuries such as air-conditioned studios and commentary boxes. On my way to this open-air, in-vision position, I walked past the armed guard at the entrance to the playing area and we exchanged a civil 'good morning'. Twenty minutes later, when I returned, my very good friend, the armed guard, had been joined by what was either a dog or possibly a large wolf, an animal approximately two metres long and a metre tall, and made of an extraordinary number of muscles and teeth. It was the original steroid dog. It was a Dobermann. Common sense dictated that I stop, and there was a very good reason for this: the Dobermann was standing between me and the entrance, or, as it was now, the exit.

We looked at one another for a considerable time. When he drew back his lips and smiled and then barked I leapt only nine inches or a foot in the air, but quickly adopted Plan B. This involved saying nothing and locking eyes with the armed guard rather than the dog. After a minute or two it worked. The guard said nothing but stood up, led the dog out on to the playing field and I made for the exit with calm assurance.

It was then I noticed several Trinidadians helpless on the asphalt, rolling around, overcome by laughter. They are nothing if not resilient in moments of comical stress however, and one of them recovered fast enough to shout, to the delight of the stand, 'Hey man, you face Wesley Hall, what for now you take a backward step? That puppy's teeth only made of rubber . . .'

One of the problems which was around when I still played cricket was the matter of common ground between media and players on the question of how much each knows about the other's job. The media know that some players flounder when asked questions; they know that some players, even captains, can be like time bombs if you allow enough silence after an answer. The media is also well aware that, given the task of writing an account of a day's play, a player might hardly be able to put thirty words together for the intro and, if he did, it would take him an hour and the edition would be gone. Some players, astonishingly, are too lazy even to write their own copy, but they are certainly agile enough to pick up the cheque.

Alongside that is the question of what cricket the media man has played, if he has played any at all, if he just likes the game and has always had an ambition to write about it, or if his father owns the newspaper. If a newspaperman, or a television commentator, is writing or talking about the game at Test level, and he has never risen above a village or an outback match, then a player might have some difficulty with the reports about his perceived lack of technique in a Test match against the ball which swings out and then cuts back between bat and pad before taking the leg bail. This is the most contentious cricket media question, without answer, that I have found over the past forty years.

These days millions of viewers of the TV screen have a first-hand sighting of what goes on, and consider they have every right to be experts on all aspects of cricket and to offer their opinions – and do so. They all have good memories for everything that happens on the field, though that has been a trait of cricket followers the world over in the past fifty years. Some cricket spectators in fact have *very* long memories. A few are brilliant with their repartee, and when they marry that with their memory, the effect can be devastating.

Forty years ago, I toured the West Indies and played in all five Tests. Led by Ian Johnson, Australia won the First Test by nine wickets, drew the Second and won the Third in Georgetown by eight wickets in only four days. When we played the Fourth, in Barbados, we made 668 and had them in all kinds of trouble at 147/6 on the third evening. The next day, the overnight not-out batsmen, Denis Atkinson and Clairmonte Depeiza, batted throughout the five hours' play. The following morning, I bowled Depeiza straight away with one that ran along the ground.

In 1991, I was in Barbados and just about to host the Channel Nine 'intro' to the one-day game eventually won by the Australians. The crowd was in high good humour at Kensington Oval and some, pre-match, were even celebrating their anticipated victory. Loudly! In my earpiece the voice of director Geoff Morris said, 'Fifteen seconds to on-air' and, at the same time, the ground went quiet.

Then, 'Hey, Sir Richard Benaud. You the son of that guy who couldn't get out Atkinson and Depeiza all the fourth day in 1955?'

Right match, wrong family connection.

'If you couldn't bowl them out, you do right to take up television, man,' he continued, just as I began my intro.

'Good morning and welcome to this delightful island of the Caribbean.' I said it through my own laughter and that of hundreds of spectators in the Kensington Stand right behind me.

You need to keep your sense of humour on television and to bear in mind a few little things to help you through commentaries. I'm often asked for advice on how to commentate, but simply copying someone else never works. You must be an individual and there are a few little notes I keep which are of some benefit in my own commentaries and general organisation. They would not suit other commentators but might or might not be of some assistance, in a general sense, to any younger people who are thinking of moving into the commentary position. In my general organisation, working in the office and in business, the approach to a day, a week and a year of work, I try to bear in mind:

Do your best, never give up.
Golf course behaviour mirrors business behaviour.
The same error twice is only one mistake, but a very big one.
Make your own luck, keep two overs ahead of the play.
Mediocrity is contagious.
Silence can be your greatest weapon.

Then, in the television commentary box, there are many aspects of discipline to be observed; it is necessary to be organised, particularly if you also have other media work to do, as happens with me. My freelance work includes television commentaries, writing for newspapers, working for radio, writing feature and special articles and doing interviews.

There are literally hundreds of things which might be said by a commentator which should not be said. Some of them find their way into journals like *Private Eye* with 'Colemanballs', some have been spotted more recently in Desmond Lynam's excellent book, and some are imprinted on the minds of those who have heard and now cherish them. Some will never be forgotten by the commentator who uttered them. They are inscribed on his or her mind for ever.

These are the ones I try to avoid. Even so they will slip through occasionally although it is a matter of lack of concentration if they do. It doesn't make me feel any better when it happens and it's then a matter of concentrating harder and trying to make certain it doesn't occur again:

Put your brain into gear before opening your mouth. Try not to allow past your lips:

He is a doyen, a guru or an icon . . .
He gives 120 per cent, or 150 per cent, or even 200 per cent . . .
At this point in time . . .
Of course . . .
You know . . .
Well, yes, you know, I mean . . .
To be perfectly honest . . .
Really and truly . . .
I really must say . . .
I must ask you . . .
As you can see on the screen . . .
Have a look at *this* . . .
The corridor of uncertainty . . .
That's a tragedy . . . or a disaster . . . (The *Titanic* was a tragedy, the Ethiopian drought a disaster, but not the fall of a wicket or a dropped catch.)

Don't take yourself too seriously!

This very short list needs to be read in conjunction with the amount of concentration needed to be a commentator: it is fierce, the same as applies to successful players and captains. One or two people I know say working on television is a 'doddle'. Not for me it isn't. If you're not prepared to concentrate and to work as hard as is required, then you are better off in another job.

But, above all, remember a job as a cricketer or a TV commentator might need fierce concentration but, just as important, you also must have a bit of fun, otherwise it just turns into an ulcer-making dirge!

One thing of which you can be certain about television commentary is the advice noted earlier, that silence is your greatest weapon. Timing is another. It is no use talking about something, making comment on a happening if there is nothing to do with that on the screen.

We were covering a Test match at Lord's five or six years ago when there was a commotion of sorts on top of a building on the eastern side of the ground. There was a small group of people having a barbecue on top of one of the rooftops and along just a little further was a lady who, even without the benefit of binoculars, I could see was dressed in slightly eccentric fashion. What there was of her garb seemed to be black. Closer examination showed it to be filmy black, possibly lace. She was standing in front of some lettering but I didn't have time to pay attention to that because the bowler was coming in at the Nursery end.

In between balls there were murmurs from the crowd who by now were paying as much attention to the lady on the roof as they were to the game. Keith Mackenzie, our producer/director, said into my earpiece, 'I'm going to have to show what's happening if nothing comes from the next ball.' I said, 'Okay' and then made a comment about the quick single that had been taken. Keith cut to the roof across the road and there she was, looking different now she was much closer on the screen from the way she did to the very naked eye. The lady, clad in black fishnet stockings and with a thick piece of string across her frontage, was draped over a well-lettered, well-planned and painted sign advertising vodka. It proclaimed, 'Fiona Vladivar loves Richie Benaud.' I said, 'And just think, that's only her mother.'

When I went through a BBC Television course in 1956, three of the commentators who were memorable were Henry Longhurst, Dan Maskell and Peter O'Sullevan. Peter is still with us, Henry and Dan sadly have left, but their influence lives on. I've always regarded them as the greatest and, although it is impossible to copy them, it was possible to learn from the manner in which they did their jobs.

Peter Alliss of the modern-day commentators is outstanding and is a master of the pause and build-up. He was responsible for one of the best pieces of sports television commentary I have heard. It was during the Dunhill Masters at Woburn several years ago when Seve Ballesteros was playing the eighteenth, which is normally the first hole for club members. It was very late in the tournament and Seve had slightly pulled his tee shot to within a yard or two of the fence alongside the road. He had been saved from being out of bounds by the ball brushing the gorse but his stance was still going to be impeded by some more gorse. Seve gave it everything when he arrived down there. He took his stance then he changed it, then he put on his waterproofs and took them off and all the time there was the camera behind him at ground level and Alliss, after telling the viewers what kind of shot Seve might be able to fashion from virtually nothing, remained quiet. There was plenty going on for the viewers to see, which is what television is all about, but there are some commentators who would have been chatting away and describing what the viewers could see for themselves. When Seve finally settled into the gorse again and wriggled around several times with a very pained expression on his face as his buttocks were scratched and torn, Alliss finally used just one sentence to add to the picture and the viewers' enjoyment. 'Ah yes,' he said, 'but how will he explain all that to his wife when he gets home!'

In 1994, Channel Nine organised a special match for Allan Border at the 'Gabba. It was a tribute to a great cricketer and the personnel taking part varied from current players to those out of the game some years, and then to one or two showbusiness personalities and footballers. It was a 16,000 all-ticket sell-out and was very successful, something which doesn't always happen with matches of that kind. They have to be done very carefully or they will quickly become run-of-the-mill. Channel Nine did it well and used a variety of experiments, with microphones on players and umpires and various other little touches, in a match which lent itself to entertainment. At the end of the game when I was racing for a taxi for the airport, with little time to spare, I was bailed up by a cricket fan who had been watching the game on television in the Queensland Cricketers' Club next door. 'Been watching all that stuff you've been doing with the microphones on the players, talking to one another and being quizzed out on the field by the commentators. Bet you're cranky you weren't able to do that in your day?'

Just shows nothing is new under the sun, because back in 1963 I played in a Lord's Taverners match at Lord's with Denis Compton and others and Brian Johnston was the BBC Television presenter for the day. He did a three-way conversation with me and with Compton, in which I was describing what I would bowl, Compton was commenting, and then, for variety, we did it with communication to Johnston and the viewers, but not between ourselves. It was said at the time by those watching the television that, 'it was wonderful to watch, great to listen to and close to unbelievable the things that can be done with modern communications.' Little did they know.

Things have changed a great deal in life, as well as in communications and television over the past thirty years, and one of the questions posed quite frequently is, 'Why don't you have more women cricket commentators?' Give me twenty bucks for every time I've been asked that and I'd be retired to some far-flung island. Why don't we have *any* women cricket commentators might be a better question than 'more'.

Channel Nine used Kate Fitzpatrick for a short time some years ago but I have always felt it was hardly a fair trial, because as she settled into her chair she was surrounded at thigh level by a mass of press photographers and journalists hanging on every word, or perhaps hoping for either a gem or an error. I wouldn't have enjoyed that any more than I expect Kate enjoyed it. Zoë Goss, who plays cricket for the Australian women's team, was used as a guest commentator one day during the Third Test between Australia and England at the SCG, in 1994–5. This was a very tough examination for her, because at the same time she was also playing in the Women's National Championships in Canberra, and had to fly to Sydney on her day off and then return to Canberra to play again the next day.

I would like to see women trying out for commentators' jobs at the same time as men, and at Channel Nine, in their auditions, they would receive the same courtesies as the men might expect. To me, the biggest problem will come when they are asked, as are the men, 'What experience have you had in playing first-class cricket?' The obvious answer is 'none' because of equally obvious circumstances.

There is no doubt one of Channel Nine's strengths is that its commentators, whether they be ex-captains of national teams or ex-Test or first-class players, have the necessary experience to talk about a particular situation in the centre of the ground. Viewers sometimes have a problem with accepting a firm opinion if it is not based on experience. For example, much as I love golf and enjoy the golf work I have done, I am not prepared to offer, on television, an opinion as to why a top-class professional golfer, say Greg Norman, has pushed a ball to the right of the eighteenth green at Augusta. I'm quite prepared to say he *has* done it and describe what happened, because that is fact.

I am a reasonably solid eleven-handicapper at the Australian Golf Club in Sydney, and I have tried to learn as much as possible about the game and the rules, but for me to add for millions of viewers that Norman hit the ball to the right of the green because his set-up was faulty, perhaps an inch or two too far to the left, he came off the ball a little, or he didn't allow for the slightly sidehill lie, would be, in my view, ridiculous. I would certainly ask Jack Newton, Peter Thomson or Clive Clark the reason and I might find out that, in fact, it was Norman's grip which was slightly faulty.

I might be prepared to offer expert golf commentary if later this year I were to pass all the PGA coaching certificate examinations, and if I managed to play as an amateur in some big tournament events so I could sample the intense pressure these players are under over the last nine holes on the final day, with a bunched leader-board and a first prize for the professionals of $200,000. Until that time, and without that expertise, I wouldn't do it.

I am quite prepared though to offer praise or criticism of Mark Taylor's or Michael Atherton's Test match captaincy, Mark Waugh's cover-drive for four or dismissal, or why Craig McDermott was slanting the ball towards the batsman's pads. That's because I've been there.

One of the great pleasures of cricket is in knowing what happened many years ago, or in trying to guess what happened. I'm completely flummoxed though by the career of E. J. Diver who played for Surrey and then for Warwickshire. My research tells me he was the first man to play for both the Gentlemen of England and the Players. He played for Surrey as an amateur and Warwickshire as a professional before the turn of the century and was spoken of, early in his career, as a possible England player in future Ashes battles. He seems to have started playing just after the deeds of Billy Murdoch and Fred Spofforth gave rise to the Sporting Times Ashes notice.

What strange circumstances do you imagine took place to have him make his professional first-class debut for Warwickshire against Notts at Trent Bridge, May 3rd–5th, 1884, return bowling figures of 30.3-14-58-6, thus ensuring his team won the match, and then not be given a bowl in the next game against his old county, Surrey? Thereafter he played for Warwickshire on more than a hundred occasions and I can't find a time where he ever again took a first-class wicket. Perhaps his captain knew something that day in Nottingham. Or perhaps it had something to do with the fact that he appears to have been a 'lob' bowler and they simply went out of fashion! When he played for the last time for Warwickshire on the Birmingham ground he made a 'pair', but at least went out in style, dismissed by Wilfred Rhodes and Schofield Haigh. I have come across a number of oddities in Test cricket over the years but this one, on the surface anyway, is one of the strangest I have seen in county cricket.

# 10

## A new structure for English cricket

English cricket is unique. No matter how one looks at it, there is no other country which plays the game under the same type of structure as England, with eighteen counties making up a professional organisation which has stood, or almost stood, the test of the past 130 years. I *hope* it stands for another 130 because, in almost all ways, it is a delightful way of life for its participants and those who form part of that structure. Whether it *does* continue in its present form is entirely another matter.

No cricket country in the world has more working committees than England. No cricket country manages to pay less attention to the important things and more attention to the unimportant matters than England when addressing the question of cricket. However, as England invented the game and happen to be the only ones to play it on a full-time professional basis, then why shouldn't they do their own thing with decision-making?

One problem is that you can get away with just about anything if you are winning but, at the moment of writing, it is quite some time since England have been in serious winning vein against any of the best teams: the West Indies or Australia, India or Pakistan. There have been blackwashes against the West Indies and some kind of green and gold washes against Allan Border's Australians on three occasions in the past six years – 1989, 1990–1 and 1993 – and then against Mark Taylor's team in 1994–5. Twice the Australian victories involved Terry Alderman and others, once Bruce Reid and friends and, in 1993, Shane Warne and his mates.

It was the 1993 series in England which struck the really cruel blow because the Australians had gone to Worcester for an early tour match and, in the heavenly atmosphere of the famous and beautiful cathedral city, Graeme Hick had thrashed hell out of them in making 187. Shane Warne had gone for 1/122 from only 23 overs and all the talk around the cricketing traps was that he was quite possibly overrated. Although he took five wickets in the next match there were still no doubts about England's ability to handle him, and when he was left out of the three Texaco one-day International teams, it was regarded as a straightforward selection-table gambit where he was simply beaten for a place. There was momentary English disquiet when, in the lead-up games to the Test, against Surrey and Leicestershire, he bowled 58 overs, 26 maidens and took 11 for 166.

As an initial statement, and in the light of events to come, 'overrated' didn't quite rank with that famous record company's original denigration of the Beatles as second-rate performers and unlikely to be a financial success, but in cricketing terms, it has so far been along the same lines. By the time Warne had finished with England's batsmen in 1993, English cricket followers began to yearn for legspin bowling to be reintroduced as a factor in their own first-class matches. There were murmurs about the need to change the structure of English cricket and more committees were set up.

I love English cricket, it has great appeal for me but, in keeping with all other things in modern-day life, adaptability is essential. There have been many changes to the game. In some ways the English county cricket championship was, and still is, quaint by the standards of world sport. Any proper competition where, as years ago used to be the case, each of the contesting teams didn't play against all the other teams and all did not play the same number of games cannot be less than quaint.

In recent times of course that has been addressed and now, with Durham in the competition and an even spread of four-day games, there is a much better structure. There is a call for the county competition to be divided into two divisions but I can't see the benefit in that. For it to be a success, there would need to be a prerequisite that spectators are likely to come flooding back to watch county cricket, which I very much doubt would be the case. At the moment the structure is geared to the members belonging to county cricket clubs and there are enough grumbles about four-day matches instead of three, and the consequent lessening of the amount of cricket played. In the days when there were three-day games at county level, the members would have a three-day match to watch starting on Wednesday and continuing on Thursday and Friday, with another one starting on Saturday and continuing on Monday and Tuesday.

In the late 1950s, a one-day series of matches, more social than competitive, was played under the Rothmans banner and it was so successful the cricket authorities decided they had to have a piece of the action.

There was a very good reason England embraced one-day cricket long before any other country. The various meetings of county chairmen and others realised county match attendances were plummeting. Then, in 1963, an unsponsored competition of one-day matches began, with a final at Lord's played in front of a packed house, and the Gillette company came in as sponsors the following year, later to be followed by NatWest. The Benson & Hedges one-day competition got under way a few years later, followed by the Sunday League.

All this was to the members' advantage but, in modern-day cricket with an emphasis on limited-overs matches, there were increasing complaints about the workload on the players. There were more and more complaints that the structure was not to the advantage of English cricket, that the County Championship should be used *solely* to produce the best England team.

This is an arguable proposition, but the best way to look at it is to pose it as a question, and the answer is that it would not be very clever if the County Championship were not to have as one of its aims the ability to produce the best England team.

My own experience with Sheffield Shield in Australia is that every year I played, from 1948 to 1964, my main desire was that New South Wales should win the Sheffield Shield, and the natural run-off from that would be that NSW would also be preparing cricketers to play for Australia. I cannot think of any time when my first thought was for myself and other NSW cricketers to get into the Test side, it being only secondary that NSW should win the Sheffield Shield.

In the past year in England there has been far more emphasis on the point about two divisions in the Championship and each time I examine it I see potential problems. The questions to ask are:

Why would you want two divisions instead of one?

What would be the advantage?

Will having nine teams in a top division improve the standard of play?

What names will be given to the divisions?

What formula will be used initially to decide on positions?

Is there, in fact, likely to be any advantage at all?

Have the administrators thought the whole thing through?

The answer to the last question is that I hope so, because one of the real problems in cricket administration in all countries revolves around matters not being thought through to their logical conclusion.

Let's start with the first question of why? I'm assured the answer is that it will increase the excitement of the County Championship so there will be one or two teams going up from the second division and one or two going down from the top division, in the same style as soccer: promotion and relegation. I can't visualise the same excitement applying to cricket. How the divisions will be first formulated, and what they will be called, will be another matter for argument. To start it off, if you are to have a first division and a second, and you decide that the first division will be based on the top nine teams from the previous season, what would you do with, say, Yorkshire who have had trouble winning the Champion-ship in recent times?

Second division for Yorkshire? Spare me, please.

Or, what about a team which has won trophies recently but last summer because of injuries happened to finish near the bottom in all events?

In fact, I don't believe you could call them first and second division, nor could you call them Division A and B, otherwise there would be dismay from the ones in the lower section, the dismay would turn to 'aggro' and the shouting matches would precede the real ones.

Just to say that automatically there would be better cricketers produced by a two-tiered system is too simplistic. The better answer, surely, is to find a way to have all the cricketers in the eighteen teams play much better and harder, and with spirit, within the current system. Technique and mental strength are very important, but simply to change the Championship to two divisions seems to me to be a bit of administrative paper-shuffling.

If there is any advantage, what would it be? There is the possible advantage already mentioned of the interest engendered in which teams would be relegated, more a kind of masochistic interest I suppose. A sudden-death soccer elimination is quite different from a four-day elimination between two cricket teams at the end of the season. The ones to gain admission to the higher competition could be more enthralled, but would they be? What would it mean, being in the top division? More money perhaps, more sponsorship? But if that were the case, would it mean that correspondingly the bottom division teams would earn less sponsorship and less money from, say, fees and hand-outs from TV rights? Would the players in the lower echelon be paid a smaller wage?

However, I do believe there is a real case for changing one aspect of the Championship, the one which specifies which county will be declared the winner each year. At the moment it is first past the post and I would like to see that change to a system of semi-finals and final which is along the lines of the system in operation in Australia in the Sheffield Shield, the comparable competition to the County Championship, although played between only six states rather than eighteen counties. The small number of participants in Australia is the reason for having a final and no semi-finals.

The best way to do it would be to have the team at the top of the table, after the seventeen matches have been completed, declared the County Premiership winners, and then the winner of the final declared the holder of the County Championship. The Premiership winners would win £100,000, the runner-up £50,000, third place £25,000 and fourth £15,000, the semi-finals to be drawn by ballot for home ground advantage. The winner of the final would receive a further £60,000 and the beaten finalist £30,000, with £15,000 for third place. That would engender plenty of interest in the County Championship of the future. It would reward the winners and it would still allow the teams finishing at the bottom of the competition to be in the same division as the better ones. And it would provide plenty of incentive for every one of the eighteen counties and, I believe, ensure that the cricket played was far more purposeful than is sometimes the case these days.

I believe it is much more important to bring in a system of semi-finals and final matches than it is to spend even a passing moment worrying about two divisions.

Even more important than that though is the manner in which the County Championship games are played. With a four-day competition being played now, there cannot be any excuse at all for contrived declarations and joke bowling. There is no doubt in my mind that *this* type of cricket, which has been prevalent in the English game in recent years, has had a great effect on the manner in which the national team has performed. The problem is that if you play soft and lazy cricket at first-class level you are not going to be in practice to play hard cricket when you arrive in the Test match arena, no matter how you might try.

Sensible declarations and hard bowling, which still allows challenging declarations to be made, should be the aim of every captain and player in the competition. Joke bowling, used simply to come up with some kind of a declaration, is boring and a waste of time and produces weak cricket and cricketers. No wonder England, at times in recent years, have had some problems when confronted by cricketers who haven't been forced to play around with the game in order to seek major points in a competition. Forfeiting an innings is not a contrived declaration, though I would regard it as being so if both captains did it in their first innings in *good* conditions just to try to ensure there would be a result obtained, with *full* points for one of the teams.

The whole thing is bound up in the attitudes of captains and players. When you find a team where the captain has a look at the pitch and then is intent from the first day on setting up something for the final day, then you know you have a real problem. When his county condones what he is doing, then you have a much bigger problem. If the cricket were to be played hard and well, it could be played over three days or four.

On the matter of three-day games against those of four days' duration, there are two arguments. The first is that English cricketers down the years always managed to finish their share of games played over three days, and at the same time they produced some outstanding cricketers for England. Four-day matches though are the sensible way to programme because there are so many limited-overs matches played these days and you need the contrast. The ideal for England, so far as I am concerned, would be the same domestic limited-overs competitions as are played now – that is the NatWest, Benson & Hedges and the Sunday League – together with the County Championship. But in England, a limited-overs match, other than the Sunday League if it remains, should always be on a knock-out basis and not in any circumstances be played on a regional round-robin basis.

There is argument that the Sunday League should be abolished to ease the players' workload. Would that be the result though, or would the players then be engaged in playing matches for the county beneficiaries every Sunday? A worthy cause, but they definitely wouldn't be having a rest as is suggested by those players who don't like the Sunday League. It is, in my view, a better idea to provide a limited-overs competition for cricket followers on a day when they are able to attend a fixture, rather than leave the day without matches.

Pitch preparation is always something of a lottery anywhere in the world but recently in England it seems to be as much under control as possible. There are strictures on the way the pitch should look and play at the start of the match and, although there are a few other instructions, really the only point necessary to make is how the pitch should be at the start.

Then natural wear and tear will take over and the spin bowlers will come into the game.

To cover pitches or to leave them uncovered is an ever-increasing argument, and one which really is only applicable to English cricket. In Australia it is impossible to have uncovered pitches at first-class level because of the texture of the soil. After being wet, they then dry like plasticine and the ball will tear pieces out of the surface and rear straight at your throat. This is due in the main to the clay content of the soil, whereas in England the soil is much finer and the ball does not jump at the batsman in such dangerous fashion off a soft surface.

I have never minded whether or not England played on covered or uncovered pitches; it is something a country needs to work out for itself. However, I've never felt that a player's technique in England has been damaged in any way by playing on uncovered pitches. It didn't do P. B. H. May a great deal of harm, or Hutton or Compton, or the county players who played with them. It is my impression though that players' techniques in recent years have *not* always been assisted by playing on covered pitches. This view is unlikely to find much support from the modern-day player, but it is one I hold because of the experience of having played under both sets of conditions: on tour in England in 1953, 1956 and 1961 when pitches weren't covered, and in Australia where they had to be covered.

The administrators, when they moved to full covering of pitches in English county cricket, claimed it was done to assist England's cricketers become more used to the conditions they could expect in Test cricket around the world. I don't deny that as an argument on paper but, so far as England is concerned, I am swinging towards leaving County Championship pitches uncovered, so long as the surrounds are properly covered.

My idea would also cost money, so it may not be universally welcomed. The cost would come from a standard foolproof covering system so that every county ground would have available the same type of covering which would be used at the discretion of the umpires in consultation with the groundsman. The Test match grounds already have excellent covering systems, even though occasionally they have not been used to the best advantage, but the basis of this suggestion is to ensure that the County Championship games are able to restart quickly after rain.

The pitch itself would remain uncovered.

The first thing is to make sure the fieldsmen and the batsmen are able to secure a reasonable foothold after rain. That may seem an unusual start but it is what I would do by covering, on the pitch square, five pitches on each side of the one being used, and then cover, at the ends of the pitch being used, *an area of one yard behind the bowling crease, the area between the bowling and batting creases and one yard in front of the batting crease.* The purpose of this would be so the umpires would be able to say, when the rain stopped, that play could continue as soon as the outer covering was removed. Batsmen would have a foothold but bowlers with long run-ups might have to wait for a while. Spin bowlers would be the ones used on the resumption of play. The umpires would be instructed that it was not a condition of the resumption of play that the faster bowlers should instantly be able to gain a perfect footing.

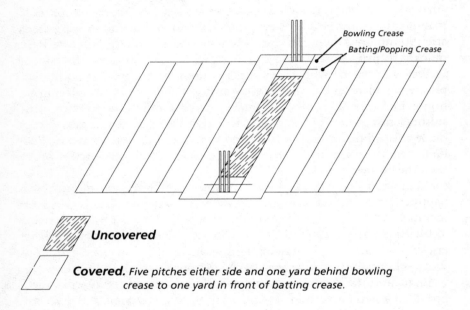

**Uncovered**

**Covered.** *Five pitches either side and one yard behind bowling crease to one yard in front of batting crease.*

My view is that this would be a perfectly reasonable rationale for county cricket in England. It would satisfy many who feel that part of the English game, and I emphasise English, has been lost through total covering, and I have personal experience of the technique aspect.

When I toured England in 1953 and 1956 they were the only times until then, other than in club cricket in Australia, when I had played on uncovered pitches. As noted earlier, playing on a wet and soft club pitch in Australia you had a good chance of having your head knocked off. Playing on a wet and soft pitch in England you had a good chance of improving your batting technique. And your bowling technique as well, for that matter.

I believe I did that in 1953 when the pitches were green and sometimes damp and gave the seam bowlers some assistance. Alec Bedser bowled magnificently during that Test series and only the most experienced Australian batsmen were able to cope with him. I certainly couldn't. But after five months of batting and bowling on all kinds of pitches, I was in no doubt my technique had improved. It should have done so, if I had the intelligence to learn. There were plenty of failures, but making runs on a damp day at Bradford, then batting for an hour against MCC on my first appearance at Lord's when Trevor Bailey and Alan Moss were in the opposition, was an invaluable lesson. So too making 70 against Les Jackson and Cliff Gladwin at Chesterfield where, after 90 minutes, my right thigh was a mass of bruises. It taught me very quickly to play more side-on!

When I was chosen to go on the tour of England I was simply a promising all-round cricketer. That was in April 1953 and we returned home in September. When I then played in the 1953–4 Australian season starting the following month, only three batsmen in the country made more runs in the summer. Two of them, Colin McDonald and Graeme Hole, were also on the 1953 England tour and benefited greatly; the other was Ken Mackay. Only one bowler in Australia, Ian Johnson, took more wickets than I did that summer of 1953–4 so I was quite happy to attribute any improvement, in part, to having a changed technique.

Neil Harvey was one who always advocated the benefits of playing cricket on uncovered pitches in England and, with his outstanding footwork, no one did it better. It was a joy to watch him. When I played in England in 1956 it was on a series of tracks which, apart from Lord's, provided a certain amount of assistance for spin bowlers and again my technique improved, though bare figures may argue against that. It was a wonderful challenge. In 1956–7 in Australia and New Zealand, and in South Africa in 1957–8 following that 1956 tour, my changed and further improved batting technique brought me more runs than ever before in a season. Purely from the personal point of view, I regarded the improvement as having partly come about through batting on uncovered pitches which required a tighter technique, although it may not have been so for everyone.

It is often said by the opponents of uncovered pitches that we shouldn't have another bowler like Derek Underwood, able to tear apart batting line-ups with some assistance from the surface. I look at it in another light. It would be a great thrill for me to see another bowler like Underwood bowling, with another wicket-keeper like Alan Knott behind the stumps. I would regard it as one of the better things that could happen to English cricket and it is possible those who go to four-day county matches might even agree.

Forget about bonus points in this hustle and bustle age of cricket. There was a time when bonus points were necessary: county cricket was sometimes slow and there were complaints about the urgency of the play. To solve this, in 1968 bonus points were introduced, but, as is the case with everything in cricket, the players find a way around any change in the Playing Conditions. Generally, the weaker teams in the competition these days score fewer bonus points and the stronger teams score more, so the bonus points tally at the end of the summer is merely a reflection of the places in the points table of the various teams. The range from the top team to the bottom team is often something like ten to twenty bonus points. Without them the positions in the Championship table would be almost unchanged.

In 1993, Middlesex won the Championship with 272 points and would still have won it with 176 without bonus points. Worcestershire were second, with 236 points, and would have been second on 152 without bonus points. Glamorgan 231 (144) and Northamptonshire 222 (128) would still have been third and fourth. It would be quite easy to continue with the same points system as is in operation now and simply delete the reference to bonus points.

Twenty-seven years is plenty for bonus points. It was one of those things which 'seemed a good idea at the time', but the changes in the way the game is played have made the concept outdated.

It's my opinion that bonus points in England have done their dash.

There are so many ideas on how best to change English cricket for the better that the first question to be asked is whether or not any change is necessary. I think so, but I don't advocate outlandish changes because, having played the game and observed it in England for forty-two years, I know that a cricket structure in any country is always more under fire when the national side is losing. You don't hear a great deal of wailing about the system being 'crook' if the national side is beating hell out of most of the teams reaching its shores, or at least holding its own.

That's not totally the story with English cricket at the moment though, because it is already going through a transition period to do with the switch from three-day to four-day cricket.

I am from the same era as Mike Smith, against whom I played in the 1961 series in England, and he was a fine cricketer. True, he doesn't very often rush around throwing his opinions on the game into the media ring, but that shouldn't be regarded as a demerit mark. I know quite a number of people who can't bear to let a journalist out of voice range, or a television commentator past an eyeline, but that doesn't mean the quality will be there when they open their mouths.

It was for that reason I was interested to read MJK's thoughts on one or two aspects of the game while he was managing the England team in Australia. He reckoned, for starters, that county professional staffs might have to be cut to, say, sixteen and that it would be difficult to cut down on the amount of domestic limited-overs matches played without affecting county and, therefore, players' finances. Also he felt that administrators would need to be very careful about any mooted plans to change the structure of club and league cricket. He offered a very good reason for this: 'having a game with your mates' was one of the main objects of club cricket. There is nothing wrong with that, because it is also the Australian way, to get out on a Saturday afternoon and play extremely competitive club cricket and later have a few drinks with your mates. I suppose one of the reasons I liked his next two comments was that I hold the same views: that *there is a shortage of attacking bowlers who have been taught to get the ball past the bat*, and that *bowlers are the key to winning matches*. No better example of the latter could have been found than the manner in which England bowled out Australia in Adelaide in January 1995.

My view has always been that simply bowling a line and length can be extremely counter-productive. The attacking bowler who takes a wicket almost always has the opposition on the defensive, for a time at least. Look at limited-overs cricket. The best way to place the clamps on a team scoring at six an over is to take a wicket. It took a while for that to sink in with some of the theorists of the shorter version of the game. Bowlers win matches and they make captains look good as well, providing they are backed up by good fieldsmen. The Australian side at present is brilliant in the field. I know from experience in 1961 that an ordinary bowling attack allied to sheer brilliance in the field can win a series and retain the Ashes. And that was just a Test series – no really competitive limited-overs cricket was played for another two years and all our fielders were merely geared to Test match field-placings where there would be three slips and a gully and a gully expert might hardly ever have to field on the boundary or in the covers. However, we did have fielders like Neil Harvey, Alan Davidson, Norman O'Neill, Bob Simpson, Brian Booth, Frank Misson, Graham McKenzie and Benaud, plus a brilliant wicket-keeper in Wally Grout. No slouches there and we won the series 2–1 because we believed in attacking methods, not defensive.

MJK pointed out that in England's two most successful periods since the war, the main bowlers were Fred Trueman, Brian Statham, Frank Tyson, Jim Laker and Tony Lock, and then, in the period 1977 to 1984, Bob Willis and Ian Botham. Nothing defensive about any of them. They knew how to bowl on pitches which might be helpful, but more important, they knew how to attack when, far more often, pitches were in favour of the batsmen. This meant they had to work very hard for their success.

A yardstick to see just how pertinent Smith's remarks are, in the context of English cricket as it stands at the moment, might be whether or not the bowlers around the counties have the ability to work hard for their wickets and whether they actually are prepared to do that. This is where the system has run down.

Competitive instincts have been submerged by attitudes geared to bonus points in the early part of a county match and set-up declarations in the latter part. Before you start leaping up and down about someone denigrating the national game, think for a moment. Is it true? My observations over the past ten years say yes, that is what is happening at county level and it is an insidious creeper which eventually affects the national game, no matter how dedicated skipper Michael Atherton might be every time he walks on to a cricket ground wearing his England cap.

One of the extraordinary things about the main domestic cricket competition in each country is that no one goes to watch. Okay, I settle for that being a *slight* exaggeration, but crowds are sparse, despite the fact that the cricket is often brilliant. The reason is that everyone's pattern of life has changed and, with the advent of the motor car and so much more leisure entertainment, and so many more sports and activities, including television, people have other things to do with their time, compared with many years ago when going to the county ground was all the rage. In Australia, people went to the Sheffield Shield cricket and crowds were significantly better than in these modern times. Elsewhere I draw some comparisons with the number of sports and recreations available to adults and, more important, to children at school. These are remarkable and give, I believe, a clear insight into why cricket struggles these days to capture and then retain a grip on youngsters wanting to play the game and on adults wanting to watch it.

The real difficulty for administrators comes in getting a share of the spectator's hard-earned pound or, in Australia, his dollar. Unfortunately, traditionalists tend to throw up their hands in horror at the thought of anyone concerned with so gentlemanly a game as cricket even thinking of taking a share of anyone's dollar. The Olympic ideal of taking part rather than winning, and of money being a dirty five-letter word, still lives in the game of cricket. More and more we are seeing and hearing criticism of what are termed the men in the grey flannel suits, the marketing men, and most times the reference is made in a sarcastic or derogatory manner. Ironically, there are many occasions when those voiced criticisms are made by people who spend half their lives trying to market their own businesses to make more money, or to market themselves to make more money. *If you were to ask them why they were doing that they would look at you in astonishment and point out that they are running a business.*

Worse things could be done than take account of the way Tony Lewis's county, Glamorgan, have managed to improve not only their image but their business performance. Sitting in the commentary box, I have followed Glamorgan's performances over many years by the looks on the faces of Lewis and the producer Alan Griffiths, who may happen to be around when the county or limited-overs match scores come over the public address system. Lewis was Chairman of Glamorgan from 1988–91 and Chairman of the Cricket Committee from 1987–91. It was a good grounding in administration after he had led Glamorgan to the County Championship in 1969, when I have no doubt the singing in the valleys, and in the pubs for that matter, was something to hear. It certainly was when they knocked off Australia in 1964, and then again in 1968, by 36 runs and 79 runs respectively. Oddly enough, Lewis didn't skipper them in their 1968 victory nor, because of a broken finger which also kept him out of the Headingley Test, did Bill Lawry captain Australia, who were led by Barry Jarman. Glamorgan have a commercial manager now and a membership in excess of 15,000. Lewis's long-term plan in the commentary box was always that the county should have its own headquarters, a ground with ample capacity to provide excellent facilities for those members and to attract for the club domestic limited-overs quarter-finals and semi-finals as well as the normal four-day county games.

They are not the only county to have plans of this kind of course but their blueprint shows imagination, involving a five-year plan of improved performance on the field and high membership with the accent very much on having members as friends rather than just cut-out images paying their annual subscriptions. The main aim has never wavered: to establish a cricket headquarters. That imagination resulted in a boost in membership of 5,000 in the months prior to the start of the 1994 season. All counties will have their own best way of doing things, and perhaps I'm closer to the action with 'AR', but I've always had a soft spot for Glamorgan from the time I walked down what seemed like a thousand steps at Swansea, got a first-baller, caught and bowled by Jim McConnon, and then walked back up what seemed like two thousand steps to the dressing-room. It was my first sighting of Wilf Wooller, who captained them fiercely and made 28 and then 71 not out to stave off defeat. I knew Wilf better as the years rolled on when he was a Test selector, journalist and administrator but I should imagine he was at his most robust and competitive when he was skipper and Glamorgan won the Championship in 1948 when Bradman's side toured England. They had come into the Championship in 1921 when Warwick Armstrong's side toured England, so there is certainly an affinity with Australians.

One of the most difficult matters to balance in England is the type of programming. The weather sometimes doesn't lend itself to assisting spectators and persuading them to make their way through the turnstiles, and there has been a changing pattern of watching as the years have passed. One of the aspects of the game which has become increasingly clear is that spectators, as we approach the turn of the century, are rightly concerned with receiving value for money and are not prepared to take anything less. Then, limited-overs cricket has changed watching patterns dramatically and, I believe, will continue to do so.

In England there are two aspects of limited-overs cricket which I find strange: the matter of the small number of limited-overs Internationals played and the insistence on continuing to take a luncheon break and a tea-time break, as well as a change-of-innings break.

There are some who delight in the fact that a maximum of three games are played between England and a touring team, or four between England and two touring teams in a domestic summer. The cry is that this is to make it clear to the rest of the world that England remains the bastion of the old-fashioned type of programming, and that only over their dead bodies, et cetera!

All limited-overs matches in England, domestic or international, should have a break of forty-five minutes between innings. There should be two drinks breaks each session and the combination of all this would allow for an even flow of play. As it is, in matches in England other than the Sunday League, something like 38 overs are bowled and the players troop off for lunch. Asked about this, administrators have told me, 'It's what we have always done, take lunch and take afternoon tea, it's tradition . . .' It sits uneasily with me that they should be mentioning tradition in the same breath as limited-overs cricket because there is no tradition about this style of game. Excitement, yes. Some wonderfully exciting finishes, yes. Taking the game to the people, yes. Capitalising on modern-day life, yes. Tradition? Careful now!

Although one-day cricket has always been played from the time the game began, in its present form it is a relatively recent phenomenon, with matches during the Second World War reduced in length because of necessity. It should be borne in mind that even in wartime it was hated by the traditionalists.

There was a perpetual sneer for those who between 1939 and 1945 found some interest in the big hitting and excitement associated with the one-day matches, and it was said the spectators who enjoyed that type of cricket were not wanted at county matches. The situation is that they don't go to county matches any more, nor to Sheffield Shield matches, even though much of the cricket played is of good quality. They have other things to do.

There are all kinds of lines peddled about limited-overs cricket, one of which has come crashing down in recent times. This was to do with the assertion that spin bowling, and legspin bowling in particular, had been denigrated and destroyed by limited-overs cricket. Shane Warne and Tim May have put a stopper on that, so too Anil Kumble and Mushtaq Ahmed. What these bowlers have been able to emphasise without saying a word, just by their actions, is that any kind of bowler will have trouble making it into a line-up if he is mediocre. A good legspinner will do well in this form of game, and why shouldn't he?

Ability and temperament will always jump all over staid mediocrity, which is what we see from quite a number of medium-pacers who find themselves trying to tie down an end in limited-overs matches.

In England the legspinner was on the way out well before limited-overs cricket began to be the financial salvation of the game in other countries. When I first worked for the BBC in 1960, there were four legspinners playing in county cricket and they were still there in 1961 when I took the Australian side over as captain. Bob Barber was the best of them, though he was a good opening batsman as well; Robin Hobbs played for Essex and England; Ian Bedford was with Middlesex and Colin Atkinson with Somerset. By 1980 there were none. In the intervening time Hobbs played at international level and there were several from overseas countries, including Kerry O'Keeffe from Australia.

They went to cricket's scrapyard in the sky because of the murmur and rumour machine around the counties which had them classed as ineffective on pitches affected by rain. This is the only thing that made me at first hesitate over suggesting a possible return to uncovered pitches, that the same remarks would almost certainly be floated.

Then I realised it didn't matter two hoots because even on the covered surfaces of recent years in England, only Ian Salisbury has been able to catch the eyes of administrators, selectors and coaches in England, and then only spasmodically. It's not going to make the slightest difference to anyone's thinking in England about legspinners. Bill O'Reilly once said he would never forgive English cricket for trying to kill off their legspinners. Once they succeeded, there was even less forgiveness from 'Tiger'.

What needs to be embraced are the desires of the spectators and potential spectators, and England's administrators have an interesting challenge here. For a start they charge spectators more than any other country in the cricket world. That is not to complain the value isn't there, but the main reason they charge as they do, and the spectators pay, is that England is an affluent country and the grounds are, relatively, very small. When tickets come on sale at £35 each – about $A80 – and there are only a restricted number for sale, they can all be sold out for the first three days of a Test in a matter of a week. This is great from the point of view of the administrators and the treasurers of the various counties, and it is also a matter of supply and demand. If the prices were too high then people wouldn't buy the tickets. Not only do they buy them, but having them is a matter of prestige, rather like someone being lucky enough to be in on the ground floor of a share-market issue.

No need for them to reduce prices for Test matches and keep up the prices for the limited-overs Internationals, as is the case now in Australia where there is perceived a need to have more people go to the Tests, even though it could result in smaller income.

The challenge will come when the administrators settle down to decide if they will have an international limited-overs tournament in

England, with the participants the two teams touring and the home side or, in the case of only one touring team, another team flown in just for the limited-overs games. This would mirror the Australian method which has been in vogue with embellishments since 1977, though it generally takes England a couple of years to agree to any innovation introduced in Australia. These days I even occasionally hear some people murmur, in England, that 'the fielding circle introduced several years ago by England for limited-overs matches has been *such* a success . . .' No one can say it's not true because England did introduce a fielding circle at home, but then you can't say either that it is true, because Australia brought it into World Series Cricket many years earlier.

There should be a triangular event in England, along the same lines as the one which started many years ago in Australia and is now copied by India, Pakistan, South Africa, Sri Lanka and New Zealand. It can only be a three-team event because of the sensible stricture from the ICC in 1994 that no competitions will in future be countenanced with more than three sides because of the consequent downgrading of World Cups. The reason this ICC ruling was brought in was the one-off competition in Australia in 1994–5 where there were two Australian teams.

The experiment, despite all the fine-worded rhetoric, was simply geared to commercial matters. I don't mind that in the slightest, we live in a commercial world and cricket needs to take advantage of every aspect of it to avoid being swamped by all those other sports and pastimes I have quoted on other pages. That is common sense. What is not such common sense is to try to convince everyone that the experiment was undertaken purely for the reason of giving Australia's young cricketers a chance they might not otherwise have had. Young stars like Merv Hughes and Paul Reiffel would have produced a slight smile at that, particularly Reiffel when he found himself playing in both the Australian team and the Australian A team. When people were talking about the A team being young and needing experience, they were forgetting that the top four in the batting order – Hayden, Langer, Martyn and Ponting – between them have hit more than forty centuries and seventy half-centuries in first-class cricket.

The concept was introduced by the Australian Cricket Board to try to make up the financial shortfall certain to be encountered because Zimbabwe were the third team in the competition. Why not say so? Zimbabwe are the ninth Test match-playing country: they are not going to be fazed by someone saying they might not be as good and as crowd-pulling as some of the top countries. What they would prefer is to be invited, to learn as much as possible and to improve, which is precisely what happened. They went back far better and more experienced cricketers than when they arrived in Australia and they were good to watch. Andy Flower, their skipper, Grant Flower, Paul Strang, Alistair Campbell and Heath Streak are cricketers of potential and the others were better for the tour. They showed this on their return to Zimbabwe when they turned in some excellent performances.

Peter Chingoka, President of the Zimbabwe Cricket Union, was in Australia during the tour and would have been impressed both by the standard of cricket played by the opposition and the improvement in his own team. He has the reputation of being a very good administrator and I hope at some stage he mentioned very quietly to Australia's administrators that he didn't mind the concept of the competition but would have preferred a more open explanation.

There is certainly no doubt it was a financial success with the public who went along to the games and the millions who watched on television. It would have been easier to explain it all though if there had been a change in the structure of the competition itself so that matches between two *domestic* teams, Australia and Australia A, were not classed as *Internationals*, and if players had not been chosen to play for both teams.

In order to explain to various correspondents and to the public exactly what the selection criterion was for the competition, I made a verbal request to Australian Cricket Board representatives for details of what would be happening with selection. In the light of what happened with players turning out for both Australia and Australia A, I'm not surprised I heard nothing in reply.

There will be other seasons where an Australian team and an Australian A team take part in a competition in Australia, perhaps with two other teams, perhaps with one. I don't mind that, so long as the Australian Cricket Board says honestly that the reasons are commercial, and so long as they address those matters of two Australian teams being said to be playing an International and swapping players between themselves. The limited-overs game is for entertainment but it would be better if the ACB didn't treat the cricket public as dumbos.

In the 1995 summer in England, England against West Indies and India would have provided a very good competition and would have been a good test for the popularity of such a three-team series. The biggest problem though is that the cricket authorities in England are well aware it would be very successful, but it would be tantamount to giving further blessing to limited-overs cricket if it were to be staged. I would suggest it is a good moment to push those thoughts aside and live with the times.

How to fit such a competition into the programme? It could be done easily by reducing the number of fixtures between the touring side and the counties, matches which these days are put into clearer perspective by the fact that the county players seem to develop mysterious ailments and strains just prior to the scheduled day and suddenly there are many new faces in the line-up handed to the touring captain at the toss.

Allan Border summed it up in England in 1993 when he was asked about future Australian tours of England and matches against the counties. 'A lot of the counties don't really want to play the game. It would be a far better idea if all the counties who did actually want to play against the tourists put up their hands and then you could build your tour programme around that,' Border said. He added, 'When we played Lancashire, Mike Atherton didn't play, Neil Fairbrother didn't, nor did Wasim Akram. Do the counties want the fixture or not, that's the question? I know when teams come to Australia we try to play our best sides against them because the blokes look forward to it as a chance to stake claims for higher honours.'

Border was also critical of matches like the touring team against an Amateur XI, Minor Counties and Combined Universities but advanced the cause of Irish and Scottish cricket, saying that taking the game there was far more important than playing against minor teams inside England. I'm pleased he spoke out in that fashion at the end of the 1993 tour of England because they *are* matters which need to be addressed. The only question is, will they be further addressed and in the proper manner?

This argument of reduced matches against counties surfaced in Australia during the Adelaide Test when the ACB put the point to Doug Insole. Previously the ACB had talked along the same lines to A. C. Smith, Chief Executive of the TCCB, and the ACB's case ran along predictable lines, first of all that they would like three weeks trimmed off the tour.

Australia generally tour England from April to September with six Tests, three one-day Internationals and a number of county games. The ACB would like to keep the six-Test and limited-overs format but reduce the number of county games by playing one four-day game between Tests. And you can be certain that if they talked in that fashion in 1995, they will do so in 1997 also because they will be coming off a

Test series in Australia and another three-Test tour of South Africa, plus one Test in Zimbabwe at the end of the South African tour.

Mr Insole, who is chairman of the TCCB's programming arm, forecast there would be many hours of discussion before any change was agreed upon. His reaction was one of disappointment, on the basis that England would prefer Australia to undertake a normal type tour.

My own view is I would like to see the English season end later, not least because in recent years the weather pattern seems to be changing and September and early October have been producing wonderful Indian summer conditions. One of the problems is that the cricket season has always been perceived to start in April and end around mid-September. With soccer commencing before the end of the final Test at The Oval, there is a feeling that it *must* be time for cricket to wind down. Football though has been starting earlier and earlier each year, training starts almost as the previous season ends and it is always cricket which seems to find it necessary to make allowances. It's not going to worry soccer and the other football codes if cricket goes on later and it could certainly be to the benefit of the summer sport, particularly if a semi-final and final series were to be introduced into the County Championship.

One of the more interesting happenings in English cricket in the past ten years was the appointment of Ted Dexter as Chairman of Selectors, but with added responsibilities for reorganising the structure of the game. Dexter went through some tough times: the Ashes were regained by Australia in 1989, then retained in 1990–1 and 1993. He stepped down in 1993, after having been mercilessly and unfairly pounded by the media, but the changes to the structure of English cricket, put into place while he was Chairman, will be seen to be beneficial as we move towards the year 2000.

In 1989 I saw one of the most extraordinary happenings of my years in Ashes cricket when twenty-nine English players were called up for duty in the six Test matches. In none of those six Tests were the England selectors able to announce their best side, injuries having complicated matters for them, then on no occasion were they able to take their previously announced side into a Test because of further illness or injury. There was total confusion in the immediate lead-up to the opening Test at Headingley when Mike Gatting and Ian Botham had to be left out, but their replacements, Kim Barnett and Robin Smith, performed more than adequately in the context of the game, Barnett making 80 and 34 and Smith 66.

That match six years ago was the start of the decline of Ian Botham's cricket at international level, with 62 runs at an average of 15.00 and 3 wickets for 241 in the series. When Australia regained the Ashes at Old Trafford, Ian was dismissed cheaply by Trevor Hohns and Terry Alderman and took two first-innings wickets. There is no doubt his back and knee problems had an enormous effect on his cricket in later years, in fact at times it astonished me how he was able to get on to the field. Like all great cricketers though, it was sad to see him not performing towards the end of his career, yet still desperately wanting to be part of the action. His time with Worcestershire coincided with the county's most successful period but his later years in England, including that 1989 series, were without the glamorous touches of earlier years, understandable I suppose when you think of the wear and tear to which he had exposed his frame. He was one of the greatest cricketers produced by England and a delightful memory is of him playing 'Boys' Own Annual' cricket alongside David Gower and Bob Willis, the latter pair playing fifty Test matches together in what was an excellent era for English cricket.

Those twenty-nine players who took part in the 1989 series included Gower as captain, after Ossie Wheatley had barred Mike Gatting from the top job. Captaincy, as David Gower found out, can be wonderful, but you do need plenty of good fortune along the way. Gatting had successfully retained the Ashes in Australia in 1986–7 after Gower had regained them from Allan Border's side in England in 1985. In the meantime, England had gone down 0–10 to the West Indies in those 'blackwashes' and the normal type of musical chairs captaincy-shuffling took place, with Gatting superseding Gower.

I loved being captain of Australia.

Being captain of England can be a great challenge, but it can also be very difficult: it is the toughest job in the cricket world. Mind you, Chairman of the England Selection Committee, when England are not doing well, runs it very close but the captaincy is, to me, the most difficult task. The media are tough, the expectations of cricket followers immense, the scrutiny intense, and that is before you even start thinking of any tactics on the field. England have had many captains disappear over the years, sometimes because of unavailability, sometimes to do with the captain's frailties, sometimes for political reasons, sometimes merely as a whim when someone disapproves of him. It should be a tough job because it is the ultimate for anyone in the cricket world, but it should not be quite as tough as it is.

It seems unusual these days, in fact, for an England captain not to play under another captain later in his career, an indication that turnover is high.

Colin Cowdrey played under six different captains after first leading England at Lord's in 1961 with Neil Harvey as his opposite number. This was the match where the 'ridge' first made its appearance. The ridge, on a good length at the Nursery End of the Lord's square, was scoffed at by some but not the batsmen who, in playing forward to a pace bowler, occasionally found the ball flying past their noses. Later Cowdrey played under Peter May, Ted Dexter, Mike Smith, Ray Illingworth, Mike Denness and John Edrich.

Ian Botham first captained England against the West Indies at Trent Bridge in 1980, and only a spirited 22 not out from Andy Roberts and two dropped catches at a crucial time deprived him of a sensational victory. Later he played under Mike Brearley, Keith Fletcher, Bob Willis, David Gower, Mike Gatting and Graham Gooch.

David Gower started in difficult fashion, taking over at Lord's in 1982 against Pakistan when Bob Willis withdrew because of a neck injury. Pakistan won by ten wickets. He captained again in Faisalabad in 1984 when Willis was ill and the match was drawn. He then went through a series as nominated captain against the West Indies, captained by Clive Lloyd, where the scoreline was 0–5, regained the Ashes in 1985 in stunning style in England, then was downed again by Viv Richards' West Indian team 0–5 in 1985–6. After making his debut as captain, he played under Bob Willis, Mike Gatting, John Emburey, Chris Cowdrey and Graham Gooch. Tough times!

Perhaps the English media had the best idea of how to diffuse matters when teams are metaphorically at one another's throats during a series. In 1991, in the Caribbean, there were moments of aggravation, with Viv Richards' team and the one captained by Allan Border playing for what was loosely termed the World Championship.

After one heated exchange on the field this was the notice pinned up in the two dressing-rooms:

Following the recent unseemly behaviour of the authorities of the Australian and West Indian Cricket Boards, the English Press Group wishes to disassociate itself from these two unruly former colonies.

Furthermore, if the matter is not resolved amicably and before the start of the next Test, we will be compelled to alert A. C. Smith, Colin Cowdrey, Tim Rice and E. W. Swanton who will take swift and decisive action. Now, say sorry you lot, *or we will invade again.*

That shows a good sense of humour and a nice turn of phrase.

# 11

# The Adelaide Academy, the ultimate in cricket?

There was a slightly hysterical edge to the news that the United Kingdom Minister for Sport, Mr Ian Sproat, intended visiting Australia around the time of the Adelaide Test in 1995 so he could learn something about the Australian AIS Commonwealth Bank Cricket Academy. The Executive Director and Chief Coach of this worthy establishment, Mr Rodney Marsh, was just the man to put him straight on that, and possibly on politics as well. How to live life to the full might even have found its way on to the agenda, providing Mr Sproat was able to spend more time on the important things and less in the VIP lounge. Mr Sproat's visit became essential when, after one or two hidings at the hands of Mark Taylor's team and Rod Marsh's Academy youngsters, Michael Atherton's England side then were kept out of the finals of the Benson & Hedges World Series limited-overs competition by Australia A and Zimbabwe, and the media showed all the symptoms of 'mulga madness'.

As Ray Illingworth had stated prior to the tour that the limited-overs competition was of less importance anyway, it seemed to be drawing something of a long bow to force the Minister for Sport to travel 24,000 miles, take the risk of sunburn and of sand getting into his contact lenses whilst on Glenelg Beach, and face the challenge of whether or not he is allergic to fresh lobster and king prawns. It was the media who organised the trip for him by constantly inferring that the Academy had rejuvenated Australian cricket, to the stage where the top team, or the Academy youngsters, were able to beat England with one hand tied behind their backs.

I think the Academy is very good, although there are one or two aspects of it that don't gel with me, mainly my preference for governments having as little as possible to do with the running of sport. I'm also not keen on youngsters leaving home to go to an academy at 18 or 19 years of age; I prefer the thought of them being with their families and achieving the same goals. However, I'm assured that, in the go-go world of Australian sport, mine are very old-fashioned ideas. Certainly in the United Kingdom adverse comments on government funding of sport are regarded as being old-fashioned, and with all UK sports administrators trying to get their fingers into the funds from the National Lottery, I suppose they have a point.

The Australian Institute of Sport is vitally interested not only in cricket but a great number of other sports as well. The Cricket Academy is constantly referred to these days as an Academy of Excellence. I was told the other day that within three years the Australian cricket team is likely to be made up totally of its graduates. That will probably depend on how many candidates make up the intake each year; if the intake is dramatically increased then, logically, there may well be a total Australian team output.

I am very happy that Marsh is there because he is a coach of old-fashioned values and method and his first aim is to keep things simple. Anyone who thinks along those lines will get my initial vote, even before I've had a chance to see what his qualifications might be. Marsh's happen to be impeccable. He was one of Australia's greatest-ever cricketers and is the only Australian wicket-keeper to make 10,000 first-class runs and collect 500 victims (11,067 and 869).

He also made 500 runs and had fifty victims five times in a season, in all captured forty victims in a season eight times in Australia and shared that wonderful on-field partnership with Dennis Lillee during the time Ian Chappell and then Greg Chappell captained Australia so successfully in the 1970s and 1980s.

When Marsh made his debut for Western Australia against the West Indies on October 26th, 1968, he made a duck. In failing, he was in quite good company because the state side, after being 22/0, then lost their next seven wickets for 17. It is a good gauge of his character that in the second innings he hit a brilliant 104. He played for Australia from 1970–1 right through until he, Lillee and Greg Chappell retired from Test cricket in the same match at the end of the 1983–4 season.

The system of cricket in Australia has changed a great deal over the years although it should be understood that while it is impossible to miss a good young cricketer these days, irrespective of whether or not he goes to the Academy, it has *always* been impossible to miss a good young cricketer in Australia. There has been a great liaison between state Cricket Associations and country cricket, though it is human nature that there was generally 'one better than the guy who made it'. Stan McCabe's brother was said to be a much better batsman but couldn't afford time off from the shop and there are many stories like that out of the bush. There were a dozen as good as Doug Walters and other Test stars from the country, so the locals always said, but most times they had a bit of bad luck when that splendid cricket administrator and former NSW player Jack Chegwyn was taking his teams on tour around country areas. 'Cheggy' and others like him missed no one.

In talking about the Academy, it is necessary to keep a clear head on these things and not get too carried away with the euphoria of beating England three times on the trot, and to bear in mind that in Australia there is an enormous difference from then to now in the way schools influence the structure of the game.

We used to play under a system which had a far greater accent on schools, partly because there were so few secondary schools. In Sydney these days there are hundreds. When I went to Parramatta High School it was one of only eight government high schools and was the only experimental co-educational secondary school in the Sydney metropolitan area. Teachers took a great interest in sport in those days; now there is very little time and the emphasis is far more on academic qualifications. Radio interviews with students who achieve an HSC (A-Level) grading better than ninety are the norm; the ones getting a hundred are guaranteed national television. There are some teachers who like sport these days but the overwhelming feeling in the education system seems to be that cricket is a waste of space, that the ground on which a match is played on a sports afternoon holds only twenty-two people plus umpires and it should really be used, instead of for such a bourgeois game, for far more worthwhile activities for something like four hundred students. Also that between people and teams *competition* is a grubby word which should have no place in the thinking of politically correct people.

Changing times. When Brian Taber and I set out to write the Rothmans National Sport Foundation National Cricket Coaching Plan in 1972, we stressed those things, and a lot more, which made it clear that the old way of producing cricketers and coaching them needed to be revised. On the first page the coaching manual said:

One key point in cricket coaching of the future seems to be that many of the teachers graduating from college and university are women and, therefore, the choice of whether or not pupils play cricket, or take one of the other sports and pastimes available, is not necessarily left to a male schoolteacher who himself may be an excellent cricketer.

There is an urgent need to produce not only male coaches throughout various areas of cricket, but also to introduce women to the game. All efforts should be directed to having both sexes going through the syllabus until a stage is reached where a female physical training instructor, or a mother taking a Saturday morning Under-13 class, can be just as efficient as her male counterpart.

A relevant point is that, if women teachers are able to learn the basic skills of the game, and therefore themselves enjoy coaching cricket, they will also be able to organise a games period of which a significant part will be some type of cricket.

Nowadays there are as many as twenty options open to school-children on what they should do with their leisure time and the days of cricket-football as the only summer-winter sports are long gone.

It is not the purpose of this National Coaching Plan necessarily to produce first-class or international cricketers. The Plan has been set up to provide more and more coaches who can provide more and more enjoyment for those taking part in what has been a great sport over the years and will continue to be a great sport in years to come.

I wrote that as Editorial Director of the project, almost a quarter of a century ago, and obviously these days it would have to be rewritten to be politically correct and talk about persons, rather than 'men' and 'women' who don't seem to exist any more. However, in 1972 it set the pattern in Australia for the problems facing cricket in the future. It was a programme which concentrated on coaching and producing coaches, not players, and from that point of view, in Australia, it was revolutionary. It also worked, to the extent that Brian Taber, who became National Director of Coaching in Australia and still holds that position, organised assistance for several other countries to do the same thing.

As a starting point it listed six basic fundamentals of coaching. A coach should be able to:

1. *Organise* a class with a safe uncluttered layout.
2. *Correctly demonstrate any skill* of the game in keeping with his coaching standard.

3. *Impart knowledge* of the technique of the game in keeping with his coaching standard.

4. *Detect and correct* errors, in individuals as well as in the total class.

5. *Conduct a practice session,* maintaining interest and participation of batsmen, bowlers and fieldsmen.

6. *Speak clearly,* not moving to another point until the previous one is understood.

That is just about as simple as you can get and it covers my total attitude to coaching: keep it simple and be able to detect errors and, more important, correct them.

There are thousands of coaches in cricket these days. It is an industry far more thriving than the game itself and, if they are all able to *correct* errors, then they are doing their job.

Detection of an error is the easy part. There are approximately a million television viewers watching a match every day and ninety-nine of every hundred of those watchers are able to detect the errors the players are making. No more than one in the hundred, if that, would be capable of proper correction.

In 1972 I mentioned there were at least twenty options open to schoolchildren as to what they might like to do with their leisure time, whereas years before it was definitely a case of the cricket-football syndrome. You might have tennis tossed in as well, and swimming, but there was really no threat to cricket and football. There was suddenly a very real threat in 1972, and a far greater one in 1995, because the choice of things to do for young people is now vast. It has risen from around twenty in 1972 to more than 120! If to the list below you add things like computers and computer games, and watching videos, it can easily be seen that cricket, which is the point at issue, has to work very hard to keep up with the rest, let alone stay ahead.

This list is taken from the *Australian Sports Directory* produced by the Australian Sports Commission and it incorporates the sports assisted by the Australian Institute of Sport, and where there are coaches or coaching made available. It is formidable! I'm sure it applies equally to England these days:

Acrobatics, aero clubs, aerobatics, aerobics, aeronautical model, aikido, aircraft sport, archery, athletics, Australian Little Athletics Union, Australian Association of Veteran Athletic Clubs, Australian football, aviation sport, badminton, ballooning, baseball, basketball, baton twirling, biathlon, billiards and snooker, BMX, bobsleigh, bocce, boomerang, bowls, indoor bowls, boxing, bridge, calisthenics, campdraft and rodeo, canoeing, casting, chess, cricket, indoor cricket, croquet, curling, cycling, mountain biking, dancesport, darts, deer, diving, driving, eight ball, endurance riding, equestrian, fencing, field archery, fishing, game fishing, futsal, gaelic athletics, gliding, golf, gridiron, gymnastics, gyrocopter flying, handball, hang gliding, hockey, ice hockey, ice racing, ice skating, ju-jitsu, judo, karate, karting, kendo, korfball, kung fu, lacrosse, marching, modern pentathlon, motor sport, motorcycling, netball, orienteering, parachuting, petanque, ploughing, polo, polocrosse, pony clubs, power boats, powerlifting, roller sport, rowing, Royal Life Saving, Rugby League, Rugby Union, school sport, shooting (sport shooting, clay targets, full bore, pistol, field and game, small bore), ski patrol, soccer, softball, squash, Surf Life Saving, surf riding, swimming, synchronised swimming, table tennis, tae kwon do, tennis, tenpin bowling, touch football, trampoline, triathlon, tug-of-war, ultralight aircraft, underwater, universities sport, vigoro, volleyball, water polo, water skiing, wave ski, weightlifting, woodchopping, wrestling, yachting. *Disabled sport*: amputee, cerebral palsy, deaf, equestrian, intellectual, paralympics, skiing, special Olympics, transplant, vision impaired, wheelchair.

When the Adelaide Academy started several years ago, with Jack Potter and Peter Spence running it in excellent fashion, they asked three former Australian captains to put in a combined submission on the type of things that might be applicable to such an establishment. Ian Chappell, Bill Lawry and Richie Benaud were the ones who wrote the notes and they might be of interest to Mr Sproat and others who are thinking of setting up an academy. There's nothing very complicated about it but what we did, in effect, was *decline* to offer advice on how an Academy should work, but provide what we believed was the way Australian cricket should work, had always been played and should be played in the future. It was a fun and worthwhile exercise. Bear in mind that it was written at a time when Australian cricket was going through a *very* rough patch and the Sheffield Shield was a much weakened competition because of the absence of some of the best players, who were playing in South Africa.

# General/Representative Cricket

## 1. Style of Play

Over the years there has evolved a distinct style of play in Australia on which our cricket has been successfully based and it is consistent with the word 'attack', whether in the form of captaincy, batting, bowling or fielding. Teams of the future should continue to have attacking batsmen with an aggressive outlook and a bowling attack based on a combination of fast and swing bowling with at least one specialist spinner and an allrounder who bowls spin. A team should preferably contain at least two genuine allrounders and it is imperative that the bowling attack be backed up by good fielding, both in catching and on the ground and, where possible, there should be a specialist wicket-keeper.

In future years our cricket should be based on the above composition with occasional adjustments for limited-overs cricket. But the emphasis should be on complete cricketers who can adapt to any type of game, any type of playing conditions and whatever tactics the opposition may employ. In addition, Australia's successful batsmen have always been able to play off the back foot as well as the front – indicative of constant practice on pitches where there is plenty of even bounce and practice on artificial pitches at junior level. In years past that would be matting or concrete, now it would be synthetic surfaces.

It should be constantly emphasised at all levels that cricket is a simple game, and the more simple you keep it, the more success you are likely to have.

A distinctive Australian style of play should be encouraged, based on positive batting, bowling and fielding, with emphasis on the development of an athletic approach particularly to fielding and running between wickets.

## 2. Captaincy

Australian Test captains over the years have always been intent on carrying the attack to the opposition. At first-class level the only encouragement in selection and style of play can come from the Australian Cricket Board, the Australian selectors, state selectors and the AIS Cricket Academy, and those groups have a vital part to play over the next twenty years. Below that, for better or worse, you are in the hands of the district or grade clubs and the selection of the right

type of captain and the fostering of attacking cricket is a much more
variable proposition.

No Australian captain should ever have to apologise for his team's
attacking and determined outlook on the game, so long as the dictates
of fair play are always observed.

Australian captains should think in attacking and aggressive fashion
and always be looking for a win. When a loss occurs they should be
able to learn from it.

The aim should be to win by playing hard, but fair, cricket. Their
responsibilities are to encourage aggressive batting and good over-
rates and demand the best possible fielding performance from
players. The aim of every first-class batsman should be to score a
century by hitting the ball through, not over, the field. To ensure
the dressing-room traditions of Australian cricket are maintained,
captains should encourage players to sit around and talk over the
game between themselves and with the opposition at the end of the
day's play.

The captain should ensure the game is enjoyable for both players
and public. He should make certain the game is flourishing for the
next generation of players.

More liaison is essential between the ACB and captains of first-class
teams and there should be a regular forum for present-day players,
umpires and administrators to have contact with those of past years.

### 3. Over-rates

Over-rates at Test level are one of the most pressing problems in
world cricket, but administrators' refusal to address the matter has
been one of the disasters of the past forty years. The time may have
passed when anything can be done about it. The cynicism which has
seen rates go down at times to fewer than seventy balls an hour has
been appalling to behold.

Everyone has missed the bus on this – it has been talked about for
years but now we are at the stage where only legislation will really
have an effect in Test matches where you would say that you require a
figure in excess of a hundred overs to be bowled in a day. Other than
for bad weather there should be no reductions in the number of overs
to be bowled.

At district or club level a rate of twenty overs per hour should be
mandatory.

## 4. Spin Bowling

There has been such an emphasis on fast bowling and deliberately slow over-rates in the last fifteen years that only lip service has been paid to introducing more spin.

If you were to say that in excess of a hundred overs had to be bowled in the day and you had harsh penalties below ninety and draconian ones below eighty, plus incentives for exceeding the figure nominated above a hundred, then teams would need carefully to consider the balance of their selection. This is one area the administrators should look at very closely.

Why not, for a start, reduce the $50,000 prize-money for a series to $25,000 and put the other $25,000 to over-rate incentives.

Add sponsorship and you could have $20,000 a Test for teams legitimately achieving the nominated figure per hour, thereby providing, within the scheduled playing hours, another hour of action for those who pay their not inconsiderable entrance fee at the turnstiles. Otherwise the game might well become one solely for television watchers who do *not* notice the actual amount of cricket provided or wasted in a day's play.

Spin bowling should be encouraged by good coaching and passing on of knowledge by captains and coaches, so the importance of the art will never be forgotten at any level of cricket.

Potential spin bowlers must be made to realise that just being a good spin bowler isn't enough to guarantee selection.

They must, as well, be good all-round cricketers. Batting against spin bowling should be improved and this can be done by educating lower-level coaches properly on the importance of correct footwork.

## 5. Support for Australian and State Teams

It is important to have a good manager. The ideal manager would be a former first-class or Test player with a good knowledge of the media, so that he could help the captain any time assistance was requested.

It has only become necessary to engage former players as practice co-ordinators because the players are not being developed properly at the levels leading up to Test cricket.

A physiotherapist is important. In the case of Sheffield Shield teams he should be of an approved standard and provided by the local association.

The Test side should always have a top-class physio travelling with them.

## 6. Approach

One of our current problems is that we seem to be over-burdened with experts who make a simple game difficult. We should get back to basic skills of batting, bowling, wicket-keeping and fielding, plus team discipline.

At the same time player development programmes should be outlined so that players may also be exposed to successful techniques which have developed in recent years to maximise potential and attain peak performance.

The introduction of sports psychology may, arguably, be a good thing, but in the absence of proper planning, with emphasis on skills, it can confuse players and divert the responsibility away from the captain who should be in complete control of the cricketers.

Unlike football, soccer and athletics, Test cricket is played over five days and, by the time the experts have their say, the cricketer who is not successful has been handed a ready-made excuse for not performing at the level required.

If stress were not talked about, half the players wouldn't even know it existed. Today, in both sport and business, people are looking for any excuse for failure to produce. There is no point in handing them that excuse.

It is ironic that in these modern times we have available videotape and all modern facilities, yet we have seen a dramatic decline in techniques and attention to the fundamentals.

Discipline both on and off the field is one answer, more than ever now that twenty-four of Australia's best are professional cricketers.

The reason for the decline in cricket standards in some states has been that the players have been sidetracked in various areas of coaching, and only recently have started to concentrate on the actual team and on cricketing skills.

Throughout Australia the standard of district cricket has slipped as the lack of dedication seeps down through the ranks. The desire to represent one's club, state or Australia should remain paramount in everybody's thinking.

The game and its coaching methods must be kept simple. If we can achieve that we will be doing the game a great service, emphasising that cricket is a most enjoyable sport and, as should be the case, success will only come when the individual is made to account for his performances. Failure should equate with the possibility of being dropped from the team or the elite group to which they belong.

## 7. Statistical Details

In most cases the local scorer should be sufficient, although a Test team on tour should have its own scorer. The team manager should set out the team's requirements for the scorer before each game. These would include scoring charts for batsmen of both teams and, in the case of limited-overs matches, all targets that are applicable to that game and those required to advance in the competition. Apart from the above, all a captain needs is the confidence that his bowlers are each capable of taking five wickets in an innings, his batsmen are capable of scoring a century and that everyone can field like Viv Richards.

## 8. District Cricket Practice/Coaching Support

Coaching and practice support at district and club level is absolutely vital. A lot of players at grade level may originally have worked very hard on the fundamentals but often forget them, simply because they have picked up bad habits and there is no one available to help them out. District teams require a practice co-ordinator to regulate batsmen and bowlers, a batting coach and a bowling coach, one of whom also runs fielding routines.

There is a need for the preparation of guidelines for clubs concerning the development of players at the district or club cricket level.

Physical fitness is extremely important; however, it doesn't specifically do anything extra for the skill of the player. It is very important that he be physically fit and at a constant peak of fitness, although one thing of which everyone should be very wary is that a cricketer should not just be physically fit – he should be physically fit for cricket.

Players should report fit for the first outdoor practice of the season and a check should be made at various times during the season to ensure that level of fitness is being maintained. But fitness training should never, in any circumstances, take up time which could be used for skills training.

While the light is good you should be practising cricket, apart from a short warm-up period before practice. Fielding practice should be a tough session so that skills are being learned and fitness is being maintained. This also helps players retain their skill level as they are tiring.

## 9. Pressure – Players and Administrators

The only way players can better learn to handle pressure is from experience out in the middle. It is not something which can be taught by professors, universities or down in Canberra, but is something which comes from the school of hard knocks, and the sooner our players and the ones coming up learn that, the better they will be.

A lot of administrators in Australia have no idea what it is like to feel international match pressure in the centre of a ground, because at that standard they've never been in the centre of a ground. They know it in theory but not in practice. You can't learn anything about pressure from theory. There is no short cut, it is just a question of acquiring experience at first-grade level, then first-class, before you step on to the field in a Test match.

### 10. Administration

One of the biggest things which in the future will hold back the development of our cricketers in Australia is this lack of recent Test, or even first-class, playing experience at the top level of the game among administrators and administrative personnel at interstate and international levels.

At present the road to becoming an administrator in Australia is heavily loaded towards having plenty of time to spare for the task. An administrative system must somehow be developed to attract present-day first-class cricketers and former leading Test and Sheffield Shield players, rather than only businessmen, into administration or the game will not advance in Australia over the next twenty years.

### 11. Practice

All practice sessions should be conducted in a competitive manner. Throughout the net session the batsman should have an imaginary field-placing in his mind and he should always be trying to find the gaps with his shots. Practice should be undertaken as though the player is in a game. The first half of the batting net session should be played like the start of an innings and the second half as though the century mark has been passed but you still play all your shots along the ground.

All fielding practice should be done competitively. The aim should be to field cleanly every ball hit along the ground and follow this by an accurate return to the 'keeper.

Slip catching is best practised on a cradle with the first player or team of two or three to drop say five catches having to buy the drinks. Regular competitive infield and outfield catching is essential. It is best to have a mix of one on one, plus team slip practice. Other types of slip-catching practice can be used to complement cradle work to relieve any monotony. There should be strong emphasis on ground fielding underlining the simple method of attacking the ball so that the pick-up and throw is made without wasting two yards – or one second.

So too the simple method of chasing, picking up correctly and returning – to save a second. Talking to experienced players, remembering the team plan and your part in it, and learning from your mistakes can help a youngster overcome pressure.

### 12. Developing Tactics and Strategies

This is more a matter of experience than anything else. You can have as many team meetings as you like but you will still find, when you get into a pressure situation, that some players, because they're built that way, will handle it better than others.

A player should practise intelligently and discuss the game in the dressing-room during and after play.

On the field players should always watch the captain between balls and think about the role they have to play in the game.

Being a good listener in the company of senior players will do no harm.

## Coaching

### 1. Role of Coaching in Australian Cricket

The sooner the ACB realise that coaching at state and junior and senior international levels should be on a professional basis, the better the game will be in Australia.

We shouldn't, under any circumstances, have physical fitness men in charge of coaching. Aiding and abetting, yes – in charge, no!

### 2. Coaching Emphasis

The major emphasis must be on the fundamentals and skills of the game. Once the fundamentals are right and players are confident in their own minds they can handle the basic skills, they have a chance.

Coaches should be reminded that fundamentals include all facets of the game and not just batting and bowling. Fielding and running between the wickets are just as important.

Coaching should be done on a commonsense basis. You take the raw talent and you teach basic fundamentals until the player could reproduce them in his sleep. You then encourage the youngster to be a good all-round cricketer, competent in every department of the game, and allow any flair or natural ability to come through.

The people in charge of the 'elite squads' from age fourteen upwards should be reconfirming the basic fundamentals, improving the cricket skills and knowledge and generally trying to develop cricketers for the highest level. This can only be done on a professional basis, using people with the experience and ability to achieve that end. It cannot be achieved by fitness trainers. It is a ridiculous state of affairs that some young players have been allowed to come through a coaching area and still have an incorrect batting grip, stance and stroke execution – certainly many of them have problems with their bowling action which often doesn't conform in any way to the fundamentals and could mean their chance of progressing to first-class level has been eroded. Remember however that a natural style of batting or bowling is a magnificent asset, even if sometimes it may seem unorthodox to a coach.

Being allowed to develop a style which only hinders the player's progress is a waste. The coaching must be on basics and skills. Then on basics plus skills whilst working under stress so that a high level of each is maintained despite weariness.

Long run-ups for youngsters are a waste of time and energy – useless when compared with the benefits of having a youngster get the fundamentals right. Why not a bowling experiment where no bowler in school, junior or lower level teams is permitted to run more than fifteen yards?

## Player Behaviour

### 1. How Should It Be Monitored?
Monitoring players' behaviour is one of the more difficult things these days where lifestyle has changed so much and the ultimate responsibility should lie with the ACB. Fines for really outlandish behaviour should start at something like $2,000 and a two Test-match suspension and be multiplied each time for each transgression, not necessarily by the same player, so that in the end you may have the fifth fellow in the season up for $10,000 and ten Test matches. You would have no more trouble with any players once they saw the Board and the various state and club levels were determined to stamp it out.

*The captain is responsible for the players' attitude to the game.* He should be able to control his players' behaviour on the field, and periodic discussion in the dressing-room after play should ensure there is no doubt what those standards are.

The umpires should be in sole charge of player behaviour on the ground and they should liaise with both captains to monitor any potentially explosive situations.

Once a player is reported the case should be heard by a judiciary comprising an ACB member, an appointed observer at the match, the two captains or their representatives, and the umpire not involved in reporting the incident. The observer should act as chairman of the committee. No legal assistance should be allowed either party involved, player or umpire, but they should be able to call witnesses.

### 2. Competitiveness and Aggressiveness

Enjoyment, competitiveness and determination, within the Laws and spirit of the game, should always be the aim of the people in charge of producing cricketers to represent Australia – it has helped make this country a great cricket nation for over a hundred years.

There must be a little 'give and take' between players, umpires and administrators because aggressive and competitive matches may produce an occasional heated discussion on the field, just as has happened since the game began in this country. Regular liaison between captains, umpires and administrators would help to keep these situations from getting out of hand.

# Pitches

### 1. Turf Pitches

Turf pitches must be maintained at a high standard for Test match and first-class cricket, although synthetic pitches could certainly be used for limited-overs matches.

Synthetic pitches should in future be used in schools and junior cricket so that the bounce of the ball is constant and batsmen will be able to develop their strokes with full confidence that the ball is going to come through truly. At the same time, bowling on a good batting track with a good, consistent bounce will, in the end, make bowlers that much better – there is nothing gives a false impression more quickly than some bowler who has been ripping through teams only because he has been able to get the ball up around the batsman's ears from a good length because of the poor preparation of the turf pitch.

From club level upwards the preparation of good turf pitches is vital to Australia's cricket future. The knowledge of how consistently to prepare good pitches must be passed from senior curators to up-and-coming groundsmen.

Consultation with councils on working hours would help improve club pitches, as turf pitches have to be prepared at the right time of the day. Consideration should be given to the curator's task in the planning of matches at first-class and international level. A Shield match closely followed by a Test match on the same ground should be avoided where possible.

## 2. Characteristics of a Good Turf Pitch

For first-class and international matches you need a pitch which bounces truly at the start of the game and, through wear and tear, starts to take spin later in the match. Each pitch will have its own character because of the different soils used around Australia and this is a good thing, but there is absolutely no excuse for not having a flat pitch which bounces truly at the start of each game.

Cross-rolling is vitally important and should be continually stressed to curators – even the disbelievers.

For the limited-overs matches a pitch of true bounce, equivalent to a third-day first-class pitch, is most desirable.

## 3. Synthetic Pitches

The ideal synthetic surface would be one where the ball will come off quickly from a good length at bail height and there should be a little spin, but there certainly shouldn't be characteristics which allow the bowler to have too much success without effort – they should be forced to work very, very hard for their wickets.

Synthetic pitches are good for indoor and outdoor practice, in the latter case when the turf pitches are too damp. It is good to practise against spinners on wet pitches as long as you don't ruin the pitch in getting your practice. Because club matches are more readily called off in wet conditions these days, players get less chance to develop batting skills to combat the turning ball.

## 4. Characteristics of a Good Synthetic Pitch

A pitch with true bounce which is more in the batsman's favour than the bowler's.

Is there currently available a suitable synthetic pitch?

Any pitch which allows true bounce is good for teaching the game to youngsters. We should always be looking at new developments which will help the game and therefore it is worth looking at any new type of synthetic pitches or ways to improve turf pitches. Outlines of required playing qualities should be drawn up for manufacturers so suitable synthetic surfaces will be available.

# Umpiring

One of the real problems is that grade umpires are not paid nearly enough and therefore it needs someone with a great love of the game to go out there for a pittance on a Saturday afternoon in a grade match and perhaps be abused by a player. There should be some form of umpiring awards for the two best and the two most improved umpires in all match competitions below first class.

## 1. How Can Umpiring Standards Be Improved?
By ensuring that senior and former umpires pass on knowledge to those starting out. By having more contact between captains, players, umpires and administrators.

There should also be more contact between former players and umpires and those presently involved in the game. The ACB could have a hospitality box at each first-class ground and invitations issued to former first-class players and umpires so they can mix with present-day players and administrators.

Sponsorship money could surely be found to cover the cost of this important link in the game's future.

Additionally, a National Cricket Umpires' Development Programme should be established with three levels of certification to provide a source of umpires at all levels of cricket, with provision for progress should ability and performance warrant.

## 2. Umpire Recruitment and Training
Far more effort should be made to attract former players to umpiring.

More thought should be given to the benefits provided for umpires, certainly monetary, and in the side benefits of the first-class and international game. The aforementioned hospitality box would help with this idea.

Sponsorship for umpires' associations should be investigated – this could be a very important aspect of improving the umpire's lot.

# Indoor Cricket

Indoor cricket has a good role to play in the development of cricket in Australia, but it is essential that the batsmen and bowlers in indoor cricket be taught, or even forced by the rules, to obey the fundamentals with regard to their batting and bowling.

It seems, though, more of an entertainment-cum-fitness exercise than a means of improving skills, other than in the art of fielding, and compressible ball (CB) cricket may have more potential to teach and improve the skills of batting, bowling and fielding, as they are used on the cricket field.

# Junior Cricket

### 1. School Cricket – Junior Cricket and Age Cricket

Schools' development over the years of Australian cricket has been good enough to keep us as one of the great, rather than good, cricket nations, but the problem we now face is the increasing refusal of teachers to take cricket to the children and encourage them to play.

It is appalling to read that competitions are to be phased out of school sport. This is the doctrine of bringing everyone down to the lowest common denominator. Kanga Cricket will keep up the interest of children and, hopefully, allow the teachers to participate, but it is essential that Kanga Cricket also be tied to teaching the skills of the game.

It is vital that in all forms of modified cricket, such as Kanga Cricket, the players be taught the fundamentals. To put on exhibitions of modified cricket, with the participants showing no knowledge of basics, is quite ridiculous.

They must hold the bat correctly, stand correctly, and bowl properly.

Consideration should be given to runs on the offside of the pitch being double value in order to restrict onside cross-bat slogging.

At primary school level the aim of the game should be to interest children in cricket without letting them get into bad habits.

There should, however, be a 1st XI which plays competitively against other schools and without restrictions, i.e. no average cricket or rules to guarantee everyone a hit and a bowl. This would require sufficient time to be allocated to achieve such a goal.

At secondary school level you should have an 'A' team for each age group, i.e. Under-13A, Under-14A, etc., which plays normal cricket against other schools and develops the most talented children, and then have any number of other teams to encourage less skilled players to experience the joy of playing the game.

*If the schools won't do this then cricket has to do it.* It is important to start developing the more talented players from about ten years of age upwards and channel them towards club, interstate and international cricket.

District clubs should be required to promote cricket in schools in each district and to develop talent identification procedures and provide the chance of progression for talented players.

## 2. When Should Children Begin Playing Competitive Cricket?

As soon as they are good enough and confident of handling the hard ball and competition – this will vary from child to child.

## 3. How Should Cricket Be Structured to Encourage Progression of Players and Development of Talented Players?

It should be organised to have the best youngsters coming through by age fourteen, so they can compete up to interstate schoolboy level.

These youngsters in state schoolboy teams should be coached by former first-class or international players and not school teachers or fitness fanatics. Where possible the coach should travel with the team.

But most importantly a senior former player wherever possible of at least first-class, and preferably international, standard should act as coach from Under-16 level upwards in all interstate and international teams.

At the end of each day's play he should discuss the happenings on the field and help to improve the knowledge and attitude of the players so they are being prepared properly for higher levels of cricket.

This procedure should apply also to our international Under-19 side in both home and away games, with the senior former player and young captain working very closely together on and off the field.

## 4. How Can Players Be Encouraged to Develop a Greater Appreciation and Understanding of the Game?

By following the above process and by much closer links between administrators, players and umpires at all levels.

Signed: Ian Chappell. Bill Lawry. Richie Benaud.

Some of that has obviously been overtaken by events in a period of nine years, but the general thrust of it remains as a fair and articulate pattern for the type of cricket we expect from young Australian cricketers, or the thinking of those who might be running an academy establishment for young cricketers. It is far more important for youngsters to play their cricket the right way than it is to set up something like an academy. Former England coach Keith Fletcher's quote in December 1994 was along the right lines.

'Whether their way is right or our way is right is open to debate,' Fletcher said. 'But really, we should have eighteen academies because we've got eighteen first-class sides and these sides should obviously produce cricketers. Each county has to look at itself and be honest with itself. We should have eighteen places of excellence, and if every county put themselves out to achieve this, we'd be a lot better off.'

There are only a certain number of things a coach is able to do with a player. Some of those involve physical activities and some mental; the Adelaide Academy is as close as possible to getting it right. The only thing not to get too carried away with is the claim that if the Academy didn't exist, then all those cricketers would be lost to the game in Australia. That is nonsense. The cricketers in question mostly play with a grade club in a city for a start, or they play with a country team and move to the city. Different from England where setting up an academy would mean the furthest a youngster had to travel would be 200 miles. In Australia you don't just go up or down the motorway, you fly from other states to Adelaide. Aged from sixteen upwards, they would still come through the Under-17 and Under-19 interstate competitions, play for their state in the Colts XI matches, represent in the state 2nd XI and then go on to Sheffield Shield. None of that would change if the Academy ceased to exist tomorrow. The one thing the elite group would miss, and it would leave a gap, is the polish put on them by Rod Marsh and the ex-Test players who cast an eye over his charges.

The Academy has slotted into the structure of Australian cricket and has done so very well, and it is worth looking at how the structure of Australian cricket has changed over the years from the time I played to the present day.

All the levels of cricket I played, or was concerned with, still exist, and these are listed, with the present-day additions:

| *1946–64* | *New since 1964* |
|---|---|
| Test Cricket | Limited-overs Internationals |
| Australian XI v. touring team | Academy v. touring team |
| Sheffield Shield | Academy v. State 2nd XI teams |
| State 2nd XI matches | Adelaide Academy |
| State Colts XI matches | Under-19 Internationals |
| City Club Cricket | State Under-19 competition |
| Country Cricket | State Under-17 competition |
| City Club Age Competitions | Much less schools coaching |
| Schools Cricket | |
| Schools Coaching | |

There is one great worry concerning club cricket, or grade cricket as it is known in Australia. I have met very few people in recent years who are totally happy with the standard of play, and with the fact that older players are leaving clubs to play in other forms of cricket because of the time frame of matches. Club cricket, where a parent wants to play in a team from 11 a.m. to 6 or 7 p.m. each Saturday and Sunday, has little relevance in the family set-up these days and it is virtually impossible for men in their thirties to do it. The younger players and the forward thinkers may say, 'So what, who cares?' They might be right, but my own view is that it's a pity this should be so, as a good mix of ages in club cricket always seemed to me to be one of the strong points of the Australian game.

The Academy has led to one problem which I believe needs to be eradicated and it involves the rating of players in the minds of the cricketing public. It is a good thing for the Academy to receive publicity, and it is a good thing for those running it to provide that publicity. It has the government agencies overjoyed when they are putting in their reports and budget forecasts to their Cabinet Minister, and they are the ones in part who fund the Academy. It keeps the sponsor, in this case the Commonwealth Bank, very happy and that is extremely important. It would be much better in my opinion though if individuals were not singled out as those who are about to take Test cricket by storm, as being the most promising young bowler or batsman in the country, or the best fielder.

We shall find out about all of that in due course and it is not a question of handing out either paper or verbal diplomas at the end of a stint at the Academy. There may be some youngsters who are unable to attend the Academy, or actually don't want to do so, preferring to spend their time with their family whilst still playing a lot of cricket. I believe unreasonable pressure has been put on some of the young players by saying they are certain to play for Australia, or that if they were in any other country they would be playing Test cricket now. That may be the case, or it may not, but first of all the Academy player named and so lauded has to remove one of the players already in the Australian team and cut short his life as an international cricketer, sending him back to Sheffield Shield, and then the Academy representative must hold his own place in the Australian team.

It seems to me unnecessary to provide such divisive praise, even though I believe individuals *should* have to account for their performances and that failure should equate with the possibility of being dropped from any team. That, to me, seems pressure enough, without stressing that one or two players are better than the others when, in fact, we all know how easy it is for bright young talent to go through rough periods.

At the time of writing, a very good young Victorian batsman, Bradley Hodge, has had a poor first-class season in Australia, which has come as a shock to his many admirers, of whom I am one. He will come back because he is talented, like many others, but no one bowling at him in Australian cricket cares at all that in 1993 he was rated around the country as one of Australia's brightest young Academy stars. In 1991–2 he was also a prominent performer in the Under-17 Championships in Australia and has been through the Under-19s as well with distinction.

The Academy is very good but all these things need to be kept in perspective, particularly by countries which are looking to grasp anything they see as a way back from losing matches.

Rodney Marsh has the best line on that kind of thing. He says, 'A drowning man will clutch at a serpent . . .'

Marsh's modern-day 'proverb' perfectly describes some of the writing and talking concerned with what England need to do as regards prospective young cricketers. It was as though everyone had far too much time on their hands between the end of the Third Test in Sydney in 1995 and the start of the Fourth in Adelaide where the Academy is situated.

The Academy has had great success in its seven years, with sixty-three players moving on to the first-class scene, up to the time the Perth Test match finished in 1995. Eleven have gone on to play Test cricket, nine of those for Australia – Brendon Julian, Michael Slater, Greg Blewett,

Justin Langer, Damien Martyn, Shane Warne, Peter McIntyre, Glenn McGrath and Michael Bevan – and two – Craig White and Martin McCague – for England.

The fifty-two Sheffield Shield players are: Darren Berry, Paul Carew, Jamie Cox, Peter Drinnen, Shane George, Stuart Law, Geoffrey Parker, Scott Prestwidge, Joseph Scuderi, Adrian Tucker, Brett Williams, Phil Alley, Clinton Auty, David Clarke, Dene Hills, Christopher Mack, Cameron Williamson, Gary Wright, Warwick Adlam, Jason Gallian, Laurence Harper, Stuart Oliver, Richard Chee Quee, Adam Gilchrist, Michael Kasprowicz, Stuart MacGill, Kevin Roberts, James Stewart, Mark Atkinson, Troy Corbett, Andrew Dykes, Shawn Flegler, Murray Goodwin, Ashley Hammond, Ricky Ponting, Darren Webber, Warren Wishart, Jason Arnberger, Simon Cook, Michael Di Venuto, David Fitzgerald, Bradley Hodge, James Maher, Wade Seccombe, Richard Allanby, Ian Harvey, Craig Howard, Craig Glassock, Shane Lee, Daniel Marsh, Andrew Symonds and Mark Harrity.

That is an imposing list, and it has been good for Australian cricket. It needs careful evaluation in England though before decisions are made, even if the idea itself is a good one.

One area where the Australian Cricket Board have recently got it right is in agreeing with Bob Simpson that there should be a separation in the jobs of coach and selector. Simpson, who has achieved good results as Australian coach, was for a time a selector, a dual job which I thought to be fraught with problems. I know Bob didn't agree with me on that because he could never see there might be any kind of difficulty with players within the side coming to him as a selector to tell him about their footwork, batting, bowling and fielding troubles. All I know is that if I were a player, and the team coach was also a selector, I would be extremely reticent about confessing to the coach that I felt out of form with the bat or ball. On the contrary, if asked by the coach-selector about my form, I would be inclined to jump in very quickly to let him know I had never seen the ball better or the ball had never come out of my hand in smoother fashion.

I *always* did that when I was a player and when one of the state or Australian selectors asked me the same question. The reply would be designed to have him wondering how he ever could have thought my form might be a little edgy at that moment. If that was my platform with a selector, why on earth would I change if the selector just happened to be the coach as well? Just because he's in a coach's track-suit, I'm not suddenly going to unzip my heart, or my lips, and tell him all my batting and bowling problems. There is a very good reason for that. If he is doing his job properly as a selector, he would take what I had said to the selection meeting and it would, and should, be the subject of extensive discussion. I would not expect anything less than that but I see no reason why I should be contributing to my own downfall. Why would I do that?

If the time comes when Bob decides he has had enough of coaching then there is not the slightest reason why he would not once more become a Test selector. He was a fine player for Australia and has had vast experience in many areas of the game, including selecting, so I could certainly see him again in that role, but not as coach as well, nor should anyone else ever be given the two tasks.

The same applied to England's Keith Fletcher. It was beyond me why he wanted to be a selector and coach. Like Bob Simpson with the Australians, he would have tabled at a selection meeting his opinion on the way various players were performing and what their technical deficiencies were, together with what they had told him regarding their skills or confidence levels at the time. If he were then relating what the players had said to him, I believe it poses a problem.

Neither Simpson nor Fletcher is likely to agree with that because they saw their dual job as something they and the players were perfectly able to handle, and they found it impossible to believe a player would not open his heart to them.

We shall just have to agree to differ.

I mentioned earlier that coaching of all kinds is a thriving business these days and it takes a form different from when I played. Then there was far more influence from the older and more experienced players in the side, and after the game you might spend an hour in the dressing-room having a few beers and moving salt and pepper shakers around the table to simulate field-placings, at the same time discussing all the strengths and weaknesses of the opposition players. That was all practical stuff and it was also a case of keeping it simple.

We are all coached in some way at some time, and when I was involved with the Rothmans National Sport Foundation, three of the most interesting speeches I have ever heard at a cricket seminar came from football coaches. Two were from Australian Rules football coaches, Neil Kerley and Ron Barassi, and the other from Jack Gibson whom I have always regarded as an outstanding Rugby League coach. In our 1973 seminar he spoke in his very quiet voice about the various aspects of player relationships, and the fact that every player you coach is to be regarded as an individual even though he might be part of a team. He said, among many other things:

- What I want in a team is the player able to look after his own game and still have something left over for his mates.
- In the teaching of players I believe the key lies in watching a man play, detecting his mistakes and then having the ability to correct those mistakes, one at a time.
- It's important to master the simple things in football, in fact in all sport.
- Eliminate your errors, that's what a game is all about.
- To win anything the team must be tough, an attribute which infiltrates into the individual. You must have a tough captain and the big test in sport is how that captain leads in adversity.
- Enthusiasm is contagious.
- To have a talent that is rarely used is a sad legacy in life.
- Last season doesn't matter. That's why it's pointless the players bringing their scrap-books to the first match.

That was twenty-two years ago and Gibson's views are still relevant today. Incidentally, he knows plenty about cricket as well as football, having been the opening bowler for the Waverley Club in Sydney for quite some time and he was certainly one of the best medium-pace net bowlers we ever had with the NSW state practice squad. He would start at 3 p.m., finish at 6 p.m., never a bumper bowled and always making the batsmen play at every ball.

As there have been great changes in Australian cricket's structure in the past ten years, and as there are now nine Test match-playing countries needing to be accommodated with fixtures, it stands to reason that programming in Australia has become more difficult. How much more difficult is something almost impossible to believe and I am full of admiration for those who do the job.

One plea, right from the heart: no more Test match nations. We have nine now and there is hardly room for all the matches they want to play. Test cricket started with England and Australia, then came South Africa, the West Indies, New Zealand and India. This made up a nice, even six-ball. When there was partition in India, Pakistan became the seventh nation and, in recent years, they have been joined first by Sri Lanka and then Zimbabwe.

There are no others immediately on the horizon but you never know. Pity the poor administrators from all countries who are charged with the task of sorting out the programming, bearing in mind that Australia and England will continue to play their Ashes series every two years, with Australia touring England every four years.

One thing on which administrators need to keep an eagle eye is tour itineraries. It's not an easy job, but it cannot be all coincidence that it is difficult to recall an England team coming to Australia and being satisfied with the itinerary originally agreed between the administrators of both countries. When England toured India in 1992–3, they arrived just after Christmas and the first match was played at Faridabad on January 3rd, followed by a game against the President's XI on January 8th, 9th and 10th. Then, in the next fortnight, they travelled from Delhi to Jaipur, Jaipur to Delhi, Delhi to Chandigarh, Chandigarh to Delhi, Delhi to Bhubaneswar, Bhubaneswar to Cuttack and Cuttack to Calcutta where the First Test was played. I suppose the fortunate thing was that during that time they only had to play a three-day game and two one-day Internationals.

The first excuse for losing which leaps to the lips of captains and players these days is that the team is playing too much limited-overs cricket. Well then, for heaven's sake, play less if that's what you want. As it happens, limited-overs cricket still provides financial lifeblood for the game in several countries, but if they want to test the market and earn the undying gratitude of the traditionalists, then give it a go and play less.

At the same time though, the tour guarantee for a visiting country would be reduced by, say, a million dollars, and the payments to players would be halved. That's fine with me, and it will sort out those who really believe what they are saying and are not merely whingeing about one-day or day-night cricket.

The question of finance also comes into programming these days. The Australian Cricket Board were convinced they would be hosting a full Pakistan tour of Australia in 1995–6 and suddenly it turned out that, because of a financially better offer, Pakistan would instead be touring South Africa on a full-scale basis and would be coming to Australia only for a short time before Christmas.

Looking at the Australian situation, the biggest difficulty lies in fitting

It is rare for one ball to have such a devastating effect on an Ashes series as Warne's first delivery to Mike Gatting at Old Trafford in 1993. It started on middle and off, swerved to outside leg stump and, when it pitched, spun back to take the off bail. The picture above tells the story of Warne who is looking at Healy, the one below, after what seemed like an eternity, underscores Gatting's complete bewilderment. Allan Border had eyes only for Gatting, he knew the effect this would have on England's batsmen.

One of England's real hopes, Graham Thorpe, is shown above sweeping at Shane Warne during his century in his debut Test at Trent Bridge in 1993. I have a high regard for Thorpe and I believe the century he made in Perth against Australia will be the turning point of his career.

Two faces of Ian Healy, a tough competitor and a fine all-round cricketer at Test level. This sweep shot (*left*) took him closer to his maiden Test century at Old Trafford in 1993 and the stumping (*below*), well, there is no better indication that he never relaxes for a moment. Robin Smith was the batsman in the Texaco limited-overs International at Lord's in 1993, and the ball was a 'wide' from Tim May. It was brilliant cricket and brilliant thinking from Healy to effect the dismissal.

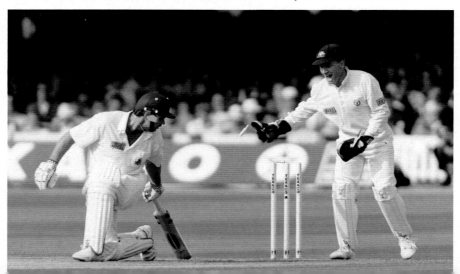

Shane Warne claims another one (*right*). Warne finished the Second Test match in 1994 with a hat-trick, eighteen months after he bowled his first ball in an Ashes battle. That ball!

And (*below*) this is the ball that started all Robin Smith's problems. I regard it as the equal of the delivery which accounted for Mike Gatting. It started on middle and off, swerved to pitch outside leg, found the outside edge and was caught by Mark Taylor at slip. Not as sensational as the Gatting wicket, but just as devastating.

Now, who would have thought in Australia in 1994–95 that the man in the centre, Michael Atherton, would have been rushing to congratulate the other two, Phil Tufnell and Angus Fraser. Fraser wasn't even in the original touring party, and Tufnell was 1000/1 to take the catch of the season which dismissed Michael Slater in the second innings in Sydney!

The Ashes retained! Unlikely batting heroes, Tim May and Shane Warne, used their brains as well as their bats during the partnership at the SCG and they were too good for England. This was the second time they had started to leave the field, having been called back when Michael Atherton correctly reminded the umpires the game wasn't over.

Darren Gough was like a breath of fresh air for England in Australia in 1994–95. Here (*above left*) he dismisses Ian Healy in the course of an outstanding bowling spell which, with his dashing batting in the same Test at the SCG, earned him the Man of the Match award. It was only a short time later that he broke down in Melbourne when running in to bowl.

I was pleased for Angus Fraser (*above right*). He's a good cricketer who has suffered some cruel blows because of injury and it looked at one stage as though he might never play Test cricket again. He bowled himself to a standstill at the SCG in 1995 until bad light meant the faster bowlers in the England side could be used no more. You don't find cricketers with more heart than Fraser.

Ray Illingworth arrived in Australia just in time to see the Melbourne débâcle. He was not impressed. The photograph below, taken at the SCG Test match, immediately following the MCG game, shows Captain and Chairman in happier times and they now have the chance to put English cricket back on track.

Graham Gooch (*left*) and
Mike Gatting (*below*),
two highly respected
cricketers who gave great
service to England at
both Test and county
level. Gatting is shown
square cutting Shane
Warne at the Adelaide
Oval in 1995 during his
splendid century. Gooch,
England's greatest run-
scorer in Test cricket, is
in typical flow during an
innings at The Oval.

A great win for England at the Adelaide Oval, victory which had Michael Atherton suggesting there was a good chance of a drawn series. That disappeared in the fielding fumbles of Perth, but Adelaide was brilliant. One of the problems with being captain these days is that you 'cop' the beer, sparkling wine, champagne and whatever else seems to be going. I suspect before they all got to him, Atherton had raised a glass of vintage 'champers' to the team and perhaps, in particular, to Devon Malcolm!

Winners and Losers! Mark Taylor and Michael Atherton listen to the speeches at the end of the Ashes series in 1995 with Taylor having led Australia to victory in his first captaincy stint in Australia. Atherton's captaincy will come on a lot for this experience, he is a good cricketer and a very strong character.

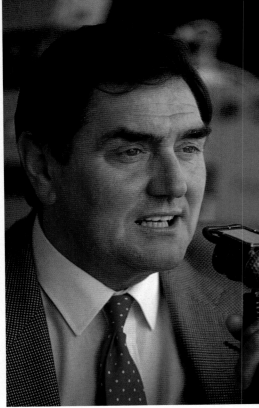

I was there! This (*above left*) is the 17th green at Augusta where I had waited for Jack Nicklaus to arrive and, by chance, the hole was directly between where I was standing and where Nicklaus's ball finished on the green. I saw the putt break to my left and then my right and dive into the hole. It was one of the great moments I have seen in sport.

Tony Lewis (*above right*), former captain of England and of Glamorgan, former Chairman of Glamorgan and Chairman of the Cricket Committee; 'AR' is the most unflappable of television commentators and the staunchest supporter and advocate for Wales. Twice, in 1964 and 1968, Glamorgan have beaten Australian touring teams. I wasn't over-keen on the drubbings but loved the singing.

Peter Alliss produced a wonderful piece of television commentary on Seve Ballesteros (*left*) on the 18th fairway, in the gorse bush, at Woburn. Seve is magic to watch, and often performs magic on the course. In 1993, in the Swiss Open at Crans Montana, he conjured something out of this little problem; first of all he had to manoeuvre the ball between two trees then clear a seven-foot wall and a swimming pool and have enough height on the ball to settle it softly on to the green. He did!

in the required number of tours, and how do you do it? Let's take the last of the two nations mentioned earlier, Sri Lanka and Zimbabwe. If they were to tour Australia either separately or together, common sense decrees in these modern times that if they played a series of Test matches and no limited-overs Internationals, the tour could provide financial problems, when you take into account the cost of air travel and accommodation, plus all the incidental expenses of the tour and payments to the players.

Or would everyone expect them to play for nothing? The only way to generate extra income would be to play a series of limited-overs Internationals, but if at the same time you are being told there are too many of those, what solution do you offer? We do need to sit back and take stock of what can be done by way of programming before we start thinking about having any more than the present nine Test countries.

It was after I had written an article critical of the programming which had denied the Victorians a proper chance to press their claims for inclusion in the opening Test of a series in Australia that Board Chairman, Alan Crompton, gave me a run-through of some of the problems associated with an Australian summer, and now he has a convert.

The first thing is that the ACB want to schedule the greatest possible number of games when the Test players are available and to provide an equal number of matches for each state when the Test stars can turn out. The fact that this simply doesn't work out is not for want of trying but because of the sheer weight of numbers of matches and tours.

There are two parts to the season in Australia – before and after Christmas – quite different from the season in England where cricket starts in April and finishes in September. There should be roughly the same number of matches played in Australia in each of the two sections but, additionally, it is a requirement that each state should have two Sheffield Shield games prior to the first Test of a series. Also, it is a further requirement that there should be two full rounds of matches prior to the Sheffield Shield final at the end of the summer.

And, where possible, there should be a full round of Sheffield Shield involving all six states in the week prior to a Test. With the introduction of the state Under-17 and Under-19 competitions, it is common sense to avoid playing a Sheffield Shield match in the city hosting those competitions, and that in itself is not an easy task. The same common sense comes into the desire not to have a Sheffield Shield game in a city the week prior to a Test or a Benson & Hedges World Series game.

There are other matters, again involving common sense but not always understood, amongst which is that the time frame for Sheffield Shield matches should be mid-October to late March and that there should be no Sheffield Shield games at the time of the Mercantile Mutual domestic limited-overs finals, and that the World Series games should be finished before February. Also, because of lack of grass growth in some states, care needs to be taken with programming matches in October and early November.

There are another dozen guidelines and it all entails a great deal of work as any computer programmer will be able to tell you, and, although I know a little about computers and cricket programming, I certainly don't envy Mr Crompton and his helpers their task – they do a great job.

This gave me a completely new insight into the vast number of problems associated with programming in Australia, problems I would suggest are unique in world cricket.

Part of my business activities take me to some strange places and, in order to write and talk about diets and food, I once did a cooking course in Italy. It certainly boosted my knowledge of Italian food because it was run by the great chef Guiliano Bugialli, who didn't hang back when extolling the virtues or otherwise of the offerings served up by his pupils. I learnt how to make my own pasta, beautifully fine in texture, something not all that easy to achieve. I was also the risotto stirrer and I can assure you stirring rice for forty people is not recommended for those with weak wrists. When Bugialli was doing the rounds, examining everyone's pasta, I was delighted he spent so much time with the $30 \times 60$ cm sheet I had made. It was as fine as tissue paper. I was prepared to hang on every word as the great man prodded and fondled the pasta but he said nothing, so I tried to help.

'Everything okay?' I asked genially.

'Quiet,' he answered, 'I was trying to count the mistakes. I'd reached seventeen and now I'll have to start again.'

Embarrassment of another kind came my way one night in London where Daphne and I had attended a splendid dinner hosted by the late David Kenning, an outstanding BBC Television sports producer. At the dinner were 'Slim' Wilkinson and his wife. 'Slim' was then Head of BBC Television Sport and a very, very VIP. They drove us home and when we arrived there, your correspondent, awakened from a doze and forgetting we were not in a taxi, thrust his hand into a pocket, pulled out a fiver and shoved it at the Head of Sport with the time-honoured words, 'Thanks, pal, keep the rest to buy a drink.'

# 12

## Shane Warne,
## the greatest young legspinner I've seen

One of the most appealing things about cricket is that there is always a turnover of players within a national team. Sometimes the turnover is fast, sometimes, when a very good team is playing, the turnover can be infrequent, but it is ever present and it is an aspect of the game which enthrals the public. They are always in on the ground floor of either an execution, a reluctant departure, the birth of a new star or the fading of an older one.

Until Shane Warne came along no better thing happened to me than to be in the commentary box over the period when those five great allrounders graced the world cricket stage. Gary Sobers was a wonderful cricketer and, with Ian Botham, Kapil Dev, Imran Khan and Richard Hadlee, joined the Test match double club, reaching 2,000 runs and 200 wickets:

## Test Match Doubles

|  | Tests | Runs | Wkts | Ct | Test No. | Date |
|---|---|---|---|---|---|---|
| R. Benaud | 63 | 2201 | 248 | 65 | 60 | 6.12.63 |
| G. St A. Sobers | 93 | 8032 | 235 | 109 | 80 | 3.4.71 |
| I. T. Botham | 102 | 5200 | 383 | 120 | 42 | 1.12.82 |
| Kapil Dev | 131 | 5230 | 432 | 64 | 50 | 12.3.83 |
| Imran Khan | 88 | 3807 | 362 | 28 | 50 | 6.12.83 |
| R. J. Hadlee | 86 | 3124 | 431 | 39 | 54 | 3.4.85 |

With Sobers and Botham each taking more than 100 catches as well, it often made a commentator's lot considerably easier as well as exciting.

All six of the players who have achieved that double have retired and that is the way of the game. It is also one of the great attributes of statistics, that we are able to see what has been done over the years and wonder about the impact of the younger players who are about to take the places of the retirees. It is interesting to look at the figures and the dates of achievement; those modern-day allrounders have turned in some sensational performances.

Kapil Dev, who became the greatest Test match wicket-taker not long before his retirement, left the stage around the same time as Allan Border, who had just gone past Sunil Gavaskar's run record. It often happens that a replacement is just around the corner. He may only be a good replacement, could be a very good one or, if you are really fortunate, he could be a great one.

It's not always easy to recognise momentous happenings.

Brian Lara's performances in 1994 were wonderful. To break Sir Garfield Sobers' record score of 365 was the pinnacle but the 501* at Edgbaston was also an outstanding innings, as much for the concentration as the runs themselves. There are many other good young cricketers around but, having had the pleasure of going through the era watching those great allrounders, I will settle in the main now for the trio of Warne, Lara and Sachin Tendulkar hopefully to take me through to the year 2000. There are others as well, notably Wasim Akram whom I think is a sensational allrounder, but those three seem a decent starting point.

When Shane Warne made his Test debut against India there was, in the opposition team, a young right-hand batsman named Tendulkar who had batted four times against the Australians for 78 runs, and although I knew he was very good from having seen him in England in 1990, I was having a certain amount of trouble in convincing my friends. He fixed that for me in the Third Test at the SCG in January 1992, and, with Warne bowling at him, made a brilliant 148 not out. He followed that with an equally good 114 in Perth in the final Test, and at the time of writing, Warne has yet to dismiss him. When they meet again it will be a battle worth watching.

Tendulkar is one of the best young batsmen I have seen in the years I have been in the game and, even before he played so well against Australia in Sydney, I had the privilege of watching him make his first Test century, this time at Old Trafford. He had hit 63 in the first innings, and with India close to disintegration in the second at 109/4, he chose that moment to produce a classic.

Tendulkar has been slightly overshadowed by Brian Lara's exploits in recent times but I have no doubt the Indian batsman will be one of the stars leading up to the turn of the century. He is a magnificent young player.

Lara is something of a contrast to Tendulkar, not merely because they bat with different hands. Lara had to wait for his chance in Test cricket because the West Indian batting side was so strong. Gifted he may have been but no one in that West Indian side was intending to step down, even temporarily, to allow him to make his debut. Very wise of them. He has already shown that, once in, he has a great liking for batting and has no intention of allowing another youngster to take his place.

Lara made his Test debut against Pakistan late in 1990 and then came to Australia. He had already been around Australia with the West Indies Under-19 side and made a very good impression as a left-hand batsman and captain. He opened the batting for them with considerable success in the World Cup in Australasia and then he came up against Shane Warne in the 1992–3 Test series. Their first meeting was at the MCG where Lara made 52 and 4 and Warne bowled Australia to a great victory with 7/52. It was a different story in Sydney where Lara made his 277, and by February 1995, as was the case with Tendulkar, Warne had not taken his wicket in a Test. Warne will have some great tussles with both of them and it is something I very much want to see: a great young legspin bowler and two of the best batsmen to grace a ground in the past fifty years.

When I interviewed Lara for BBC Television at The Oval in June 1994, he was flying home to Trinidad for a brief holiday. This was on the Tuesday evening after he had hit a brilliant 70 from 73 balls for Warwickshire against Surrey, with Warwickshire needing 268 to win the limited-overs semi-final. They won with five balls to spare and were on their way to Lord's for the Benson & Hedges Final.

The fee Warwickshire paid Lara to play for them had been repaid several times over by the time the English summer was one-third complete. Lara, the day before the semi-final, had gone from 111★ to 501★ against Durham to eclipse Hanif Mohammad's previous record first-class score of 499, and when he said he was homesick, no one thought of suggesting he play on. 'Come back next week with your batteries recharged,' they said, which was not quite what county bowlers around England wanted to hear.

He had been doing nothing but make runs for the previous few months: first the wonderful performance in Antigua which took him past Sir Garfield Sobers' Test record 365★, followed by the string of centuries in county cricket, and then the 501★. Just thinking about anyone making 500 is tiring, but he has one distinct advantage, in hitting more boundaries than other players. In that B & H semi-final, in 73 balls he hit more boundaries than the whole Surrey team in their 267 total. When he made his 501 he hit more boundaries than any other player in any innings in the history of first-class cricket. I suppose the latter record is understandable in the context of someone making half a thousand runs in one innings but, in general terms, his ratio of boundaries to runs is astonishing.

Lara is a champion, but even champions will blink occasionally when records come their way. His Test record, when he went past the previous best held by Gary Sobers, was a wonderful effort, bearing in mind that only a week earlier England had beaten the West Indies in the Test in Barbados. Here was a chance for Lara to take some form of revenge for that defeat, perhaps by making a Test century. He doubled that, trebled it, and then set out for the record; he should have been thinking along those lines: he is an ambitious young batsman and a wonderful entertainer.

Sir Garfield said something about him even before he made his 375 and it should be pasted on the inside lid of the cricket bag of every cricketer in the land, imprinted on the mind of every captain and definitely emblazoned on the pages of every coach's manual: '*Brian Lara is a batsman who plays cricket the way it should be played, he rarely uses his pads but hits the ball with the bat. He is a pride and joy to watch.*'

There is only one statistic which is really relevant to that Test innings: the fact that he broke the record. That he did it in style and with wonderful flair is a bonus.

In his innings for Warwickshire though there are many landmarks which are relevant. The statistics will allow us, in later years, to relive what happened that day at Edgbaston, even if we weren't able to make it to the ground on Monday June 6th, 1994. He had reached his century the previous evening in 144 minutes, 138 balls and with 14 fours.

111  Resumed batting, Warwickshire 210/2 after Durham had made 556/8 declared
148  Personal best for Warwickshire
150  201 minutes, 193 balls, 22 fours
200  224 minutes, 220 balls, 30 fours and 2 sixes
248  Highest score made against Durham (previous best Chris Lewis's 247 for Nottinghamshire in 1993)
250  246 minutes, 245 balls, 37 fours and 5 sixes
278  Highest score by a Warwickshire batsman at Edgbaston (previous best 277 by Roger Twose versus Glamorgan earlier in the season)

285 Made 174 in the morning session (previous best 173 by Reg Santall versus Northamptonshire, 1933)

297 Highest partnership against Durham (314 in 55 overs with Trevor Penney, 44)

300 First player to score a triple century at Edgbaston, 280 minutes, 278 balls, 44 fours, 7 sixes

306 Highest score made for Warwickshire (previous best Frank Foster 305★ versus Worcestershire at Dudley, 1914)

323 Highest score by a West Indian in England (previous best 322 by Viv Richards for Somerset against Warwickshire, Taunton 1985)

325 1,000 runs in seven innings, equalling Don Bradman's 1938 achievement. Completed 1,000 runs in a season faster than any Warwickshire batsman (Jim Stewart reached 1,000 on June 12th, 1962)

350 319 minutes, 311 balls, 49 fours, 8 sixes

376 Highest score by a West Indian, beating his own world Test record 375 against England in Antigua two months earlier

386 Highest score by a left-hander (previous best Bert Sutcliffe 385 for Otago versus Canterbury at Christchurch in 1952)

400 367 minutes, 350 balls, 53 fours, 8 sixes

406 Highest score in England this century (previous best Graeme Hick 405★, Worcestershire versus Somerset, Taunton, 1988)

411 Nineteenth player to score 300 in a day

418 384 minutes, 365 balls, 54 fours and 9 sixes and became the first Warwickshire player to make a century in each of the first two sessions on the same day

425 Highest-ever score in England (previous best Archie McLaren, 424 for Lancashire versus Somerset, Taunton, 1895)

429 Warwickshire's new county record total, beating 657/6 versus Hampshire in 1899, and 657/7 versus Glamorgan in 1994

450 430 minutes, 398 balls, 55 fours, 9 sixes

453 Second-highest scorer in history (overtaking Don Bradman 452 for NSW versus Queensland, 1930)

457 Highest individual score in a day (previous best 345, Charlie Macartney, Australia versus Nottinghamshire, Trent Bridge, 1921)

459 Final 20 overs begin, Lara 459 (40 behind Hanif Mohammad's world record 499, Karachi, against Bahawalpur in 1958–9)

494 Most boundaries in an innings, beating 68 by Percy Perrin (Essex versus Derbyshire, Chesterfield, 1904)

501 Hit John Morris to the extra cover boundary to reach 501★

It was a remarkable day and a remarkable innings, something that will live in the memories of those who watched it all unfold and those who are interested in the records of cricket.

That kind of batting keeps people talking; often they can be people who have little affiliation with the game itself but who are captivated by the publicity given to an outstanding achievement in any sport. There was a time when only the written word would provide a record of such matters, some film would exist, but mostly it would be the beautiful prose which would bring back memories.

Shane Warne is the best *young* legspin bowler I have ever seen. My hope is that he becomes the best *mature* legspin bowler I have ever seen as well, because then I will have had a most enjoyable time in the commentary box observing one of the great talents in the game engaged in exhibiting one of the great arts of the game. Warne only came into the first-class scene in 1991 but prior to that, at the start of the summer, he had toured Zimbabwe with an Australian 'B' team captained by Mark Taylor. There were two legspin bowlers in that Australian side, Warne and Peter McIntyre, the latter also from Victoria.

McIntyre played for the Vics up to 1990–1 but then transferred to South Australia, wisely so because there was little chance of Victoria playing two legspin bowlers in the one Sheffield Shield match. That Australian team to Zimbabwe was managed by Australian selector John Benaud and he was impressed with both Warne and McIntyre, though it was Warne who bowled out Zimbabwe in the main match of the tour. McIntyre, in 1994–5, played for the Australian A team in the Benson & Hedges World Series and then was chosen in the team for the Test match in Adelaide. He suffered a little from nerves in that game but took two first innings wickets, then was omitted from the Fifth Test team in Perth against England when the Australian selectors needed an extra pace bowler.

There had earlier been some trouble for Warne at the Cricket Academy in Adelaide and he was suspended from action at one point for what was termed inappropriate behaviour. Brian Taber and Steve Bernard, who managed the Under-19 Australian team to the West Indies after that little dispute, devised a method of control which was to have beneficial effects on Warne. They made him 'senior pro' in the team, gave him responsibility, and when I later talked to Taber about him, he was thoroughly impressed by Warne's reaction. Warne then started to make an impression with the Victorian side. He made his debut in 1991 against Western Australia in a lacklustre game at the St Kilda Oval; oddly enough, in the same match Irish-born Martin McCague made his debut for Western Australia. Three years later the Australian Test player Warne was being talked about as the future holder of the Australian wicket-taking record at Test level, and the England Test player McCague had flown home from the 1994–5 Ashes tour of Australia, maybe pondering whether his future would involve ever playing again for England.

Warne's progress thereafter was rapid enough. He finished that summer in Australian cricket and, in the following one, made his Test debut in the Sydney game against India. It was hardly a success because he took 1/150. It wasn't that he bowled badly but the Indian batsmen, led by Ravi Shastri and Sachin Tendulkar, brought up on legspin and offspin, played him well. It was a matter of lack of experience outweighing natural skills.

He didn't bowl badly against Lara either the next season and he will bowl better and better as the years go on, though I do add one proviso: *providing he stays fully fit!* I have considerable and painful knowledge of shoulder injuries and the fact that Warne has had some minor problems in this regard is by no means good news. The most dangerous aspect of it is the manner in which he sustained his injury, which was to go to the nets and bowl forty-five wrong 'uns to Ian Healy when they were trying to work on one aspect of technique. Very dangerous and you can be guaranteed he won't do it again.

There was another example in Australia, in 1994, when Steve Waugh damaged his bowling shoulder fielding during the tour of Pakistan and had to be flown home. He was unable to bowl throughout the 1994–5 summer in Australia, and it was said he would not be allowed to bowl during the West Indies tour, something which completely altered the balance of the Australian team. It was even more disquieting to learn that as the summer had progressed his shoulder became worse rather than better, despite it being rested, and it sounded very ominous to me, having gone through a similar injury in the period 1961–4. It didn't affect his batting physically though it may have done so mentally, but it certainly affected his throwing and his bowling, and had a dramatic effect on the Australian selectors.

Australia needs cricketers like Steve Waugh, players who excel when the going is hard and who improve as it becomes tougher and tougher. His batting against England in 1989 and 1993, and in other Tests in between those tours, was exemplary. It is true during that time he wasn't doing as much bowling as in years past, but in 1994 he turned the Newlands Test with a great bowling performance, as he had done only weeks earlier in the Test against South Africa in Adelaide. Tough, resourceful cricketers are what a captain needs, and when Waugh came back from injury in Adelaide in 1994 and made 164, and shared a match-winning stand with his captain, Border would have derived great comfort from seeing him at the other end. He then took 4/26 in a high-class spell of medium-pace bowling, and matched all that at Newlands where a very good 86 and 5/28 tore the game away from the South Africans. However, he hasn't bowled since the Pakistan tour and it is possible he may never again bowl effectively.

Shoulder injuries are awful for bowlers. That high-class left-arm pace bowler Bruce Reid, who sustained a back injury and then had severe shoulder problems, had to have a silver plate inserted in his back and, in one of the saddest of stories, unless something extraordinary happens, will not play again for Australia.

My own shoulder problems stemmed from bowling one wrong 'un to Tom Graveney on April 30th, 1961. Later I was to find out I had torn fibres off the super spinatus tendon which runs along the top of the shoulder and is apparently connected to the third finger, which was my spinning finger.

Dr Brian Corrigan was the man who arranged special treatment for me with Dr Alan Bass, the Chelsea Football Club doctor. It involved a lot of work but eventually it came right, or right enough to share in that last-day triumph at Old Trafford. During each interval Dr Bass treated my shoulder in the physiotherapy room attached to our dressing-room, and he might easily have been Man of the Match in modern-day cricket.

People tell me how lucky cricketers are and they are right, it is a great game to play. It can also be very cruel and overnight injury can cut short the career of even the best of players so that the following week they are out looking for a job. There is very little security of tenure in cricket; you are only as good as your next match and, if that never happens, there is always someone to take your place. A famous Australian administrator once said that to Rodney 'Bacchus' Marsh in 1976 at the SCG, when the wicket-keeper, nicknamed after a small town in Victoria, was comment-ing on the record gate-takings ($A1 million, for the first time) for the Australia–West Indies series and was suggesting players' very low match fees and security might be improved by the ACB.

'If you don't want to play, there are 50,000 people who would play for Australia for nothing,' was the answer Marsh received. The administrator received only a brief, though pithy, reply and his necktie, attached to Rodney's fingers, shortened an inch or two!

If Warne and Waugh are able to stay fit for spin bowling and batting respectively, Australia's chances of continuing to win will be correspondingly improved. One other cautionary note about Warne and Lara is that legspinners, traditionally, are not at their best against left-handers. Bill O'Reilly, President of the Legspinners' League, was of the opinion that left-handers should be barred from the game, but that is possibly an extreme view. Possibly!

Warne is something of a freak bowler. He is unlike other legspinners I have seen and, in fact, in one or two aspects has rewritten the technique book on over-the-wrist spin bowling. For a start he walks part of the way to the bowling crease; the rest is more of an amble than anything else until the last yard. The ball is only held loosely in his hand but he has exceptionally powerful fingers, wrist and forearm and he utilises sidespin much more than I did. Watching him I have come to the conclusion that, given my time over, I would try to copy him and use a bit more sidespin, though I found the overspin part of the delivery of immense value bowling in Australia, or anywhere where the pitches are hard and the ball will bounce.

He is a great one for experimenting and, providing his fitness holds up, we will see a variety of different balls, the like of which have not been sighted since Clarrie Grimmett was learning his trade. Best of all, not only are the crowds who watch him bowl enthusiastic about legspin bowling, but he is extremely enthusiastic as well. You might be inclined to think he should be as it is his trade, job and recreation, and anything less than enthusiasm would hardly be common sense. It is very easy though to fall into the trap of becoming blasé, particularly if success has come your way, and to slacken off as regards practice and experimenting.

Warne doesn't do that. The amount he spins the ball tends to inhibit the batsmen, even the good ones, from coming down the pitch at him unless they are absolutely certain they will be to the length of the ball. There is no doubt he is deceptive in this regard and I've talked with Graham Gooch about it, without ever quite being offered the definitive answer. Gooch played Warne as well as anyone but he too had difficulty in getting down the pitch to him. Gooch says it is the amount he spins the ball which makes him difficult, though he adds that the swerve is definitely a factor.

Because Warne is such a great young bowler, and has already done so many extraordinary things on the field, there are many column inches written about how best to play him. English newspapers during the

1994–5 Ashes tour were even running stories from players who had faced him on how little or how much trouble they had with him:

- South African Hansie Cronje said he liked to try to dominate from the start using a much more open stance and the sweep or the slog-sweep.
- New Zealand captain Ken Rutherford also looked to get on top of Warne and sweep him, used his feet as much as possible but stressed you must be careful because he turns the ball so far.
- Ravi Shastri pointed to using either bat or pad, as he said Graham Gooch does, but not necessarily bat and pad together.
- Brian Lara said play him on merit and attack as much as possible, and it is an advantage to be a left-hander.
- Salim Malik plays the ball very late and uses his feet to get either right back or right to the pitch of the ball.

They were the overseas batsmen, there was also a poll of former Australian batsmen renowned for their skills against spin bowling:

- Greg Chappell said his philosophy would be the same for Warne as any other high-class spinner he had faced: he would take him on. He would be prepared to hit him over the top, and good use of the feet was imperative. 'Defend from your crease and you are a sitting duck! Warne is by far the best spinner I have ever seen. Bill O'Reilly must have been a great bowler, but he couldn't have been better than Shane.'
- Neil Harvey said you must get down the pitch and attack him, there can only be one boss in a situation of this kind. 'The ball can't spin if it doesn't bounce.'
- Ian Redpath: 'I can't imagine anyone bowling better than Warne, but you must have good footwork to combat him.'

They also asked Mark Waugh. A note on an innings he played against Warne possibly sums it up: Waugh, in 1993–4, played one of the great innings of the year in a Sheffield Shield match, batting for NSW against Victoria and Warne. The game finished in a thrilling draw, with NSW 275/9 needing, in all, 306 to win. Warne took 5/77 in the first innings and Waugh's century was a triumph of skill, judgment and brilliant footwork against a great bowler.

Perhaps that's all you need: skill, judgment and brilliant footwork!

In his fascinating book, *Grimmett on Getting Wickets,* published in 1930, Clarrie Grimmett didn't fool about with his opinions on the merit of different styles of bowling.

Grimmett said, 'Bowling may be divided into three classes, fast, medium and slow, the latter two being the most interesting.' Never had much time for those off a long run, our Clarrie.

He went on: 'This spin bowling, and, in a lesser degree, swerve bowling, is a most fascinating branch of cricket.' Swerve bowling?

It certainly took me back to that first match I ever watched at the Sydney Cricket Ground, but I can't recall now whether or not Grimmett swerved the ball. It would be unusual had he not done so, and his chapter on this aspect of over-the-wrist spin gives an insight into what a great cricket brain he must have had. When he was writing sixty-five years ago about various methods of spinning and swerving the ball, he described the way to bowl the leg-break, overspinner and wrong 'un and then said, 'I have a very fine method of demonstrating this wrist work which I use in lecturing. It enables anyone immediately to grasp the importance of altering the position of the wrist to get the various classes and degrees of break. The value of this is that there is no necessity to change grips etc., the ball being spun the same way each time and made to stop, gather pace, or turn from the leg or the off.'

Made to stop? Do I hear those of scientific bent chuckling in disbelief?

That last paragraph of Grimmett's is fascinating, and there is another which in the light of various discussions, mild and otherwise, about reverse swing also seems pertinent.

The ball or sphere which is perfectly round and has no seam swerves because it is affected by the pressure of the atmosphere. This is dependent on the way in which the ball is spinning. Take, for instance, a ball spinning in a horizontal plane from right to left. That is if you were to put a chalk mark around a sphere similar to the seam on a cricket ball, it would be spinning round at right angles to the line of flight, parallel to the ground. The ball would then be travelling much faster on the right side than on the left because it is spinning forward. On the left side, the ball is spinning back, and, consequently, not going so fast as on the other side. Hence the different sides of the ball are differentially affected by air pressure. It is therefore easy to see that the ball must tend to travel or swerve to the side on which there is most resistance.

However, in 1926, four years before Grimmett wrote his book, M. A. Noble, the great Australian allrounder and medium-pace bowler, wrote a short treatise on bowling in his book, *The Game's the Thing*. He said, when talking about what he called spin-swerve:

> If a sphere revolves from left to right while travelling through the air, it creates a vacuum at the spot directly opposite to the point at which the greatest air pressure is encountered. That vacuum, particularly if there is wind blowing in the opposite direction to that taken by the ball, makes it alter course where there is least resistance. The spin imparted causes the vacuum and creates what is called 'drift'. Spin from left to right causes swerve and also makes the ball turn back off the pitch in the other direction after it touches the ground. Overspin, on the other hand, creates a vacuum underneath the ball and thus is an aid to gravity making the ball drop quickly in its flight through the air.

Noble told the story of being approached in the Sydney Cricket Ground nets one day by an American visitor who was an expert on baseball pitching. He asked Noble if he was aware he was swerving the ball in the air like a baseballer and Noble said, 'No.' The American explained what was happening and added, for Noble's benefit, a short talk about learning as well how to make the ball 'drop'. This was in keeping with part of the baseball pitcher's armoury, the 'outcurve drop'. Noble wrote in 1926:

> From that day on I bowled for hours and hours every different ball of which I was capable until at last I saw a slight swing *with a drop in it*, and then I concentrated on that particular ball until I could do it at will. With this spin–swerve the ball goes straight along for about half the length of the pitch, then the swerve begins from right to left, that is from the leg to the offside of a right-hand batsman, and at the same time drops quickly.

I have tended to shy away from reverse swing, possibly because the scientists are the ones who have been most interested in it, apart, that is, from the bowlers who are able to control it.

Cricketers and cricket followers tend to be confused by diagrams and paragraphs relating to wind tunnels and peripheral air pressure on the seam of the ball. The best explanation I have read though comes not from a scientist but from a pace bowler, Simon Hughes, with whom I have enjoyed working on commentary with the BBC when he has not been playing for Middlesex or Durham.

He wrote in the London *Sunday Telegraph*, 'What is meant by reverse swing?' He went on to say that, without getting too technical, there is an accepted MCC coaching manual method of swinging the ball away from the right-handed batsman with the shine positioned facing the *legside*, the seam angled at second slip.

In certain conditions the ball becomes ripped and scarred in natural fashion from normal wear and tear and it starts to swing in the opposite direction; in other words, a ball held as described will swing into the batsman instead of away from him.

Reverse swing *only* materialises on dry, cracked pitches where the leather on the ball becomes scuffed when it lands.

Hughes said bowlers usually know if reverse swing will be possible after bowling a couple of overs with the new ball which, on such surfaces, looks as if it has been in contact with sandpaper. Oddly the ball doesn't start reverse swinging until it is thirty or forty overs old.

No layman quite knows why this phenomenon happens, but the most likely theory is that sweat rubbed into one side of the ball and small bits of leather falling off the other side cause a weight imbalance which makes the ball curve and dip. Some believe rubbing dirt or soil into the little nooks and crannies on the rough side of the ball will exaggerate the difference between the heavy or polished side and the scuffed side, a thought that could catch the attention of match referees.

Reverse swing appears to be more consistent and easier to control than orthodox swing, for which you should keep the ball in shiny condition on one side and keep your body in the correct position.

That is definitely a layman's guide and it fits in with my ideas of keeping things simple, and it seems to work, which is the best thing.

When Shane Warne runs in to bowl and spins the ball out of his hand and then swerves it, he is embodying all the strictures and lessons laid down by both Grimmett and Noble as far back as seventy years ago. From the legspinning point of view, Grimmett's are the most important for comparison because he was rightly recognised as being the greatest legspin bowler of all time. Then Warne came along and turned the cricket world of Australia and England upside down in 1993.

It is rare for one ball to dominate an Ashes battle but the first ball Warne bowled in a Test match in England has monopolised discussions to this day, partly because of television, partly because of what the ball actually did. I was commentating at the time at Old Trafford when he came on to bowl to Mike Gatting. Warne was at the Warwick Road end and the ball was a beauty. It had all the virtues of swerve and spin espoused by Grimmett sixty-three years earlier, starting on middle and off and then swerving to pitch just outside leg stump. It then whipped back and took the off bail. There have been other balls as good as that bowled by legspinners over the past ninety-five years, but not necessarily on television and not a bowler's first ball in an Ashes battle. Millions watched it, gasped at it, were enthralled by it and told their friends who then watched it on videotape replay, some of them time and again. Many have said it spun two feet and was unplayable. In fact, it only spun about fourteen inches and was almost unplayable!

I have seen it probably fifty times and I don't tire of it. The one who may be tired of seeing it in TV titles and replays is Mike Gatting himself! But then 'Gatt' wouldn't exactly be falling about every time he sees the World Cup reverse sweep either.

There is no doubt the Gatting delivery was just about perfect but I said that the one which dismissed Robin Smith soon after at Old Trafford was just as good, though receiving far less publicity. Perhaps it was that people were getting used to it. The ball was little different from the one which bowled Gatting. It just happened, instead of having the impact of bowling him, that it found the edge of the bat and was caught by Taylor at slip. It was a beautiful piece of bowling and certainly was a ball Smith is unlikely to forget.

Warne has done some remarkable things for Australian cricket in the short time he has been in action as a member of the national side. For a start, he has temporarily put fast bowling on the back burner. Fast bowling is great, and in the section with Ian Chappell and Bill Lawry, I advance the opinion that Australian cricket will always be best served by a bowling attack based on quality legspin and quality fast bowling. But fast bowling was dominating things too much; youngsters couldn't be bothered with legspin bowling because there was no one to watch doing it on television. You could watch fast men and listen to the tales about Dennis Lillee and Jeff Thomson, but there was no one bowling over-the-wrist spin and ripping it across the right-hander to take the off bail.

There is no doubt Shane Warne bowls very well with Tim May at the other end, and they work well together. One team of great bowlers in years gone past was Clarrie Grimmett and Bill O'Reilly, although there is no intention here to compare the two pairs. However, what I am able to say with certainty is that Warne and May are the best duo of spin bowlers to take the field for Australia since O'Reilly and Grimmett prior to the Second World War. That is a long time because Grimmett didn't go to England in 1938, much to O'Reilly's chagrin, being left out in favour of Frank Ward and Ted White, Ward a leg-break bowler and White the left-arm spinner from NSW.

Ward played in three of the Tests in the 1936–7 series in Australia and he took 53 wickets in the season, more than either O'Reilly or Grimmett. The previous season, 1935–6, he headed them with his 50 wickets and, in a lead-up to the choice of the team for England, he took 51 in the 1937–8 season in Australia, again more than either O'Reilly or Grimmett.

What seems to have given him the jump on Grimmett though was his bowling in a four-day match, October 9th–13th, 1936, a game regarded as a Test trial and played between Don Bradman's XI and Vic Richardson's XI at the SCG. It was a testimonial match for Jack Gregory and Warren Bardsley. This took place just as the England team, or MCC as they then were known, arrived in Perth for the start of their tour of Australia. Ward took 7/127 and 5/100 and it was said that the only batsmen to play him in any comfort were Stan McCabe and Bill Brown.

That would have caught the eyes of the watching Australian selectors. When the 1938 team toured England, there were arguments about whether it would have been stronger with Grimmett at the end opposite O'Reilly and, of course, there is no real answer to that except to say that Grimmett would almost certainly have played in the Test team, which was something Ward and White didn't, to any extent, Ward playing only in the opening encounter at Trent Bridge (0/142 from 30 overs) and White not being used in any of the five Tests.

O'Reilly never wavered in his opinion that, given Grimmett at the other end in 1938, Australia would have won.

The table of wickets taken by O'Reilly and Grimmett at different stages of their careers makes interesting reading, and may be found in Appendix II on p. 265.

There is always conjecture when you have a pair of bowlers and one is taking wickets and the other is not. Sometimes it is because the one not having success is just an ordinary bowler, occasionally feeding off the outstanding one at the other end. That's not the case with May and Warne and I certainly hope the Australian selectors don't fall for it. To my mind, it is very important to put a balanced side into the field, depending always on the type of pitch provided for the match. If it is a green-top then there is a good chance May wouldn't play although Warne definitely would. In that case you would have three pace bowlers, Warne and an allrounder who might bowl some spin, but more likely medium pace.

There is a clear case to be made for the fact that Warne is more successful when May is in the team spinning the ball in the opposite direction and, possibly more important, providing a balanced bowling attack. Their figures are significant, and may also be found in Appendix II.

I never really had one particular spin bowler at the other end when I was playing Test cricket. There were, in fact, quite a variety, all of them good but never quite certain of their grip on the position. Bob Simpson was there all the time as a second spinner, because he was sure of his place as a batsman. What I did have at the other end though was one of the greatest bowlers ever to step on to a field, and I can assure you Alan Davidson was responsible for many of the wickets I took at Test level. He took 186 Test wickets, at an average of 20.53 runs per wicket, the best bowling average of any of the great allrounders produced by Australia. His strike-rate was a wicket every 62 balls and his economy-rate 39 runs for every 100 balls bowled.

It wasn't until the 1957–8 Australian tour of South Africa that Davidson and I were in fully responsible bowling positions in the Australian Test team – before that we were 'bit' players. However, from that moment in South Africa, we played thirty-two Tests together; Davidson took 170 wickets and I took 163. Many of mine came because of the biting swing, movement off the seam, accuracy and left-handedness at the other end and I was both lucky and grateful that he was there. It was in the same way Grimmett and O'Reilly worked best together, and I'm sure Warne and May do too, the only proviso being that they are bowling on the type of pitch suited to a balanced attack. That is, until Warne came along and slightly upset those theories because he is such a good attacking *and* defensive legspinner.

There was no real shortage of legspinners in Australia from the time Grimmett and O'Reilly finished, but keeping them in the team for long periods was another matter. After the end of the Second World War, there were many fine spin bowlers in the five states, starting with Colin McCool and Doug Ring, both of whom toured England with the 1948 side, as did Ian Johnson, the offspinner. Two who missed out were Bruce Dooland and George Tribe, both of whom briefly played against touring teams in Australia, with moderate success, before working out that there was so much competition it might be better to take up a career in league cricket in England and then move into the county scene.

George Tribe was a very good left-arm over-the-wrist spinner, Dooland an outstanding leg-break and googly bowler who developed the flipper, having been shown it by Grimmett. Dooland then showed it to me in 1956, at a time when English county batsmen were finding batting against him a confusing business.

Straight after the 1948 tour, Doug Ring was the best legspinner in Australia and he gave me a lot of excellent advice on the 1953 tour of England. I played through to 1964 and in the latter part of my career, Bob Simpson was in the Test side; Peter Philpott played in 1964 and 1965; and after that came Kerry O'Keeffe, Terry Jenner and John Watkins during the time Ian Chappell was captain of Australia. Jim Higgs in the early 1980s and then Peter Sleep, Bob Holland and Trevor Hohns completed the list of legspinners. Hohns was one of Australia's very good first-class cricket allrounders, as is shown by the statistical table in Appendix III on p. 269.

The unorthodox spinners were John Gleeson in the 1960s and, before him, Jack Iverson who, in the late 1940s and early '50s, came on to the scene like Warne bowling that first ball at Old Trafford. Iverson only took 21 Test match wickets, costing him 15 runs apiece. Because he didn't know a great deal about bowling but was a manufactured bowler, it was possible to put Jack under pressure. I've always believed NSW cost Australia the Ashes in 1953 by belting Iverson out of a game in 1951.

It might even have been a change in programming which came against Iverson because, although he had his problems against NSW, he bowled brilliantly against England in the Test matches in 1950–1. He took those 21 wickets against the Englishmen from only 138 overs and his strike-rate of a wicket every 52 balls was remarkable. More so when you consider that in the Fifth Test, which England won and where Reg Simpson made 156 not out, Iverson's figures in the first innings were a perfectly respectable 2/52 from 20 overs.

This ended Australia's run of twenty-five Tests without a defeat and was a significant moment in post-war Tests. It was also the last time Iverson played Test cricket. During that season, along with another young cricketer, Jim Burke, I had been chosen for the Australian XI game against England at the SCG but broke a bone in my right thumb fielding the final ball in a grade match at Cumberland Oval a few days before the game. That was in late December and, unusually, we had already played our match against Victoria in Melbourne where they took first innings points.

It was after this match that Keith Miller, Arthur Morris and Jack Moroney decided that the one way to beat Iverson was to attack him. In the NSW innings of 346 in that game in Melbourne he bowled 36-15-52-2. I made 55 in the innings and can testify that he was very difficult to play. Because of that broken thumb, I then watched the whole of the return match in Sydney from outside the boundary and I had a great view of the way in which the three NSW batsmen dealt with Iverson. His figures were 20-5-108-3 and, after he bowled five maidens early in the innings, they then hit 108 off 15 overs. It was brilliant to watch but it was the beginning of the end of Jack's first-class cricket career and, although it was good for NSW, it certainly didn't do Australia's Ashes challenge in 1953 any good at all. He would have been close to unplayable in England on the pitches we encountered.

In that period of the late 1940s and very early 1950s there was another dimension which reacted against spin bowling: the 40-over rule or, as it was in England, the 55-over rule. It was one of the more bizarre administrative decisions ever made, that a new ball could be taken after that number of overs. I love the wording that went with the Playing Condition in England, that 'after the 45th over the scorers shall display a small white flag which shall be replaced by a yellow flag after the 50th over. At the commencement of the 55th over both signals shall be exposed and left exposed until the new ball is taken.'

I imagine Sir Donald Bradman could hardly believe what he had read when he and his fellow selectors, Jack Ryder and Chappie Dwyer, sat down to choose the side to tour England in 1948. The games were on uncovered pitches in those days and England's pace bowling attack consisted of Alec Bedser, a great bowler, Bill Edrich, whose career figures were 41 wickets at 41 apiece, Charlie Barnett, Alex Coxon, Dick Pollard, Ken Cranston and Alan Watkins, all medium-pacers. Australia had Ray Lindwall, Keith Miller, Bill Johnston, Ernie Toshack and Sam Loxton.

When I made my debut for New South Wales the following summer, I was batting at number three for my club, Central Cumberland, and gained Sheffield Shield selection because I scored 160 against Gordon on a Saturday afternoon. In the NSW team I was able to bowl overs number 38 and 40 before the second new ball was taken by Lindwall, Miller, Alan Walker, Alan Davidson and Tom Brooks.

It was a crazy law change which killed off spin bowling for a time and it was repealed quickly enough once it was realised the administrators hadn't thought it through.

Legspin bowling is back to a certain extent in Australia in 1995 but I doubt it will ever return in England. One of the reasons it is the 'in thing' in Australia these days is that the ACB recognise its value.

The ANL Spinners are Winners programme, instituted by the Board in Australia and involving Warne and Tim May, is brilliant. The youngsters love it. They all want to bowl leg-breaks like the one that did for Gatting at Old Trafford.

However, despite the modern-day success, the pioneers shouldn't be forgotten, certainly not those who went to England to carry the legspinning message. Dooland and Tribe were very good cricketers and they and other Australian cricketers like Bill Alley, Colin McCool and offspinner Vic Jackson had a great impact on English cricket in the 1950s when they played with Nottinghamshire, Northamptonshire, Somerset and Leicestershire. Those five are in a group of Australian allrounders who have scored 5,000 runs and taken 250 wickets in first-class cricket; Alley, Jackson, McCool and Tribe all made 10,000 runs and took 500 wickets, as did Rodney Marsh, the wicket-keeping allrounder who was an outstanding cricketer and played from 1968–9 to 1983–4, making 11,067 runs with 869 wicket-keeping victims. Named 'Iron-gloves' by England's media in 1970 at the 'Gabba, he showed them all from that moment. Lists of the achievements of these Australian allrounders may be found in Appendix III on p. 269.

Correspondence is a good reflection of interest on the part of the general public, and since Warne has been playing in international cricket, my correspondence on the subject of legspin bowling has greatly increased. Scores of letters come in every week through Channel Nine and the BBC; they used to be letters asking for general advice, now the writers stress they would like to be able to bowl the flipper and leg-break, and in that order. One thing in which I have always believed is that cricket should remain a simple game. It is a battle between bat and ball, and coaching which complicates either aspect is just a waste of time. That's the manner in which I work when asked for spin bowling advice by young players and I have a standard short reply. Just one A4 page. The matters on that sheet of paper can of course be expanded if necessary, but for any youngsters interested in the art of legspinning I think the advice, though brief, could prove useful as a starting point. The notes are for right-hand bowlers:

> For over-the-wrist spin, grip the ball so that the seam runs across the first joint of the index finger and the first joint of the third finger.
> For the leg-break, and the overspinner or topspinner, the ball is spun off the third finger. The wrist is cocked, but definitely not stiffly cocked which would prevent flexibility.

In delivering the ball, you look at the spot on the pitch on which you wish to land the ball, the bowling hand starts level with the face and then describes what could loosely be termed an anti-clockwise circle to the point of delivery.

*The position of the bowling hand dictates in which direction the ball will spin.*

At the moment of delivery the positioning of the hand is as follows:

*Leg-break* – in delivery, the back of the hand is facing the face. (The ball will spin out with the seam rotating in an anti-clockwise direction towards slip.)

*Overspinner or topspinner* – in delivery, the back of the hand is facing the sky and then the batsman. (The ball will spin out with the seam rotating in an anti-clockwise direction and towards the batsman.)

*Wrong 'un* – in delivery, the back of the hand is first facing the sky and then the ground. (The ball will spin out with the seam rotating in an anti-clockwise direction towards fine leg.)

You should be side-on to the batsman and looking over your front shoulder as you deliver the ball and then your bowling hand will finish up going past your front thigh. This means, if you have done it correctly, your body will also have rotated anti-clockwise.

This 'pivot' is of great importance. If you bowl a ball that is too short, you can be almost certain it happened because your body was 'chest-on' to the batsman, rather than side-on.

When you are bowling in a net, make a white shoe cleaner mark the size of a 20 cent piece, on what seems to you to be a good length; that is with the ball pitching where *you* would not like it to pitch if you were batting.

Never *have your bowling arm at or past the perpendicular when you deliver the ball; it should be* at least *a few inches lower than the perpendicular*.

Don't even think about learning the 'flipper' before you have mastered the leg-break, topspinner and wrong 'un.

My father, Lou, was a very good legspin bowler with Central Cumberland at the same time as Bill O'Reilly and Hughie Chilvers played in Sydney, and he was a great teacher. His advice on legspin bowling was always to keep it simple and concentrate on perfecting the stock ball, the really hard-spun leg-break with a lot of overspin. I have been influenced in these notes by him and Grimmett and that little book I read some fifty years ago, also by the fact that it was Grimmett I first saw bowl at the Sydney Cricket Ground way back in 1940. The point about it is that not much changes in legspin bowling, there are only a small number of things to do and to do well, and the best advice remains to keep it simple. That in itself can create problems because, after sending that one page of advice, I have then had letters saying, 'Is that all?' in a tone best described as aggrieved.

Keep it simple is the answer. Get the basics right first; if you can't do that, then the more complicated things will be impossible anyway. It is possible to extend some of those points but the one thing of which you can be guaranteed is that common sense will always outweigh rhetoric and complication.

And, no matter what I might say is the best way to bowl legspin, there are many examples which show that natural ability can be more important than anything else. My learning curve was based on Grimmett's writings and my father's excellent advice, yet it would hardly be common sense to say that is the only way to do it, although many of the things they both suggested remain part of modern-day bowlers' techniques.

I do have one additional page of advice, though it is to do with attitude, not technique:

1. Patience: bowling is a tough game and you will need to work on a batsman with your stock ball, sometimes for several overs, before putting a plan into action.
*(If you take a wicket on average every ten overs in Test cricket, you will have a better strike-rate than any of O'Reilly, Grimmett and Benaud. If you take a wicket on an average every eight overs, you will have the best strike-rate of any modern-day Test bowler, fast or slow.)*

2. Concentration: anything less than a hundred per cent concentration running in to bowl is unpardonable. The spot on the pitch where you want the ball to land should be the only thing in your mind from the moment you turn to run in.
*(If someone offered you $10,000 to hit, with a ball, an object nineteen yards away, in trying to do it would you look at someone standing close by, or at some other object?)*

3. Economy: this is a war between you and the batsman.
*(Is there some reason you want to give him more than two runs per over?)*

4. Attitude: calm, purposeful aggression and a clear mind are needed, plus a steely resolve that no batsman will ever get the better of you over a long period of time.
*(In other walks of life you want to be mentally strong and on top of the*

*opposition. Is there some particular reason why this should not be the case with your battle with the batsmen?)*

5. Practice: all practice should be undertaken with a purpose.
*(You think hard before doing most other things, why should cricket practice be allowed to be dull and boring?)*

Even Warne, who is something new in the world of over-the-wrist spin bowling and who does things differently, adheres to many of the old-fashioned traits. It is sensible to do so. He has, as the basis of his bowling, a standard, hard-spun leg-break which he tries to bowl on a perfect length. This serves two purposes. First, he is able to take wickets with it, and secondly, just as important, if anyone is threatening to hand him a belting, he is able to fall back on it as a defensive measure. Let's say, for example, someone has just pulled his flipper to the mid-wicket boundary, or driven his wrong 'un and back-cut a topspinner. The next over Warne's skill gives him the chance to bowl six hard-spun leg-breaks, pitching on, say, middle and turning to outside off stump. The odds are it could be a maiden and suddenly he is back on track again and it is the batsman who is on the defensive.

There is also another stage for a legspinner, or any successful bowler for that matter, to go through. Take Warne as the example. He comes on the scene, makes a name for himself and is threatening to curtail permanently, or temporarily interrupt, the international careers of some opposing batsmen. These days that may mean the mortgage payments are in jeopardy, the thought of buying a Lexus is put on the back-burner, holidays need to be local rather than international. The answer they come up with is to try to belt that bowler into submission so that his career in fact is the one threatened.

It is for that reason I constantly stress the importance of a legspinner having as his basic delivery the fiercely spun leg-break, bowled accurately, which can be used as an attacking ball. When under pressure, it is also a wonderful defensive delivery. It is a marvellous safety net!

I am in the very good position of not having had anything to do with coaching Shane, although there are many who have. I have had dinner with him, Tim May and Ian Healy, and will do so again. In the course of the dinner and a most interesting discussion I learnt a great deal about legspin bowling, offspin bowling, wicket-keeping and modern-day cricketers, and have been able to relate it to the era in which I played and the cricketers with whom I mixed. Healy is an interesting character, a fine wicket-keeper with a competitive attitude and a good cricket brain. He is a very good vice-captain to Mark Taylor.

A captain can't do it all, he needs a good vice-captain, a third selector with common sense if on tour, and it is very handy if the wicket-keeper does more than stop the ball and take the catches which come his way.

Mark Taylor is lucky to have Healy in his team because Healy is one of the more astute cricketers in the game, reads it well when he is batting, I should imagine is a good reader of it in the field as well and is a splendid allrounder. Far too often minor consideration is given to the all-round deeds of a wicket-keeper when those of batsmen-bowlers are trumpeted to anyone who cares to listen. Why should only a batsman-bowler allrounder be regarded as an allrounder for statistical purposes and a wicket-keeper, on the rather weak premise that he is not actually credited with the wicket, have his all-round efforts given a wave of the hand?

I put them together these days and it's not as though there are a great number of wicket-keepers to be taken into account, but there are certainly some very good ones. Clever too. When the Australians played their final limited-overs International on the South African tour in 1994 in Bloemfontein, Damien Fleming was given the task of bowling the final two overs from the City end. This was no easy task. Australia had to win the match to square the eight-match series, and Fleming had only just arrived in the country to take the place of McDermott who had been flown home for surgery on his knee. In the commentary box I was saying it seemed there was something wrong with Fleming's run-up in his second-last over which cost 12 runs; he appeared to be straining to make it up to the crease. Fleming walked in from his fielding position to bowl the vital last over and was handing his cap to the umpire when suddenly Healy arrived. He told 5' 9" Fleming that he looked to be struggling, possibly under the pressure of the game. He added that Fleming should check his bowling mark because it was very close to the one 6' 6" fast bowler Glenn McGrath had been using earlier and it was possible Fleming had got them mixed up.

Sure enough, that was what had happened. Fleming bowled a very good last over where South Africa needed four to win off the last ball. They only made two, with Tim Shaw run out off the third run, and the Australians were home. Very bright of Healy. As wicket-keeper he is well able to offer Warne advice in the same way as Wally Grout was of great assistance to me.

Healy's all-round figures in Test cricket put him into the 2,000 runs and 200 victims category. They form a select group of top-class cricketers:

|              | Tests | Runs | Wkts | Test No. | Date    |
|--------------|-------|------|------|----------|---------|
| T. G. Evans  | 91    | 2439 | 219  | 42       | 27.7.57 |
| A. P. E. Knott | 95  | 4389 | 269  | 30       | 26.1.75 |
| R. W. Marsh  | 96    | 3633 | 355  | 25       | 2.12.79 |
| P. J. L. Dujon | 81  | 3322 | 272  | 30       | 16.4.89 |
| I. A. Healy  | 69    | 2430 | 238  | 36       | 20.3.94 |

The only advice I have offered Warne in response to a question was that he should pursue and perfect the idea of the hard-spun leg-break as a stock ball. It was at a golf day, hosted by the Victorian Cricket Association at the Royal Melbourne Golf Club, and we were walking from the barbecue brunch to the first tee and chatted on the way. He asked if I had any advice and I just said two things: 'Keep it simple, and develop a hard-spun leg-break which you can bowl on a perfect length and make that your stock ball.' There was nothing revolutionary about that, nor anything clever, nor was it my idea. It was Grimmett's and my father's basic philosophy and advice. I added that it would take him *at least* four years of extremely hard work to perfect it.

He did it in two.

Since then I have had a few interesting conversations with Warne where he may have some queries about different aspects of his game, but as I would do with any cricketer I have always tried to deflect those into an area where he has to do the thinking for himself.

If the question relates, say, to a bowler bowling a short delivery in just about every over and he asks, 'What am I doing wrong?' the easy way, but the incorrect way in my view, is to offer an opinion. He might finish up with ten different opinions, depending on how many people he asks, and the odds are he would be totally confused. Far better to send him away to work it out for himself by pointing out that 'often the flight of the ball will be totally influenced by the positioning of the body in delivery. Go away and think about that.'

The answer to this piece of lateral thinking is that, when a full toss is bowled, probably the bowler's body is side-on to the batsman and the ball leaves the hand a little later than would be the case with a good length ball. When a short ball is bowled it is, to my mind, a much clearer proposition, that most short balls are bowled because the bowler's body, at the moment of delivery, is definitely front-on to the batsman and the ball is then dragged down into the pitch. I believe this is the best way to offer advice on cricket: to exercise the mind of the player concerned and to make him go away and think about it for himself. Once he has done that, the cricketer will never forget the information he has gathered. If he has would-be coaches nagging him all the time, it can often be a case of going in one ear and then straight out the other.

I am against mass coaching, though I am certainly in favour of assimilation of ideas for individuals. We all have some form of coaching in our careers but theoretical coaching leaves me cold. It is quite an industry these days; everywhere you look there is a coach doing something, but I guess it is in all sports and not only cricket. Much of it is to do with politicians and government departments, because it would be just about impossible to have as many coaches as we do these days without government funding. The government sets up a sports body, funds it, calls for applications for prospective coaches and we are away with an expanding industry. The politicians take the credit if players and teams are successful; others always take the blame if there is a lack of success. I know we have a real problem if I see a media hand-out which begins, 'Research into sport has shown . . . '!

Forty-two years ago, Doug Ring and I shared the spin bowling roles in the Coronation series, when England took the Ashes for the first time in twenty years. I was twenty-three then, as Warne was when he made his first tour of England in 1993.

He has the ability, the nerve and the desire. That's close to an ideal combination but not quite all that is needed. You need an enquiring mind, an ability to sift good information from mediocre – and a genuine liking of hard work. The hard work is essential because the first requirement of those odd people who bowl out of the back of the hand is that they must develop that hard-spun stock ball.

Show me someone who just rolls it out of his fingers and bowls accurately, and you can almost guarantee a steady bowler of county or Sheffield Shield standard. But show me someone who spins it hard, with overspin as well as sidespin, and then develops accuracy through sheer hard work – and you have a young bowler with a real chance.

The other vitally important aspect is that he had the complete confidence of his captain Allan Border and, when Border retired, exactly the same applied with his new skipper, Mark Taylor.

Warne, Brian Lara and Sachin Tendulkar are three great new cricketers. Lara and Tendulkar strode on to the arenas of the world around five years ago. Shane Warne was slightly later than that. Their cricket is magnificent, as is that of some other modern-day players who are set to captivate us over the next five years. It has great appeal for me and I intend to enjoy every moment of it.

Shane Warne is one of the most exciting things to happen to the game in fifty years, and I just hope he continues to play until he can reach that point I mentioned of becoming the best *mature* legspinner I have seen.

# 13

## *Kapil Dev, Allan Border and a few other greats*

One of the reasons the game of cricket is such a delight, as well as a sadness, is that young cricketers like Warne and Tendulkar and Lara keep arriving just as others like Border and Kapil Dev are leaving. No one ever really wants to retire, though I suspect I did it with less regret than most because of the shoulder problem and, in any case, I was hoping to be part of the game in another capacity. Those plans can often go wrong but in this case I've been fortunate, and not only have I seen the young ones arrive threatening to be great, but the great ones disappear, having already been so.

The all-round scene I mentioned earlier provided me with some wonderful watching over the years and it was in the 1980s when most of the action took place, with Botham, Kapil, Imran and Hadlee turning in such wonderful performances. In the space of twenty-eight months all four reached that double of 2,000 runs and 200 wickets in Tests. Fancy being lucky enough to be around when that happened. Malcolm Marshall was another who would have reached it had he continued to play; Wasim Akram might still do it providing he gets his head down and bats as we know he can. He already has 1,000 Test runs and 200 wickets.

Richard Hadlee was a magnificent cricketer who held New Zealand cricket together for many years. It was a travesty that he was never made captain of his country. In 1980 he reached the 1,000 run, 100 wicket Test double against the West Indies in Christchurch in only his twenty-eighth Test, having become New Zealand's greatest ever wicket-taker in the previous Test in Dunedin.

Imran was not only a champion batsman, bowler and fielder, but he had the gift of man management as well. It's not easy to handle a team of volatile individuals, many of whom are also brilliant cricketers.

Two greats who did disappear in 1994 were Border and Kapil Dev, both of whom retired with a world record, Border's for runs, having beaten Sunil Gavaskar's record, and Kapil having gone past Sir Richard Hadlee's Test wicket-taking record.

Nothing could have been more humble than Kapil's start in Test cricket at the Iqbal Stadium, Faisalabad, on October 16th, 1978, when he made the trip under the captaincy of Bishen Bedi. It was a high-scoring match with four centuries, one each to Zaheer Abbas, Javed Miandad, Asif Iqbal and Gundappa Viswanath. Kapil was carted for 71 in 16 overs and most of the bowling was done by the spinners – Prasanna, Chandrasekhar and Bedi. In the Indian second innings he took the wicket of Sadiq Mohammad but it would have been an early lesson that Test cricket is a step up in class. One of the more abiding memories might have been the argument between Gavaskar and the umpires concerning Amarnath being warned for running too close to the line of leg stump. The remaining two Tests of that series thankfully were result matches, though Kapil may not have relished that fact. Pakistan won both, the margin on each occasion being eight wickets. Batting performances of 15, 43, 59 and 34 started him off in the right way in a Test match series but 7/446 with the ball would have confirmed the thought that Test cricket could be a tough business.

He was only a name in the newspaper to me at this stage but suddenly he became a well-known figure in cricket, just by making 26 not out. It was a match against the West Indies in Madras, such a low-scoring event that only 759 runs were scored for the loss of 37 wickets, and when Kapil came in on the fourth afternoon, India were 84/6 needing 125 to win, with Sylvester Clarke, Norbert Phillip and Vanburn Holder doing extraordinary things with the ball. He saw it out amid great tension and a few bruises and, as he took seven wickets in the match as well, it could be said to have been the proper start of his great all-round career. It certainly boosted his confidence because in the next match at Delhi he hit his maiden Test century. It wasn't your normal, grinding century but one where only 124 balls were faced in his 126 not out and he reached his hundred with a six off Norbert Phillip.

I first saw him play in 1979 when India toured England and I was working for BBC Television. There were four Tests in the series that year and in the First, at Edgbaston, Geoff Boycott made a century and David Gower a double, with Kapil Dev taking all five wickets in an

England score of 633/5. As he only made 45 runs in six innings there was little chance to gauge his batting potential, but two things were clear. He was the fastest bowler I had seen from India and, as well, one of the more enthusiastic, but it was an inconclusive series from which to draw firm conclusions.

When Kim Hughes took the Australians to India in 1979, India won the matches at Kanpur and Bombay very easily, the latter with a day to spare, and Kapil played a big part in both victories. The Australians came back with a healthy respect for him, particularly as he was doing a pace bowler's job in a country which had never actually produced an assembly line of fast bowlers. In his young days, when chided for some misdemeanour at a coaching camp, he said in his reply that he intended to become a fast bowler. The response he received from the administrator who was upbraiding him was that this was a ridiculous thing to say because India had never produced any fast bowlers.

Well, Kapil showed them.

He came to Australia with Gavaskar's side in 1980–1 and, for starters, had the dubious privilege of being part of a three-day Test match at the Sydney Cricket Ground. The SCG has given short shrift to touring teams on many occasions over the years and this one didn't get away to a great start for India when Gavaskar was out without a run on the board to that great combination, c. Marsh b. Lillee. Kapil Dev took 5/97 though in the Australian innings of 406, where Greg Chappell made a masterly 204, and not even Chappell completely dominated him.

The next Test in the three-match series, this time in Adelaide, produced an extraordinary draw, with Karsan Ghavri and Shival Yodav hanging on for the final half-hour in dramatic circumstances. Nothing in those two Tests had prepared me for what I was to witness in the Melbourne Test. Nor did the first two days seem likely to be any different from the mayhem and chaos of the first two matches so far as India were concerned, despite the fact that Greg Chappell had given Australia the chance to bat last on the MCG pitch, which had anything but a great track record at that stage for teams batting fourth.

Shades of Michael Atherton in 1994–5 when he put Australia in to bat but then didn't have the batting firepower to take advantage of it. It was a move fraught with danger in 1981, and thirteen years later the odds were no better.

In the event India made 237 and faced a first innings deficit of 182, after Australia compiled 419 with Allan Border making 124, and then, in the second innings, although they made 324, Kapil contributed a zero to that figure, being bowled by Bruce Yardley. Chappell's side needed only 143 to win and they failed in dramatic fashion after a wonderful and courageous bowling spell from Kapil Dev and a magnificent early breakthrough from Dilip Doshi and Ghavri. As Doshi was bowling with a broken bone in his foot and Kapil had torn a muscle in his thigh, it was some performance.

Kapil finished with 5/28 from 16.4 overs, India won by 59 runs and they shared the series with Australia. It was one of the more astonishing results I had seen in Test cricket and it has always stuck in my mind, for the result and for two other matters which took place on the field.

Sunil Gavaskar, who is a delightful person but occasionally has a short fuse, walked off the field at one stage in the Indian second innings, during the fourth day's play shortly after mid-day, and took Chetan Chauhan with him. They made it to the players' gate where team manager, Wing Commander S. K. Durrani, had managed to position himself between them and the dressing-room. I was in the commentary box at the time and the television pictures of the action were difficult to describe. Sunil didn't quite have steam coming out of his ears but that was only because it was evaporating before the camera could zoom in. Sunil had 'done his nana'. That is a peculiar Australian expression which means 'blown his top', stemming from the Australian slang, 'to do your block'. Gavaskar did all three that day in Melbourne.

It happened when he was given out lbw to Dennis Lillee and believed he had got an inside edge on to the pad. It was one of those explosive incidents which happen from time to time in Test cricket and I was musing in a newspaper column the following day on what the result might have been if I had tried the same kind of walk-off in a Test match in India:

Even onlookers must retain their senses of humour in situations of that kind. Mine ran instantly to thinking what would have happened to me, or to any other Australian captain had he tried the same caper on an Indian Test match ground, in front of a 50,000 crowd including politicians who, in India, are cricket lovers. Because of the sensitive nature and general hypocrisy of world politics, I, or any Australian captain, would have been asked to apologise to . . . well, not just to the Indian team, or the umpire I had made a fool of, but to the Indian nation as a whole for behaviour which, at its very best, could be classed as highly insulting.

Now, I'm not saying this is what should have happened to Sunil, who is among the most pleasant of men, I'm just saying what I, or any other Australian captain in such a hot seat, would have been asked to do. The sequence would have been an invitation to see the Australian High Commissioner and to discuss with him the cable which undoubtedly would have just come in from the Australian Prime Minister!

The other incident, and one which tended to be lost in the aftermath of those dramatic few minutes, was that Dennis Lillee, when he had Chetan Chauhan caught at point by Bruce Yardley, became Australia's greatest Test wicket-taker, 249 to Benaud's 248.

The final day, when Australia started at 24/3 and then disintegrated, came after Kapil Dev had been off the field for two days after straining that thigh muscle and it had been stated he would certainly not be able to bowl. His thigh was bruised and he had been limping the previous evening when the Indian team had a curry and tea party at the home of a prominent Indian doctor, who offered his opinion that Kapil might well be able to bowl on the morrow.

That he did, and magnificently too. 'How much pain you can stand depends on the situation,' was his statement after the match. 'There was a build-up of blood in my thigh and it was badly bruised and very sore, but we won.' True, they won very well too, and the Australians were beaten chasing a small target for victory, something which continued to plague them for many years, culminating in the 1995 loss to England in Adelaide.

It was only slightly less than a year since Kapil had become the youngest cricketer ever to take 100 Test wickets, achieving that in one year and 105 days at the age of twenty-one years and twenty-five days. In the same match against Pakistan in Calcutta, he became the youngest to do the double of 1,000 runs and 100 wickets in Tests. Quite an achievement, or series of achievements, and he didn't by any means stop there.

One of the things I have always regretted missing was in 1983, when Kapil was captain of India in the World Cup played in England and he hit 175 not out against Zimbabwe at Tunbridge Wells after his team had been reduced to 17/5. BBC Television covered another match. Had India lost that game they were out of the reckoning in the Cup but they won it and then won the final at Lord's. I saw him captain them that day, and a splendid victory it was too, but it would have been great also to have been at Tunbridge Wells to see those six sixes soaring away over the rhododendron bushes and the sixteen fours smashing into the boundary boards.

I always enjoy watching cricketers with a bit of style about them, not in the sense that they look good but that they show some flair to the paying public, and it makes it more enjoyable. Kapil certainly had plenty of flair. Having been there when he was one of the main factors in the victory in Melbourne, I was also there when he almost saved a Test for India at Lord's. It was in 1990 when Graham Gooch made 333 for England in a total of 653/4 and then India, after Shastri had made 100 and Azharuddin had hit a glorious 121, were 430/9 and needed 24 to save the follow-on. Narendra Hirwani, a genuine number 11, was the last man in and Kapil was 53 not out. He watched Hirwani survive the last ball of Angus Fraser's over and then carefully played the first two balls of Eddie Hemmings' next over. The next four he hit for six. Well, if you need 24 to save a follow-on, and probably only have four balls in which to do it, is there some better way? I doubt it. And they weren't just ordinary sixes, they brought the spectators to their feet and the commentators as well. In the end India lost the match, being bowled out on the final afternoon, but the audacity of Kapil Dev on the Monday of that game is unforgettable.

He was a fine cricketer and a graceful winner and loser, and when he retired after 131 Tests, he was the only cricketer in the history of the game to have made 5,000 Test runs and taken 400 wickets. Not bad for a cricketer who, when a youngster, had to convince others that he had the required dedication for the game. My favourite quote about Kapil is one of his: 'God gave me the outswinger – the rest I had to learn.'

Kapil played his cricket in the same era as Allan Border. Kapil's Test debut was on October 16th, 1978, Allan's on December 29th the same year. Border came into the Australian side in the second year of World Series Cricket and after their opponents, England, had won the first two Test matches of the series. It was to be a coincidence that when he assumed the captaincy of Australia six years later, it was after the West Indies had also won the first two Test matches of the series.

In 1978, even more odd was the fact that Border tasted victory in his first game as an Australian player, odd because England won all five of the other Tests in the series and won them by hefty margins. Graham Yallop was captain of Australia at the time and Border's experiences at the hands of England in that series would have influenced his attitude towards Ashes battles in later years.

Border played well enough in his debut season against both England and Pakistan, and for the next two seasons, but it was on his first tour of

England that he started to show real signs of what a fine batsman he would become. This was the tour where Kim Hughes was skipper and everything disintegrated after England were asked to follow on at Headingley. It was Botham's match, the game where England's players were so certain they would be beaten that they booked out of their hotel on the second last morning. Some indifferent bowling, uninspired captaincy and slipshod fielding, allied to panic induced by Botham's beautiful clean hitting, undid the Australians to the extent that Mike Brearley, with his captaincy, and Bob Willis, with his fast bowling, were able to destroy them on the final day. Botham was magnificent.

That disintegration of Australia then continued through to the next Test at Edgbaston where Botham took 5/1 in 28 balls, and to Old Trafford where he hit a brilliant 118, one of the greatest innings I have ever had the privilege of watching. And all this happened after he had either relinquished the England captaincy or had been told he was being 'stepped down', whichever version you care to believe. This was character building for Border, at a time when the Australian Cricket Board did some very strange things in their programming, and not only sent a team to the Caribbean in 1983–4, but also brought the West Indies back to Australia just a few months later. The West Indies were right at the peak of their form at the time.

In the same way as I wished I had been at Tunbridge Wells in England to watch Kapil Dev hit his magnificent century in the World Cup match, I'd have loved to have been in the Caribbean when Border made 98★ and 100★ against the West Indies, and against an attack which included Joel Garner, Malcolm Marshall and Wayne Daniel. Clive Lloyd was out of the West Indian side because of a torn hamstring, Viv Richards led them and nothing has been more strange in Australian cricket than the fact that Terry Alderman batted with Border for the last 105 minutes of the Test to achieve a draw. Alderman's nearest and dearest might be of the opinion that this is par for his batting but they are definitely in the minority.

That day in Trinidad, at the Queen's Park Oval, is one Border will never forget and it goes down in the annals of Test cricket as one of the finest of rearguard actions. Border batted 634 minutes in that match and faced 535 balls. It was a wonderful exhibition, according to all who saw it, and I'm certain that match had a big effect on his career. Jeff Dujon said it was the best batting he had seen in a match. Border knew from that moment he could do it, that nothing was impossible for him, and that was the way he carried on for the next ten years. He had all the traumas of being made captain of the Australian side after Kim Hughes' tearful resignation at the 'Gabba, but I thought his first overseas tour as skipper, to England in 1985, was the making of him as a captain.

In 1989 he completely and deliberately changed his on-field captaincy methods, including determining that he would take the blame for his own mistakes, so it would be better if he were the one to make the decisions.

1985 though was the year which was responsible for the steel coming into his captaincy in later years.

That may seem unusual because England won the series after Australia had squared at 1–1 with the victory at Lord's, then came two draws at Trent Bridge and Old Trafford, the latter due to a splendid fighting innings from Border who made 146 not out. England then won the next two Test matches by an innings; the first of those, at Edgbaston, was an absolute hammering, by an innings and 118, so too the final game at The Oval which was by an innings and 94, with Australia bowled out for 129 to finish the series, Border top-scoring with 58 and only two other double-figure scores in the innings. All kinds of records were established in that final Test, the sixth of the series, none of them to Border's liking, and it was this crushing defeat at the hands of David Gower which, more than anything, set the pattern for the 1989 Ashes battle in England.

There is no doubt England were without luck as regards injuries and illness. In fact, until I saw the 1994–5 England team battling their way around Australia, their 1989 side was the unluckiest I had watched in that regard. England, though, didn't do themselves any favours in the manner in which they chose their side, starting with the captain. When the announcement of the captain was made, the name conjured out of the hat was David Gower.

There was a very good reason for David's name appearing. Mike Gatting's appointment had been vetoed by Ossie Wheatley, not because of his cricket, which was excellent, or his captaincy, which had been outstanding in Australia, retaining the Ashes in the five-match series. No one actually said if it was a veto to do with the spat with Shakoor Rana involving Gatting leading England in a Test in Pakistan, or the evening drink with the young lady at the Nottinghamshire hotel and the following media rumpus. What we do know is that Wheatley instituted the veto and everyone tried to keep it a secret, which just shows how much cricket administrators know about real life. When eventually, later in the summer, news of it leaked out, there was hell to pay because Gower, quite rightly, had assumed he was the first choice of the England

Committee. Not so. When during the summer there was a meeting of the Cricketers' Association, questions were asked about whether or not there was a veto and, if there was, had it been used?

There were all kinds of contortions from the people being asked the questions but still there was no answer given and the truth didn't escape until weeks later. I should imagine a veto is a very difficult thing to use. You would need to be very certain of yourself in the first place before using it, even if you had the right to do so, then you would need to be asking yourself what would be your reaction to other captains at later dates if they did something which, in your opinion, required action to be taken.

Mike Atherton, for example. If, on the one hand, you had the power of veto in the case of Gatting, would you feel it necessary to speak up about what happened at Lord's in the 1994 Test against South Africa? You would need a very clear mind, as well as complete faith in your own ability not to be too pious, and you would need the knowledge that fairness had to be the most important aspect of any decisions you intended to make.

None of the veto business was known to Border at the time of that Lord's Test and the Australians only found out about it at the same time as the rest of the cricket world, with which they shared their surprise.

There's not much fun in an Ashes battle if you are on the receiving end of successive innings defeats, particularly if it is the first time it has happened for thirty years. England also made their highest total against Australia in a single day for forty-seven years and there was a new series aggregate for a single batsman, Border's opposite number and good friend England skipper Gower, who made 732 runs. Border himself played a superb innings in the Second Test at Lord's, the one where the Australians were victorious.

Two superb innings in fact, although the second, when you look at the records, will seem ordinary enough. His first innings of 196 gave the Australians a lead of 135 and they struggled home by four wickets, with Border 41 not out batting at number 5, with him Simon O'Donnell on 9. It was a day unlikely to be forgotten by any Australian present because Border's team needed only 127 to win and they lost their first three wickets for 22, Ian Botham taking two and Paul Allott one. When Kepler Wessels was run out with the score at 63, and David Boon went to Phil Edmonds two runs later, half the team were back in the dressing-room and there were still 62 needed. Wayne Phillips and Border put on 51 for the sixth wicket and you would have thought then it would be a certain win for Australia. Phil Edmonds though proceeded to bowl quite superbly from the Nursery end and O'Donnell, who hits the ball as hard as most good strikers I have seen, couldn't manage to get him off the square.

It was then that Border pulled one of the best psychological ploys of his short captaincy life. He called O'Donnell to mid-pitch and focused his gaze on the sightscreen at the Nursery end. 'If it's up . . . let him have it,' he said quietly. When Edmonds teased O'Donnell next over with a beautifully flighted delivery, it fairly whistled away over the sightscreen for six and that was the finish for England.

After that Test series in 1985, the first thing to happen with Border was the steely resolve that in future there would be a good bowling attack available to him, taking into account that this 1985 side was very inexperienced and lacked the services of Terry Alderman who had gone on tour to South Africa. The bowlers were Geoff Lawson, Craig McDermott, Dave Gilbert, Murray Bennett, Jeff Thomson, Bob Holland, Simon O'Donnell and Greg Matthews. There were only two experienced bowlers, Lawson who had played twenty-eight Tests, Thomson forty-nine, but this was the finish for Thomson and he never played again for Australia after the Edgbaston match. Six support bowlers, with only nine Tests between them in 1985, made a deep impression on Border when it came to choices for the 1989 tour of England where Laurie Sawle was the Manager, as well as being Chairman of the Australian Selection Committee. The team was carefully, if controversially, chosen. Neither Craig McDermott (26 wickets at 34 runs apiece) nor Michael Whitney (58 wickets at 23) could make the final touring party, but only twelve players were used in the six Test matches played in England, the hallmark of an excellent original selection.

Greg Campbell was chosen at Headingley in the First Test but from that point the tour selectors went for a balanced attack in every match, almost irrespective of pitch conditions. The bowlers were Terry Alderman, Geoff Lawson, Merv Hughes, Steve Waugh, Trevor Hohns and, in the opening Test only, Campbell. They bowled to a plan and to excellent field-placings and they were too good for David Gower and his men.

Border's triumph in the 1989 Test series was complete and, after what had been a real drought, the Ashes were regained at Old Trafford. It was the first time in fifty-five years Australia had regained them in England; Bill Woodfull's 1934 team was the last to do it straight after the Bodyline tour. It was one of the best moments I have experienced in fifty years of watching Ashes battles.

Border had driven the team to great heights with his own very disciplined performance and it was a good double for him, the World Cup in 1987 in India and Pakistan and then the Ashes regained in England. Then, to follow that with the retention of the Ashes in Australia in 1990–1, and again in 1993, was a great effort and it was a pity his retirement came in such awkward circumstances with the ACB and the Australian selectors. It was all eventually sorted out with the Australian Cricket Board but it was sad it should have been done as it was.

It wasn't the first time Border had clashed with officialdom because he was fiercely proud of his team and intensely loyal to them. He was also always inclined to call a spade very much a spade, as honest as they come. It seemed to me this admirable trait did not always sit easily with some of his critics who would have preferred a more kindly approach. For example, the news that the Australians in 1989 were mixing less with the opposition than had been the case in 1985, when they took a beating, was regarded in some quarters as beyond the pale. They would have been happy to see Australia lose, but to win, and to do it with a hard-nosed approach, was not regarded as quite the right thing. They may be right but Border, who played ninety-three Test matches more than I did, and would have played many more had he been allowed, started his Test cricket in much the same way as I did, losing to England. The two series, in 1978–9 in Australia and 1981 in England, hardened his resolve about Ashes battles, as did the fact that England refused to put up the Ashes in 1979–80.

He had the good fortune to play under Greg Chappell's captaincy in the 1982–3 series against England in Australia, when the Ashes were regained, and resolved it to be a case of 'never again' after the 1985 series disintegrated. The toughness during the 1989 tour was probably no more than anything I ever exhibited towards England because that was precisely the way I was brought up to play my cricket. I would never have thought of fraternisation on the field to the extent Border did in 1985, but he got it right in 1989. Hard but fair and enjoy the battles and the drinks at the end of the day's play is the way to go in Ashes cricket, and that was what happened with Border in 1989, but it was a change that was definitely noticed.

He had made his statement to the team that, 'Okay, this time I intend to be a lot tougher.' The team followed and certainly approved; David

Gower noticed but didn't approve, to the extent of mentioning it in his autobiography. The answer he was given at a convivial barbecue was said in friendly enough fashion but it carried the message firmly: 'David, when I came here in 1985 I was a nice guy who ran last and everyone in England loved me. I've been through all sorts of good and not so good times with this team and this time we had a bloody good chance to win. I was prepared to be as ruthless as I could to stuff you up.'

Can't have anything more honest than that.

There are many books about Border, he's written some himself, and he was a great cricketer for Australia. The statistics show how good he was. Anyone who plays sixteen years in Test cricket, and at the end of that time has made 11,174 runs at an average of over 50 an innings, has regained the Ashes once and successfully defended them twice, is a great in the game. The other and more important aspect in my mind is that anyone who captains Australia at cricket over any length of time should leave a legacy for those who follow and Border did that. He also lifted Australian cricket from the despair of the 1980s and for that he deserves a place in any Australian Hall of Fame.

Two great retired cricketers and Test record-holders: Kapil Dev, 434 wickets and 5,248 runs and the only Test cricketer in the history of the game to make 5,000 runs and take 400 wickets; and Allan Border, who played more Tests than anyone else, played more limited-overs Internationals than anyone else, scored more Test runs, 11,174, than anyone else. Two wonderful cricketers whose presence on the field lifted their team-mates and enhanced the game for its followers at the ground, watching on television, listening to radio, reading the newspapers or perusing a variety of journals.

Not long before Kapil Dev and Allan Border retired, so too did David Gower and Ian Botham of England and Viv Richards of the West Indies. It's no wonder England have been struggling a little in recent times when you think that not only is the structure of county cricket posing problems, but they have also lost players of the quality of Botham and Gower. To have all those things happening simultaneously is very awkward and, in fact, not totally dissimilar to the problems Australia had in 1983 after Greg Chappell, Dennis Lillee and Rod Marsh retired at the same time from the Test arena. There is really not a lot to be done about it if cricketers are reaching their 'use-by' date so far as they or the selectors are concerned. Whether Gower had reached that is another matter, although it seemed to me Botham was struggling towards the end of his career and, to a lesser extent, Richards too. All three were also coming up against problems with the national selectors in their respective countries. Botham's protestations that he was fully fit were not met with universal acclamation by the selectors at Lord's; Richards still wanted to be part of the West Indian scene but was eased aside without actually being rebuffed; Gower was both rebuffed by England and eased aside, though there were many of his supporters who were of the opinion that he was mugged.

The latter little contretemps resulted in meetings at Lord's, protests to Lord's, petitions, but the one thing which didn't happen was that Gower made it back to the England team. As much as anything it was a reaction to the 1990–1 tour of Australia where Gower was fined by the team management for taking part in a flying escapade over a cricket ground on which England were playing in Queensland, and his dismissal in the Adelaide Test of that series caught off the last ball before a luncheon interval, after falling into a trap that was no less obvious than the 21-gun salute at the same ground each Australia Day. I was never over-worried about the Tiger Moth escapade, far more about the stroke Gower played when he had been set up and fell for it – that either showed stubbornness beyond reason or a certain lack of concentration; the Tiger Moth job was having a bit of fun.

In fact, I have always had trouble reconciling the penalty for that fly-past with what happened when Ted Dexter flew from London to France in the 1960s to attend a race meeting. The reaction of the Australian team to that was no more than half a raised eyebrow, even though it was on the rest day of the Test match, something we had in those days. Ted's escapade made a headline or two but it was really no different from going up the motorway to a race meeting, having a glass of champagne in the evening and then an early night. It didn't affect his performance in the Test, nor did Gower's affect his. Gower once said, 'When they complain about my attitude, I'd like them to explain how I compiled my Test record.' He eventually made it back into the England team against Pakistan, made runs at Old Trafford to go past Geoff Boycott's then run record, and went on to play very well at Headingley where, in a second-innings partnership with Mark Ramprakash, he guided the younger player and England to a victory. It seemed to me at the time to be churlish to ignore Gower after he had played so well and the England selectors appeared to lose their way – policy one day was unrecognisable as such the next.

Gower was one of the best batsmen I ever watched and it wasn't only because of his graceful ability. A lot of cricketers have beautiful batting styles or close to perfect bowling actions, but at the same time they can be shallow performers. Gower was worth every penny of the admittance money at the turnstiles and he gave those who paid that money great value. He had well-documented problems with Gooch but I liked Gower's reply to that when taxed about his age. 'To be told you are too old at thirty-five by a man of thirty-nine who is batting better than at any time in his career gives the impression there must be some other reason.'

Botham also was one who provided great value for those who paid their money at the turnstiles. It was his batting I liked best of all, though I fully appreciated his ability to swing the ball and the match as well. His batting filled grounds and emptied the bars and excited commentators, none more than me as I watched him play from his debut through to the time his fortunes started to wane in 1989. His first match at Trent Bridge in 1977 showed his bowling to full advantage, and the best quality he had so far as I was concerned was that he was an attacker. I can't ever recall seeing him bowl defensively, in fact I'm not even sure he had the ability to do that; it doesn't sit well with a charge to the crease and constant confrontation with the batsman. Although he could be fast at times I always thought him at his best at fast medium pace and bowling the outswinger. Because he had been taught well and assimilated the lessons, that outswinger was generally on a driving length for the batsman. This is what made for the attacking cricket: he not only gave the batsman a chance to drive, he encouraged him to do so.

Gower made his Test debut against Pakistan at Edgbaston in 1978, Botham had already played for England against Australia in 1977, and Willis, the longest-serving of the trio, was a replacement player in Ray Illingworth's 1970–1 team which toured Australia.

They made a formidable trio in Tests against all countries through to 1983–4 when Willis retired. It was one of England's best five-year spans in Test cricket since the end of the Second World War, the other being when P. B. H. May captained England after Len Hutton's retirement.

Viv Richards was another wonderful cricketer. I first saw him in 1975–6 when he came out to Australia with Clive Lloyd's side and with a reputation of being slightly difficult to handle, something which had come about because of stories to do with one of his early appearances in Antigua where he had animated discussions with the umpire who had just given him out.

On that Australian tour Richards had such an ordinary time in the first four Tests (147 runs in seven innings) that Clive Lloyd and Lance Gibbs decided to let him open the innings in Tasmania, and he hit 160 and 107★. He followed that with a brilliant 101 in the Adelaide Test and then 50 and 98 at the MCG, each time opening the innings with Roy Fredericks.

Some of the best and most competitive cricket I have ever seen was in the time of World Series Cricket which followed Richards' wonderful tour of England in 1976, when the tempers of the West Indian team were not improved by suggestions that England might prove too much for them, although the phraseology was a little different from that. His reply was to hit 829 runs in the series with a top score of 291, and he made a century and two doubles in the Tests.

From the time his career was resuscitated in Australia in 1975 to the moment he retired, Richards was marvellous value for money. I don't believe anyone could ever have hit the ball harder in all the time cricket has been played and there was always this delightful air of arrogance about his batting that said he didn't believe anyone could bowl. He was one of the batsmen for whom I would be prepared to pay my own money at the turnstiles instead of using my media pass. He was the great entertainer for millions of cricket followers and no one has batted better in my time of watching cricket.

A question: is it correct that the scorers of England and Australia adopt a different procedure on wides when totalling the number of balls faced by a batsman? In Australia, if a batsman scored 100 and faced 25 balls and 3 wides, he would, I've been told, have faced 28 balls. This appears to be on the basis that he is able to be dismissed from any of those 28 balls, including the 3 wides. The problem for me comes in the fact that the batsman is not permitted to score from those three deliveries.

As an example, let's say that a batsman playing for Team A hits 100 from 25 balls and there is a prize of $100,000 for the fastest century of the season. In the final game, Team A is playing against Team B and a batsman in Team B is a renowned hitter and has stated his intention to attack the record.

The first twelve balls he faces are smashed out of the gound and he is 72. The captain brings on his man who holds the record and is looking forward to pocketing the $100,000. The first four balls all result in magnificent sixes and the batsman is 96. The next nine are wides. The tenth is hit for six. Does that mean the batsman has taken 26 balls to reach his century, or 17? Is it something which needs to be looked at?

# 14

## *Why I bet on horses and not humans*

The players could, of course, back themselves against others or against a
score or number of wickets. We shall look at this in the chapter on gambling
when we must consider the question of players throwing the game.

John Ford, *Cricket, a Social History*, 1972

The best book I have ever read on the game is Ford's *Cricket, a
Social History 1700–1835*. I always recommend it to those who ask
me about the origins of the game and why various things
happened in its evolution. As noted in the title it only goes up
to 1835, but it is a very well-researched and documented book for
the layman.

John Ford was Bursar of the English Campus of the United States
International University when he wrote the book and, although the
written word sometimes disappears in the mass of videotape and film of
the modern game, this is a worthwhile 180 pages for all cricketers who
are keen on the history of sport.

Dan Jenkins, an American sportswriter and friend of ours, knowing
little about the origins of cricket, came through Australia some years ago
and wanted information. I didn't give him a 'How to Play' manual but
instead loaned him Ford's book which he described later to me as one of
the most outstanding of its type he had read.

It also suddenly assumed a great deal of relevance in 1995 when stories
of gambling and attempted bribery began to surface around the cricket
world.

The first thing to come under notice in the rumour mill was that,
supposedly, the Pakistan team members named on November 11th,

1994 for the tour of South Africa and Zimbabwe had to sign an affidavit that they had not been involved in gambling. The curious bit was that they should have even been asked to do this but things became clearer in February 1995 when they were said in fact to have sworn on the Koran, rather than signed an affidavit, and what they were required to deny was not gambling, but betting on cricket matches in which they were involved. There is a difference.

Pakistan's team manager, Intikhab Alam, was quoted as saying it was not a source of worry that this had been necessary: 'It's not worrying at all. We just wanted to make sure because there are so many ugly rumours. Once they have sworn on the Koran how can you suspect people?' he said.

All this came shortly after an Australian newspaper had published details of Shane Warne, Tim May and Mark Waugh allegedly having been offered bribes to perform badly in a Test series between Pakistan and Australia, and Mushtaq Mohammad had announced he was the man who had mentioned $A1,000,000 to Allan Border, but it was a remark made in jest.

There was another angle to that the following day when Tim Zoehrer, the former Australian wicket-keeper, was quoted in the *Sydney Morning Herald* saying he was the one who took the message to Border that Mushtaq would like to see him during the Test match in England.

The Manager of that Australian team in Pakistan was C. J. Egar, former Chairman of the Australian Cricket Board and former Test match umpire. On February 12th, 1995 he was quoted in News Limited newspapers in Australia as saying he had heard of the attempted bribing of May and Warne.

Mr Egar said the players rejected the bribes out of hand. He believed the offer to each was 'more than $US50,000. I was informed that it was knocked back and the blokes, whoever they were, turned around and said, "Piss off." '

Short Australian sledge, but to the point and probably no need for the match referee to step in with a fine for bad language.

Mr Egar said there was a tremendous amount of betting in Pakistan but only with people outside the cricket scene. He said he did not discuss the attempted bribes with the players concerned and he wouldn't discuss it with them because the offer had been knocked back, so why open it up in such a bloody good cricket team. They were doing well and he knew just a couple of players were involved.

He said his information did not come from within the team, he had no proof it went on and his major concern was, by airing the issue publicly, it would open a can of worms.

Mr Asif Ali Abasi, a member of the Board of Control for Cricket in Pakistan, was also a member of a committee which investigated claims of betting on matches during Pakistan's tour of Sri Lanka in 1994 which coincided with Australia's visit to Sri Lanka for a triangular limited-overs series.

Mr Abasi, on February 15th, 1995, blamed ICC Chief Executive David Richards and his organisation for the imbroglio. His quote did seem to me to be odd from the point of view of the time frame. Mr Abasi was quoted as saying, 'If someone in Pakistan tried to nobble two of their players, why is it reported five and a half months later?'

He added that ACB Chief Executive, Graham Halbish, had told him Richards had known of the allegations for more than five months. The Pakistan–Australia Test in Karachi started on September 28th, so something doesn't add up.

Newspaper reports also alluded to the allegation that the ICC knew of umpires who had been the recipients of offers of $A100,000 to influence matches.

After that enquiry Mr Abasi said, 'I cannot pass judgment on these allegations.'

The Pakistan captain, Salim Malik, said, 'There is no such thing as Pakistan's players betting on matches!'

Until there is any hard evidence to the contrary that is where matters will rest: that there is no such thing as Pakistan players betting on matches. Or so we thought at the time.

Then the next day Aamir Sohail was quoted in an Australian newspaper, in an article by Adam Shand and Australian Associated Press, as calling on the cricketing authorities to stamp out illegal betting on Test matches, claiming members of the Pakistan team took bribes from bookmakers to lose. He was further quoted in the same story as saying he would like to see several members of the Pakistan team dropped because of their involvement with betting syndicates, and that it was becoming so bad it was getting all the guys who didn't do it a bad name also. If he were not bound by a Code of Conduct, he would be prepared to name many players in the national team who had been bribed to lose matches. There were plenty of quotes from other team officials. Colin Egar's remark about the can of worms was sounding more accurate, but I have found it difficult to believe how any player can

set out to throw a cricket match, because his team-mates could change
that by making a century or taking five wickets. The allegations sounded
strange to me. They seemed even more strange a few weeks later.

My normal thing is only ever to bet on racehorses, with a maximum
bet of $A10. I never bet on human beings because they seem less reliable
and certainly less attractive, as Les Carlyon once so beautifully described,
than a black stallion with a great sloping shoulder and huge girth and
rein, a steed with its neck stretched and nostrils flared, surging to the line.

There was a time when a mate of mine, Bob Gray, and I splashed out on
a couple of racehorses, Santa Claus and Homeward Bound, and we pulled
off the Derby–Oaks double in 1964. Keith Miller reckoned Santa Claus,
ridden by Scobie Breasley, was a good bet for the Derby and Geoff
'Flipper' Lewis said he liked the look of Homeward Bound for the Oaks,
but only if the track was soft, as she couldn't run at all on firm going.

The First Test was being played at Trent Bridge the week of the
Derby which was run on the Wednesday, the day before the Test began.
Between us we had an ante-post wager of £10 at multiplied odds of 7/1
and 25/1. The bookies, generous to a fault, gave us a point above in each
case, 8/1 and 26/1, which meant we had the double going for a return of
£2,080. Santa Claus was backed down to 6/4 and duly obliged the day
before the Test, on very firm going. The Oaks was to be run on the
following Saturday but we needed rain. We got it. Storms swirled
around London, there was a cloudburst before the start of the Oaks, the
going changed from firm to very heavy in an hour and Homeward
Bound bolted in by two lengths. The rain hadn't missed Trent Bridge
either and there was no play during the Saturday of the Oaks race but I
was working on TV for the BBC and Gray was across the other side of
the ground in the press box.

When Homeward Bound flashed past the post I was on a ladder in the
grandstand with a radio earpiece in my ear and cheering. Gray stopped
the press box in its tracks with a yell of 'Pigsarse it is, it's Homeward
Bound for Gray and Benaud.' No one had the slightest idea what he was
yelling about but, in fact, he was merely replying to Peter Bromley, the
racing commentator, who, in Gray's ear, had just shouted, 'It's Homeward Bound for England . . .' A number of hardy spectators waiting for
the cricket to start were in no doubt that all Australians were mad!

I once tried to bet on human beings and it was a lesson to me. It was at
Headingley in 1981, when Lillee and Marsh actually did bet on the
opposition and made a lot of money after England had been asked to
follow on and Ladbrokes put up the odds of 500/1 on the scoreboard.

Bookmaking is a perfectly legal operation in England at cricket-matches, and every morning of that summer Ron Pollard and Godfrey Evans came into the BBC commentary box with the odds of the day. Some mornings I would have a couple of one-pound betting slips made for the 3.30 at Sandown, but on this particular morning, Ted Dexter and I decided, just for the hell of it, that we couldn't possibly miss the 500/1. Whichever of us was not on commentary would give Godfrey £20, £10 each as the stake, because those odds were irresistible in what was a two-horse race. Neither of us expected to collect, nor *did* we. Ron and Godfrey, for the first time in their lives, didn't come to the commentary box. Instead, they packed their bags and hot-footed it down the motorway to London because they knew the odds were really 10,000/1 against England. It was, as I say, a lesson in human unreliability and something to write off to experience.

Lillee and Marsh, who took the odds for the same reason we tried to take them, because they were irresistible, made many thousands but also copped a great deal of flak, which they deserved for betting on the opposition. Since that day I have stayed with the $A10 maximum bet, mostly for a place, so I doubt that I would be of very much use to the Bombay bookmakers who are being so freely quoted at the moment.

Not least of the strange things about the bribery allegations was what fun would you get out of doing something where you knew the result beforehand? The money, I suppose, but one of the charms of being in a contest is that only by playing your best can you come out on top. If there are those out there who take bribes, and know the result beforehand, they must lead awful lives, starting with looking in the mirror each morning.

In recent times there has been no shortage of incidents which seem to have a shadowy background of betting or gambling. Some have had overseas connections, some Australian, and there has been talk of Bombay bookmakers even though in theory they don't exist. That is to say they are not legal, something along the lines of illegal starting-price bookmaking in Australia.

There are official bookmakers in Australia and, in 1994, there was a definite problem with one of the events on which they were offering odds, the Rothmans Medal for Rugby League in Sydney, a best-and-fairest award. It was a slight contradiction in terms – 'best and fairest' – when somehow someone got wind of the name of the player who was likely to win and backed him with the bookmakers for good money. No one was able to establish criminal liability but it was a nasty business.

In Australia as well there have been enquiries into various areas of alleged corruption in sport and the Senate is conducting its own enquiry into soccer. When the cricket bribery allegations surfaced in Australia, the Chairman of the Senate Committee, Mr John Coulter, said it was quite possible submissions on cricket allegations might be invited to coincide with the soccer hearing.

There have been other bribery and corruption allegations in Australia including one, in 1994, in which the NSW Major Crimes Squad cleared the South Sydney Rugby League team of fixing an August 14th premiership game with Wests following claims that some players had backed the opposition to win. The players were completely exonerated of any wrongdoing and are reportedly taking legal action against those who publicised the stories.

Outside Australia, Malaysian soccer has been in turmoil with ten players charged with match-rigging and another fifty under investigation. 'Socceroo' Warren Spink said players at his club, Perak, were approached by a local betting syndicate to throw games.

In France the outstanding team, Olympic Marseille, were relegated and banned from European competition after a soccer bribery scandal. There was a suggestion that two Marseille European Cup matches in 1991 may have been rigged.

Soccer goalkeeper Bruce Grobbelaar was alleged to have taken a bribe of £40,000 to concede goals in a 1993 match, and to have tried to throw three other games.

English county cricket players, Don Topley and Guy Lovell, claimed in 1994 that their team, Essex, was handed a County Championship victory by Lancashire in return for throwing a one-day Sunday League match. Essex investigated immediately but the general feeling seemed to be one of mystification.

Seventy-six years ago, in 1919, the greatest sports scandal to that time took place when Chicago White Sox players threw the baseball World Series to benefit gamblers. The cheats, including legendary outfielder 'Shoeless' Joe Jackson, were banned and one of the most famous quotes was born, with a tearful young White Sox supporter standing in front of Jackson and sobbing, 'Say it ain't so, Joe . . .'

John Ford's book traces the birth of gambling in cricket, which was actually part of the game, along with local public houses and inns, some of them famous. As far back as 1774, Ford explains that gambling was very much in the minds of those revising the Laws of Cricket. The *Morning Chronicle* of that time said:

Cricket has too long been perverted from diversion and innocent pastime to excessive gaming and public dissipation. Revision of the Laws of Cricket was made at the Star and Garter Inn, Pall Mall, by a Committee of Noblemen and Gentlemen of Kent, Hampshire, Surrey, Sussex, Middlesex and London. Particular reference is made to the requirements of gambling. Ball between five and a half and five and three quarter ounces; lbw for the first time; short runs; visiting side gets the choice of pitch and first innings.

Ford goes on to say:

Before that, however, in 1727, when there was no generally agreed code of rules, the Articles of Agreement of a match between the Duke of Richmond's side and that of Mr A. Brodrick of Pepperharowe went into the greatest detail with regard to methods of dismissal, etc. It was essential that they should. Money was at stake and the complexity and variety of rulings given in lesser friendly games required codification. The first codifications then of the Laws came in the Articles of Agreement for individual matches promoted by the individuals or groups as a form of gambling.

In the early 1820s MCC banned the bookmakers, or blacklegs, from the pavilion at Lord's as a few years earlier they had banned William Lambert, the greatest of the professionals, for accepting money to throw a game for England against Nottingham.

We know that the blacklegs made a habit of visiting the Green Man and Still where the country cricketers stayed for the big matches, and no doubt on a number of occasions they were successful in adjusting the odds to their benefit. Lambert was made a scapegoat but it was widely known that there were others. John Nyren, writing in 1832, compared that time to his youth: 'the modern politics of tricking and "crossing" . . . were as yet a sealed book to the Hambledonians.'

When such a match is played for money, it is particularly important to have the right man as umpire. Indeed in many matches until well into the nineteenth century it was the umpires who chose the pitch and tossed for innings.

The big matches, which for the last decade of the eighteenth century were usually played at Lord's, attracted the best players from Hampshire, Surrey, Kent and Sussex and these players required accommodation for several days at a time. 'Silver' Billy Beldham,

one of the greatest of all cricketers, described to the Rev. James
Pycroft in memorable words these country bumpkins coming to the
metropolis and staying at the Green Man and Still in Oxford Street:

> There was no mistaking the Kent boys when they came staring into
> the Green Man. A few of us had grown used to London, but Kent
> and Hampshire men had but to speak, or even show themselves,
> and you need not ask them which side they were on.

It was said also that at the Green Man and Still the blacklegs would
come to improve the odds by bribing the country boys to throw the
game.

It could be that Ford's book will need updating in the light of what has
already happened in 1995 and what may be waiting for us in years to
come.

# 15

## Darren Gough, Michael Slater and Mark Taylor, Bradman and Australian cricket

Having talked about the appeal of cricket, the great players who have graced the stage and others who have provided much watching pleasure, it came as something of a shock to the system to be confronted by a bribery scandal, though, as John Ford's writing almost a quarter of a century ago indicates, nothing is new under the cricket umbrella.

More pleasant then to think for a moment of two young players and one other, new to a position of responsibility: Darren Gough, Michael Slater and Mark Taylor. I've had fun watching all three of them, but unfortunately during the Ashes tour, twice there were injuries which temporarily set back the careers of Gough and Slater. Gough's was the most serious.

I've seen plenty of cricketers break down on the field – I've done it myself – but one of the toughest to watch was Gough stumbling in agony out of the 1994–5 Ashes series in Australia. Gough had been like a breath of fresh air for England on the tour, bowling well, batting in effervescent fashion and with skill and being very smart in the field. He also captivated Australian audiences at the grounds and, more important, millions of television viewers around the cricket world. That is not to put less importance on those who pay their money at the gate than those who watch in their living-rooms, but to carry the cricket message around the world, it is essential to have flair of this kind appearing on the TV screen as well as at the ground.

It is not usual to hear about these things, but I'm told there were tears from people who were down between the players' gate and the England dressing-room at the MCG, as Gough was carried off by his team-mates that afternoon. I'm not surprised. He had just given a striking exhibition of batting, played some unorthodox strokes which brought the crowd to their feet and was running in to bowl the first ball of the innings against Australia A when he fractured a bone in his foot.

It looked awful. I'm sure it felt awful too.

He was flown home to England, which in itself was hardly what he wanted because his wife, Anna, baby son Liam and his wife's parents were due to fly to Australia the next day to join him for the last part of the tour. There seemed little point in him staying though; the main thing for him then was to get the best possible treatment from his own doctors and we knew he was to be on crutches for at least a week.

That was before he left Australia, but when he arrived back in Yorkshire and talked with the specialist who is also retained by Leeds United Football Club, it was established that more comprehensive treatment was needed. It was clear to everyone, including Gough himself, that it was pointless just having him on crutches and telling him not to walk on the injury for fear of making it worse. He is, to say the least, hyperactive. The upshot was that Gough's left leg was put in plaster up to his knee and a very thick sponge rubber pad was placed on the base of his foot so he would be able to get around without doing any further damage. Sensibly, after talking with the specialist, he went off to Barbados with his wife and family for a short break and some mental relaxation.

It was confirmed for me that he was a young cricketer with a bit about him the evening after the accident as I watched Channel Nine's television news, and he was shown making his way slowly and painfully through the airport on his crutches when an autograph hunter came bustling up to him. He looked hard at him for a moment, put his crutches against a potted palm, signed the auto-graph, smiled, picked up his crutches and again moved painfully ahead. Great control!

It is a chilling reminder that cricket is a game where, no matter how good you are, how much potential you may have and what you have already done on the field, injury can stop you in your tracks overnight.

The good news came around the middle of February 1995 when the specialist told him he was rapidly improving. The big plaster came off and, instead, a small ankle pot plaster was put on, and then that was removed before the end of February. It also gave Gough the chance to make a sensible plea for English cricket followers not to expect too much from him. 'First I am recovering from a broken foot and, secondly, I have only played seven Test matches and I'm not even an allrounder, just a bowler who can bat a bit,' he said.

I first heard of Gough in a roundabout way in 1990 when a friend of mine, John Robson, from Yorkshire, mentioned him as a player who had a bit of fire about him but was all over the place with his bowling. He had been watching a Yorkshire NatWest Trophy victory over Warwickshire at Headingley which had pleased him no end and Gough had apparently bowled half a dozen lively overs before the batsmen got at him towards the end of his spell. He had, however, claimed the wickets of Andy Moles and Geoff Humpage, which had been a setback to Warwickshire and a boost to the 'Tykes'.

Gough did very little for Yorkshire in county cricket over the next six weeks, though his experience was broadened when he came up against overseas players Mark Waugh, for Essex, and Desmond Haynes, for Middlesex, in the space of a fortnight in August. Waugh made 207★ for Essex and Haynes 131 for Middlesex, which would have been enough to tell Gough that this could be a tough game if he were intending to step up in class.

Nothing of any great significance seemed to happen to him for most of the 1991 season but I noted an all-round performance he turned in during the Roses match, played at Scarborough right at the end of the summer. Gough made 60★ and 5★ and took 1/79 and 5/41, excellent figures, but the thing that was eye-catching was that Yorkshire had bowled out the Red Rose county to win by 45 runs in a very tight game. It was his first five-wicket haul in the Championship and, according to the press reports of the match, he did it with a 'hostile spell'.

In 1992 not much seemed to go right for him, though once or twice he appeared again to bowl in hostile fashion, without luck; at other times reports had him as being very inaccurate. Richie Richardson wasn't playing with Yorkshire then but was to have a significant effect on the youngster when he arrived at Headingley in 1993. The pressure was on Gough to bowl accurately and I can imagine the heartburn of that because I've not seen anyone who looks less like a boring, accurate medium-pacer. Richardson, early in the season, told him simply to get stuck in and bowl fast, which he did. Oddly enough, the first time I actually saw him bowl was at Headingley and the teams were the same as when John Robson had mentioned him to me: Yorkshire versus Warwickshire, again in the NatWest Trophy competition, and this time BBC Television covered the match.

Rain early in the day meant the players had to come back on the second morning, but as I had already made other business arrangements, I wasn't there to watch Yorkshire bat. I had been there, however, to see Gough bowl on the first day and it was worth watching. I was commentating with Ray Illingworth at the time the innings finished, with Gough having Allan Donald lbw, and I said to him, 'Raymond, I think you might have one there.' He just smiled and walked out of the commentary box.

Gough finished with 55 wickets for the season and a place in the England A team to South Africa, and he did look to have a great deal of potential. That potential isn't exhausted yet for the boy from Barnsley whose tour of Australia finished in such sad fashion. It's not his first injury so England will need to keep an eye on him. He strained a muscle in his side in the limited–overs International against New Zealand at Edgbaston in 1994 and, if he is to be a spearhead of the England attack and a genuine lower-order allrounder, he will need to be looked after, though not mollycoddled. Not all bowlers are intelligent – nor batsmen – but I think it is significant that he has looked at both Wasim Akram and Waqar Younis and tried to learn from what he has seen them do. The result has been the ability to bowl the inswinging yorker with the old ball, and when he bowled it in Australia it looked a great delivery. That, and two good slower balls, an offspinner-type delivery and a leg-break, the latter earning him two Test wickets in Australia, completes the armoury at the moment.

It is great to see young cricketers with style and verve come on to the international scene. Not everyone is able to do it and get away with it but Gough is a natural. For heaven's sake though, why can't people let him remain Darren Gough? Everyone seems to be asking whether England have found the new Botham. Botham was a magnificent all-round cricketer with a very distinctive personality. Why can't people let Darren Gough just be Darren Gough?

Michael Slater is the one Gough has copied in the kissing of the national emblem; for him it is the three lions rather than the kangaroo and emu, but the meaning is the same. He looks *genuinely* pleased to be playing for England. Can't ask more than that at the moment.

When Gough becomes fully fit again, it is Slater against whom he will be bowling the next time England meet Australia, in the Ashes battle of 1997. Slater and Taylor actually, barring accidents, and that should be something of a contest, because if Gough is fit and has improved as much as I expect him to, he will test the two Australian batsmen. It is the right-hand, left-hand combination that he will find most upsetting, as many opening bowling combinations have already discovered.

Slater is like Gough – he always seems to be marvelling at his good fortune in playing for his country. There is hardly a time when Slater is not smiling: during a hurtling save at cover, diving to save a four on the boundary, throwing after a slide and quick pick-up. It is this ability of players to bring the crowds into *their* game which so captivates the people who have paid their money at the gate and those watching at home on television.

A wide variety of correspondence comes to our postbox. It can be about batting, bowling, fielding, people, Laws of cricket or the way in which television viewers see the game. A lot of the letters in recent times have been to do with Michael Slater and, before he returned to England, Darren Gough. The letters talked about how wonderful it was to see cricketers looking as though they were enjoying themselves. I know they do enjoy themselves but not everyone is able to show it and it looks as though both Slater and Gough have extrovert genes.

Although Slater and Mark Taylor both play for New South Wales, Slater didn't begin his career with Taylor but opened on his Sheffield Shield debut with Steve Small and then was left out of the side when NSW played WA in the Shield Final of 1991–2. It wasn't until the following summer in Australia that they opened the batting together for the first time and Slater made a duck in the Centenary match against South Australia at the Adelaide Oval. He made up for it in the second innings with a very brisk top score of 82 and NSW won the match by nine runs on their way to another Sheffield Shield title.

Even though he had missed games early in the season, Slater still made 1,000 runs in the first-class season in Australia, leading up to the selection of the Australian team to tour England, and his performance in the last match before the final against Queensland would have done him no harm in the selectors' eyes. He made 53 and 143 and followed it with 69 and 18 in the final itself. The Test players were away on tour in New Zealand at the time, which was good for young players like Slater who had a chance to make their mark and he was the one who beat Dean Jones for a place in the team to tour England in 1993.

Once in England, the tour selectors preferred Matthew Hayden to Slater in the three Texaco one-day matches in 1993. Australia won all of them but Hayden wasn't able to do much and the selectors decided to go with the left-hand, right-hand opening batting method which had served them so well with Taylor and Geoff Marsh in 1989. It was to be another inspired decision.

There had been several wet days prior to the Test at Old Trafford, which was to be known later more for the ball with which Shane Warne bowled Mike Gatting than for the 128-run opening stand between Taylor and Slater, after England had won the toss and put Australia in to bat. Taylor made 124, Slater 58 and 27. Graham Gooch was out handled the ball for 133 and Australia won with nine overs still available. It wasn't your ordinary old humdrum game of cricket, nor was the next at Lord's where Slater hit a magnificent 152, and with Taylor put on 260 for the opening stand.

Lord's was the first time I had really appreciated how good Slater was likely to become. He played quite magnificently, with many wonderfully orthodox strokes and quite a few which he thought up as he went along. It was exhilarating stuff. He continued in that vein right from that first Test century, hit two more in the first three Tests against England in Australia in 1994–5, another one in the final Test of that series in Perth, and seems to be improving all the time.

He slaughtered England's bowlers in the opening Test at the 'Gabba – in fact, I have not seen many better innings played in my life than that 176. It was his highest Test score and involved complete dominance of the England bowling attack, so much so that in the course of his splendid partnership with Mark Waugh, Waugh remained quietly in the background. Slater showed that day he has no inhibitions and he is a refreshing breeze in the cricket world. He has a wonderful defensive technique but uses it only when attack is completely out of the question, preferring to launch himself most of the time into an all-out onslaught on the opposition bowlers. He was marvellous to watch. He certainly launched himself at the first ball of that Ashes series and it set the pattern of the day for Australia, England, the good crowd at the ground and the television viewers. When he walked off it was to a standing ovation from the crowd and one from my small section of the commentary box as well. It was great to be there to watch it.

This is the kind of entertainment so necessary these days in cricket, although of course it cannot be done all the time. If it were, then there would be no bowlers left. They are, or should be, already plotting how to get rid of Taylor and Slater next time they come to England. Prior to that, the Australian pair had the problem of making it through the tour of the Caribbean against a group of fast bowlers just itching to get at them.

Taylor has already made a great fist of the captaincy he inherited from Allan Border. It's no fun taking over from someone as good and as successful as Border but Taylor's approach to the job is different. Already he has stamped his mark on the team and he has led well, both from the batting and the tactical point of view.

He had an interesting start in captaincy at first-class level. It was in the final of the Sheffield Shield in 1989–90 and it came after the regular captain, Geoff Lawson, ruled himself out of the game after a fitness test on the morning of the match. The game was against Queensland, who have never won the Shield since coming into the competition in 1926–7. In their first-ever Shield game, in 1926 against NSW, the Queenslanders led on the first innings and then managed to lose by eight runs. It was Archie Jackson's debut in first-class cricket, none of the NSW players from the tour of England had yet returned, and Alan Kippax led NSW, making a century in each innings of the match.

A century in each innings is exactly what Taylor produced on being appointed NSW captain that day in Sydney, a performance which marked him down as a cricketer of great temperament. The Queensland captain, Greg Ritchie, put NSW into bat and Taylor and Steve Small made 160 for the opening partnership.

Taylor is one of those players who seems to grow in stature with responsibility such as captaincy. He is level-headed, articulate and has his own firm views about the manner in which things should be conducted. He runs, or has run so far, the Australian team very well since taking over from Border, and his partnership with Slater at the top of the batting order has been something special, not just for the team but for cricket followers as well.

I have only one piece of advice for him, gleaned from many years of playing and observing: *take all the credit you can for victory in the sure and certain knowledge that you will be given all the blame in defeat.*

When I first came into the game forty-seven years ago as a player, Lindwall and Miller were letting fly with some short-pitched bowling, then came Tyson, Statham, Trueman, Adcock, Heine, Hall and Griffith, followed by Snow, Lillee and Thomson and the four-pronged pace attacks of the West Indies. I refuse to believe more bumpers are bowled now, or were bowled in the '80s, than when I played. I was either on the receiving end of a lot of them or watching from slip or the pavilion.

I've thought for many years that the use of the helmet has had a big effect on the technique of combating the short ball. For a start, it gives the batsman a false feeling of confidence that he won't be hurt, and it stops him concentrating on getting himself into the right position to play the short ball. Two of the best examples I know of improvement in technique against the short ball are Steve Waugh and Graeme Hick, both of whom, for a time, were so correct and side-on that they made life very difficult for themselves. When Steve Waugh concentrated on getting more front-on to the short ball, he played it much better and was a sounder batsman against the one coming at him between waist and shoulder. The same applied to Hick: that until he began to move more front-on in defence and in playing the pull shot he had nowhere to go with his footwork.

Geoffrey Boycott, who played the short ball from a side-on position, remained unconvinced by my ideas on this, but I agree with Bradman and Sobers who seem to be of the opinion that playing the pull or hook from a perfectly correct side-on position was difficult, and that batsmen could be best served by being front-on to play those strokes or, alternatively, to keep both eyes on the ball while evading it.

In my time there was no more intimidating pair of fast bowlers than South Africans Adcock and Heine. Neil Adcock wasn't as fast as Tyson or Thomson, may or may not have been quite as fast as Wes Hall and Ray Lindwall, but was decidedly quick. No more pleasant companion could be found in the dressing-room after the game; on the field he was a tiger. Peter Heine wasn't as fast but he had this thing about hating batsmen who played off the front foot. His follow-through took him on a direct line towards your left ear. He was constantly trying to eyeball you while posing personal questions about your mother and father.

He had plenty to say. I found the best way to counter this was to ignore him, though I did manage to offer a couple of suggestions that would have made him a gold medallist in the sexual Olympics. The thing that annoyed him most was to keep your back to him and decline to catch his eye. It made for some very unusual shuffles in the crease at the Wanderers ground in Johannesburg in 1957–8.

This was around the time Frederick Sewards Trueman was bowling quite beautifully for England and, at the same time, establishing himself as even more of a character. No one has ever been faster with the answer to a possible put-down than 'FS', something that can also apply to ordinary cricketers who mask some lack of sporting ability with repartee. But Fred had every right to be quick off the mark because he was a great bowler, and he had a heart the size of his backside, which was not inconsiderable.

I first saw Fred in action when he played for Combined Services against the Australians at Kingston-upon-Thames in 1953, on one of the best batting pitches I have seen. In a way, this was a Test trial for Fred, who was doing National Service at the time. After his performance against India the previous summer he had a real chance now of playing in the final match at The Oval. He had bowled out the Indians in 1952 and made his celebrated remark to Alec Bedser: 'Keep 'em quiet at that end, Big Al, and I'll bowl 'em out . . .'

As it turned out, he did so, and then in 1953 was instrumental in bowling out Australia in that Oval Test for a reasonable total, which had a real bearing on England regaining the Ashes for the first time since pre-war days.

At Kingston, though, it was a flat track. Even so, Fred never stopped trying. He ran in and bowled fast and it was this effort, as much as anything and in spite of 0/100, that did him no harm when the selectors met and gave him his first Test cap against Australia.

The Combined Services side was captained by a squadron-leader who was a good cricketer; there was a major, a lieutenant-commander, a couple of midshipmen, including Colin Ingleby-Mackenzie, and Air-craftsman Fred Trueman was there at number ten on the list. After the game, when we were having a drink, and sweat was still pouring off Fred's brow, he was approached and castigated by someone adorned with gold braid for not having taken a wicket. Fred kept it short and to the point but the general gist of his suggestion would have involved some very difficult contortions. He then got the biting reply that, if that was his attitude, he would never again play for Combined Services. 'Bloody right there, china,' was the much more cheerful reply. 'I'm being demobbed tomorrow morning.'

Fred will tell you, and I agree, that not much is new in the game of cricket, but one aspect in 1995, half-a-team matches, certainly is. Six-a-side cricket stems from the successful seven-a-side Rugby competitions and it is an interesting concept.

Cricket needs to live with the times and one only has to look at the evolution of the limited-overs game and its wide acceptance by the public to have confirmation that six-a-side matches will also become popular. I believe, however, it would be better as seven-a-side. There have been some sporadic attempts to play this type of cricket in Australia in recent years but the ones who do it best are the organisers in Hong Kong.

At the end of the 1994 season in England, I went to Hong Kong for their annual Sixes tournament and was thoroughly impressed with their organisation and with the cricket. There were teams from all of the main cricket-playing countries, the beautiful Kowloon Cricket Club ground was ideal for the event and some spectacular cricket was played. The small ground was perfect for the many sixes hit but it had one disadvantage for the organisers in that only 6,000 spectators could be fitted in, and therefore potential income was not fully utilised. They will have to strike a balance between the need to keep the wonderful atmosphere provided by a small ground and the maximising of income to pay expenses, including fees to the players. It will not be an easy decision.

The one decision they and other such organisers should make is to increase the number of players on each side to seven. With six-a-side, you have the bowler and the wicket-keeper and two fielders on the boundary on either side. Having watched the many matches over the two days, there is no doubt in my mind that you need three fielders on one side, the third obviously at the discretion of the captain, but almost certainly he would be placed close in on one side of the pitch to stop easy singles. That would tighten up the run-making and add a new tactical twist to proceedings.

It was a great pity the attempt to play a similar series in England at the end of 1994 was such a dismal failure, particularly from the financial point of view, with some overseas players stranded in England when no finance was forthcoming after rain washed out the tournament. As soon as I read several days before the event that the organisers were intending to pay expenses out of the gate-takings, I knew there was trouble in store. A six-a-side cricket competition in England in September, with profits coming from the turnstiles? The only way that kind of thing can be run successfully is as they do in Hong Kong, at the right time of year, with multi-sponsorship and very efficient organisation.

I shall be very interested to see what is done with the 1995–6 World Cup Playing Conditions in regard to the rain rule. Rain is a bore at any time in cricket; it is one of the few games which cannot start in rain and then probably will be stopped by anything but very light rain. It is bad for spectators at Test matches, and for television viewers, because the odds are it will contribute to a drawn match.

There is very little that is able to be done about it in Test match playing conditions. Limited-overs matches have a similar problem, but there is a difference in that there has always been some kind of a built-in Playing Condition to try to ensure a result. There are several methods. The one operating for some years meant the side batting second merely had to score at the same overall rate as the side batting first, and it also meant that the side batting second would always win and win easily and spectators would be streaming out of the ground, totally dissatisfied, well before the scheduled finishing time. Then there was the condition used in Australasia in the World Cup of 1991–2, which was later amended by five per cent, which makes it harder for the side batting second. This one works very well with that adjustment and is now accepted in Australia. There is the one used in India in the Hero Cup which was said to be quite good, other than for the fact that you could have a situation where the side batting second, after bowling out the opposition for 30, would themselves face a target of 56.

The Australasian Playing Condition came under fire in the semi-final between South Africa and England at the SCG when South Africa deliberately bowled only 45 overs of their required 50 in the allotted three and a half hours. They were clever enough to have worked out they too would have 45 overs. That loophole has now been changed in Australia so the side batting first will, in fact, receive their full 50 overs and the side batting second will only get the number they themselves had bowled at the three-and-a-half-hour cut-off point.

Australia will always be different from every other country as regards run-rates in limited-overs Internationals played as day-night games. It is the only country where a day-night limited-overs match must finish no later than 10.15 p.m. EST. The same does not apply in South Africa where they could play until 2 a.m. if they liked, so too in India and Pakistan. With no restriction on finishing time, and so long as they make certain the Playing Condition in regard to the full fifty overs for the side batting first is in place, there will be no problems in 1996 in the World Cup matches in Sri Lanka, Pakistan and India.

Australia's problems in this regard lie with strict local and city council ordinances, environmental groups and local residents' associations in Sydney and Melbourne. Don't ever think of having a confrontation with them on allowing night-time finishes to go past the agreed time. It simply doesn't work and administrators in Australia are well aware of the fact that if they try it they will be hit by an injunction before they can whimper, 'Yabba.'

I hope there is no rain in the 1996 World Cup but the task of the side batting second in a rain-affected match should remain difficult because limited-overs matches are for entertainment. All these matters will be closely noted I should imagine by Mark Mascarenhas who holds the television rights to the World Cup and who will have a great interest in what time the matches finish for prime time television, and in how much excitement is engendered by the agreed Playing Conditions concerning weather delays.

It will be quite a competition, and with Pakistan the World Cup holders, there will be enormous pressure on them to do well, not least because of controversial and unfavourable publicity in recent months. The last time the Cup was held on the sub-continent, the Australians won a magnificent battle with England in the final on November 8th, 1987, the day of the Mike Gatting reverse sweep!

If the ICC get themselves into Law-changing, experimenting or thinking mode with limited-overs rain rules, they could do worse than look at experimenting with the lbw Law. I receive scores of letters from viewers and readers suggesting the Law should be widened to include the ball pitching outside leg stump. Although such a move would have benefited me as a leg-break bowler and certainly would benefit Shane Warne, I believe it would create negative cricket, with bowlers of all types being too good for the batsmen and the game becoming a very low-scoring affair; fast bowlers would start bowling around the wicket, batsmen would have to stand more front-on and, in all, it would be very much to the detriment of the game as a spectacle. Warne, around the wicket and into the footmarks to a right-hander, might almost bring scoring to a halt!

The present lbw Law – Law 36 – states that:

The striker shall be out lbw in the circumstances set out below:

*(a) Striker Attempting to Play the Ball*
The striker shall be out lbw if he first intercepts with any part of his person, dress or equipment a fair ball which would have hit the wicket and which has not previously touched his bat or a hand holding the bat, provided that:

(i) The ball pitched in a straight line between wicket and wicket *or on the off side of the striker's wicket,* or was intercepted full pitch. and

(ii) The point of impact is in a straight line between wicket and wicket, even if above the level of the bails.

*(b) Striker Making No Attempt to Play the Ball*
The striker shall be out lbw even if the ball is intercepted outside the line of the off stump, if, in the opinion of the umpire, he has made no genuine attempt to play the ball with his bat, but has intercepted the ball with some part of his person and if the other circumstances set out in (a) above apply.

By simply deleting my italicised words in (a)(i), the Law would continue to penalise the player who makes no genuine attempt to play the ball outside off stump but just shoves his pad at it, and it would put less emphasis on inslant bowlers. I would anticipate more offside back-foot and front-foot attacking play with this revision of the Law.

On a scale of ten, it was very close to maximum disappointment that Don Bradman retired the season I started, 1948–9. I once offered the thought to Keith Miller that of all the things which had happened to me, this was one of the saddest, that I never had the chance to bowl at him. Miller said nothing for a while then suggested, in as nice a way as possible, that I might have been extremely fortunate.

The Bradman phenomenon continues in Australia and the establishing of the Bradman Trust and the Foundation at Bowral, together with the scholarship award to send a young cricketer to England each year, is interesting, and in 1994 there was a televised Bradman XI versus World XI match played at the SCG.

A glance at the Australian first-class run-makers over a period of sixty years leaves 'The Don' with more runs than anyone else, at almost double the average and in ridiculously fewer matches. Greg Chappell was a great batsman, and Neil Harvey was the most difficult Australian batsman I ever bowled against; they made 74 and 67 first-class centuries respectively against Bradman's 117. It is significant that when the modern-day players loudly claim cricketers today are at least as good and probably better than in every other era, they always except Bradman.

I was fortunate that my period of captaincy coincided with Bradman's tenure as Chairman of Selectors, with Jack Ryder and Dudley Seddon as the other two committee members. They were the best selectors I ever saw: thorough, consistently aggressive with their selections and their attitude to the game, and approachable. I had captained Australia in the series against England in 1958–9 and then in India and Pakistan in 1959–60, but although there was great enthusiasm over beating England and the crowds were bigger than since 1946–7, there were complaints about the tempo of the game.

When we came to the series against the West Indies, I had to pass a rigorous fitness test before being allowed to play in the First Test and Bradman addressed our team meeting the night before the game. He delivered a message to every player in the side that the selectors would be looking in kindly fashion on players who played aggressively, who thought about the people paying their money at the turnstiles, who made the game attractive, and who won doing those things. This is the way selectors should work with players, although Bradman's chat the evening prior to the Test was the first time it had ever happened in Australian cricket.

Fifty-six years ago Bradman wrote an article for *Wisden* in which he made a plea for cricket to adapt itself to the quickening tempo of modern life, for administrators to consider ways of speeding up the game, to provide more modern scoreboards, especially in England, and to keep abreast of financial problems.

Nine years ago he wrote another article for *Wisden* commenting on the great stadiums of Melbourne and Sydney with their huge electronic scoreboards costing millions of dollars and providing a wealth of information for the spectators, light towers turning night into day and the use of coloured clothing and a white ball instead of a red one.

He didn't seem to be fazed by all of this, in fact commented that, despite his deep feeling for the traditional game and his conviction that a vast majority of players and the public still regard Test cricket as the supreme contest, it is necessary to accept that we live in a new era. The public is primarily interested in entertainment. He said he was satisfied that one-day cricket, especially day-night cricket, is here to stay. He added that if there was a threat to the survival of the game of cricket, that threat lay in the first-class arena, and it behoved the administrators to understand the challenge and face up to it.

On another aspect of cricket he had this to say:

Inevitably one sees the odd umpiring mistake, graphically portrayed by the modern marvel of the instant replay on television. With this new and available technology, I should see no loss of face or pride if umpires were to agree, when in doubt about a decision, to seek arbitration from 'the box'. This could never apply to lbw, but for run-outs and, on odd occasions, for stumpings or a disputed catch, it would seem logical.

That was all written nine years ago, before anyone else was even thinking about a third umpire with television replays, let alone writing about it!

Bradman had a remarkable influence on Australian cricket from the time he came into the game as a player sixty-seven years ago and then continued for many years as an administrator. It is one of the more extraordinary aspects of the great game that in 1995 people in Australia still seek 'another Bradman' whenever a young cricketer shows a good deal of batting potential.

Pressures on Australian cricketers these days include adapting to the change from tradition to the modern-day whiz-kids who control our lives. In Canberra, for example, the politicians and others say that Australian cricketers will soon be playing under a new flag. That apparently will happen as soon as a referendum can be set up to allow people to decide on a republic or continuing traditional ties with Britain. That will be interesting. I played for Australia for twelve years, in sixty-three Tests, twenty-eight of them as captain, and I played hard and with enthusiasm and a tremendous amount of pride for Australia and the Australian flag which came into existence on September 16th, 1901. I was proud to be part of it. Although the Benaud family originally came from France in the early 1800s and married into the Saville family, who came from England in 1856, I have never had any problem feeling very Australian. As a player and captain I wouldn't have tried less hard, and definitely no harder, if it had been for a multi-coloured flag or flags and some politically correct politician who had been voted in by the people as President of Australia. We'll have to wait and see how it affects everyone in years to come.

Whenever I go past Belmore Park and the Richie Benaud Oval just a few hundred yards from where I lived with my parents, I never fail to think of the days when the park was more like a paddock, where the pitch was concrete and missing the ball meant quite a chase to fetch it. Now the Parramatta area is a city, not just a town, the steam trains to Central Station and the toast-rack trams from Eddy Avenue to the SCG and Coogee are no more, as the transport system is run by computers. You might be able to score by computer these days but cricket itself has remained a contest between a bat and a ball, as was the case when I watched my first matches.

*In the thirty-five years over which my memory sweeps, cricket has undergone many changes. The game we play today is scarcely like the game of my boyhood. There have been silent revolutions transforming cricket in many directions, improving it in some ways and in others robbing it of some elements of its charm.*

As you sit reading that paragraph, you may say to yourself that it is the best, most incisive summing-up you have come across in the game of cricket.

I think so too. I just wish I had written it.

In fact, it was written by W. G. Grace in 1899 when he was in the process of introducing his *Cricket Reminiscences and Personal Recollections*, a book published by James Bowden the year before the turn of the century, the same year Victor Trumper first toured England with an Australian team. My time span is fifty-five years rather than WG's thirty-five, but the message is the same.

There have been many changes since then. Great players and great team men, ordinary players and ordinary team men have taken part in splendid or mediocre matches. There have been changes to the Laws and the Playing Conditions, and stubbornness and ignorance ensure that in some areas no change will take place. There have been generous incidents and bitchy behaviour, joy and despair. This is, in part, what makes cricket such a great game, a game that should be taken seriously, although we shouldn't take ourselves too seriously. Involved is a stern test of character for everyone: players, umpires, administrators, media representatives and cricket followers. More than anything else, this is the appeal of cricket.

# APPENDIX I

## *Breaches of the ICC Code of Conduct*

## Individual Breaches

| Player | Series and Match | Offence/Action | Referee |
|---|---|---|---|
| Aqib Javed | Eng. v. Pak. 3rd Test at Old Trafford, 2–7.7.92 | Violated Codes 2 and 3. Fined 50% of match fee. | C. C. Hunte |
| Javed Miandad | " " | Failed to control Aqib Javed on field. Reprimand. | C. C. Hunte |
| Intikhab Alam | " " | Violated Code 8 by speaking to Press. Reprimand. | C. C. Hunte |
| Rashid Latif | Eng. v. Pak. 4th Test at Headingley, 23–27.7.92 | Violated Code 3. Dissent at umpire's decision. Fined 40% of match fee. | C. L. Walcott |
| Allan Border | Aus. v. WI 1st Test at Brisbane, 27.11–1.12.92 | Violated Code 3. Dissent to umpire. Fined 50% of match fee ($A2,000). | R. Subba Row |
| Merv Hughes | " " | Violated Codes 3 and 5 by showing dissent and using abusive language to umpire. Fined 10% of match fee ($A400). | R. Subba Row |

| Peter Kirsten | SA v. Ind. one-day Int. at Port Elizabeth, 9.12.92 | Dissent after run out, plus offensive language. Fined 50% of match fee (R1,000). | C. H. Lloyd |
|---|---|---|---|
| Manoj Prabhakar | SA v. Ind. 3rd Test at Port Elizabeth, 26–30.12.92 | Showed dissent. Fined 10% of match fee (R1,000). | M. J. K. Smith |
| Aqib Javed | NZ v. Pak. one-day Int. at Napier, 28.12.92 | Violated Codes 2 and 3. Suspended from next one-day International (30.12.92 in Auckland). | P. J. Burge |
| Desmond Haynes | Aus v. WI one-day Int. at Brisbane, 10.1.93 | Dissent at umpire's decision. Fined 50% of match fee ($US350) and warned as to future conduct. | D. B. Carr |
| Allan Border | Aus. v. WI 5th Test at Perth, 30.1–1.2.93 | Violated Codes 3 and 5. Severely reprimanded and warned as to future conduct. | D. B. Carr |
| Merv Hughes | " " | Violated Codes 3 and 5. Severely reprimanded and warned as to future conduct. | D. B. Carr |
| Vinod Kambli | SL v. Ind. 2nd Test at Colombo, 27.7–1.8.93 | Dissent against his dismissal. Severe reprimand. | P. J. Burge |
| Andrew Jones | Aus. v. NZ 1st Test at Perth, 12–16.11.93 | Dissent to umpire after bat/pad catch refused. Severe reprimand. | S. Venkatara-ghavan |

| | | | |
|---|---|---|---|
| Peter Kirsten | Aus. v. SA 3rd Test at Adelaide, 28.1–1.2.94 | Dissent to umpire about lbws against team-mates. Fined 25% of match fee (R750). | J. L. Hendriks |
| Peter Kirsten | " " | Dissent after given out lbw. Second offence of match. Fined further 40% of match fee (R1200). | J. L. Hendriks |
| Shane Warne | SA v. Aus. 1st Test at Johannesburg, 4–8.3.94 | Verbal abuse of SA batsman. Fined 10% of match fee (R1,000) and severely reprimanded. | D. B. Carr |
| Merv Hughes | " " | Verbal abuse of SA batsman. Fined 10% of match fee (R1,000) and severely reprimanded. | D. B. Carr |
| Curtly Ambrose | WI v. Eng. 4th Test at Barbados, 8–13.4.94 | Breach of Article 2 for knocking stump out of ground after being bowled. Fined $US1,500. | J. R. Reid |
| Nayan Mongia | Aus. v. Ind. one-day Int. at Sharjah, 20.4.94 | Dissent against catch not given. Fined $US750 and one-match suspension. | A. M. Ebrahim |
| Dion Nash | Pak. v. NZ one-day Int. at Sharjah, 20.4.94 | Breach of Codes 2 and 5. Fined $US350. | A. M. Ebrahim |
| Michael Atherton | Eng. v. SA 3rd Test at The Oval, 18–22.8.94 | Breach of Code 3, showed dissent at umpire's decision re lbw. Fined 50% of match fee (£1200) | P. J. Burge |

| Fanie de Villiers | " " | Breach of Code 3, showed dissent at umpire's decision re caught behind appeal turned down. Fined 25% of match fee. | P. J. Burge |
| Jo Angel | Pak. v. Aus. 1st Test at Karachi, 28.9–2.10.94 | Dissent against rejection of caught behind appeal. Severe reprimand. | J. R. Reid |
| Guy Whittal | Zim. v. SL 1st Test at Harare, 11–16.10.94 | Breach of Code 3, showed dissent at umpire's decision after being given out caught behind. Fined 25% of match fee. | P. van der Merwe |
| Brian Lara | WI v. NZ one-day Int. at Goa, 26.10.94 | Breach of Code 3, showed dissent after being given out stumped. Fined 50% of match fee, suspended for next match in triangular competition and severe reprimand. | R. Subba Row |
| Phil Tufnell | Aus. 'A' v. Eng. one-day Int. at Melbourne, 13.12.94 | Breach of Codes 2 and 3, bringing game into disrepute by throwing ball in aggressive manner after caught behind appeal turned down. Fined 30% of match fee. | J. R. Reid |
| Arjuna Ranatunga | SL v. NZ one-day Int. at East London, 18.12.94 | Breach of Code 3, showed dissent after being given out caught behind by indicating that the ball came off his pad. Fined 25% of match fee. | P. J. Burge |

| | | | |
|---|---|---|---|
| Ken Rutherford | " " | Breach of Code 4, attempted to intimidate umpire by moving towards him with hands raised, shouting, 'That's out.' Fined 50% of match fee ($NZ500). | P. J. Burge |
| Ken Rutherford | SA v. NZ 4th Test at Cape Town, 2– 6.1.95 | Breach of Codes 2 and 3, clear dissent at umpire's decision after being given out lbw. Fined 75% of match fee ($NZ750) plus two-match suspended sentence. | P. J. Burge |
| David Richardson | SA v. Pak. 1st one-day Int. final at Cape Town, 10.1.95 | Violation of Code 2, hit a stump out of the ground after being given run out. Severe reprimand and 20% suspended match fee for remainder of series. | P. J. Burge |
| Chris Lewis | Aus. v. Eng. 4th Test at Adelaide, 26–30.1.95 | Breach of Codes 2 and 4, after dismissing Craig McDermott, he 'gestured' him to the pavilion four times. Fined 50% of match fee. | J. R. Reid |

## Team Breaches

| Team | Series and Match | Offence/Action | Referee |
|---|---|---|---|
| South Africa | SA v. Ind. one-day Int. at Port Elizabeth, 9.12.92 | Warned of appalling behaviour. | C. H. Lloyd |
| India | " " | Warned of appalling behaviour. | C. H. Lloyd |

| New Zealand | NZ v. Pak. Test at Hamilton, 2–6.1.93 | Cautioned for ill-tempered behaviour. | P. J. Burge |
| Pakistan | " " | Cautioned for ill-tempered behaviour. | P. J. Burge |

## Over-rate Fines

| *Team* | *Series and Match* | *Offence/Action* | *Referee* |
| --- | --- | --- | --- |
| Pakistan | Pak. v. SL 3rd Test at Faisalabad, 2–7.1.92 | Team 9 overs short of target. Fined 45% of each player's match fee. | D. B. Carr |
| England | Eng. v. Pak. 2nd Test at Lord's, 18–22.6.92 | Team 3 overs short of target. Fined 15% of each player's match fee. | R. M. Cowper |
| Pakistan | Eng. v. Pak. 3rd Test at Old Trafford, 2–7.7.92 | Team 8 overs short of target. Fined 40% of each player's match fee. | C. C. Hunte |
| Pakistan | Eng. v. Pak. 3rd one-day Int. at Trent Bridge, 20.8.92 | Team 3 overs short of target. Fined 15% of each player's match fee. | D. L. Murray |
| Pakistan | Eng. v. Pak. 4th one-day Int. at Lord's, 22–3.8.92 | Some leeway allowed for adverse weather, extra wickets and batsmen coming to crease and tense finish. Team fined 5% of each player's match fee for being one over short. | D. L. Murray |
| Pakistan | NZ v. Pak. Test at Hamilton, 2–6.1.93 | Team fined 10% of each player's match fee for slow over-rate. | P. J. Burge |
| West Indies | Aus. v. WI one-day Int. at Brisbane, 10.1.93 | Team two overs short of target. Each player fined 10% of match fee ($US70 each). | D. B. Carr |

| England | Ind. v. Eng. 1st one-day Int. at Jaipur, 18.1.93 | Team fined 5% of each player's match fee for slow over-rate. | C. Smith |
|---|---|---|---|
| England | Ind. v. Eng. 3rd one-day Int. at Bangalore, 26.2.93 | Team fined 30% of each player's match fee for slow over-rate. | C. Smith |
| India | " " | Team fined 15% of each player's match fee for slow over-rate. | C. Smith |
| Pakistan | WI v. Pak. 3rd one-day Int. at Trinidad, 27.3.93 | Team fined 20% of each player's match fee for slow over-rate. | R. Subba Row |
| Pakistan | WI v. Pak. 1st Test at Trinidad, 16–20.4.93 | Team fined 50% of each player's match fee for slow over-rate. | R. Subba Row |
| Pakistan | WI v. Pak. 2nd Test at Barbados, 23–8.4.93 | Team fined 25% of each player's match fee for slow over-rate. | R. Subba Row |
| South Africa | SL v. SA 2nd one-day Int. at Colombo, 4.9.93 | Team 4 overs short of target. Fined 20% of each player's match fee. | J. R. Reid |
| South Africa | SL v. SA 3rd Test at Colombo, 14–19.9.93 | Team 3 overs short of target. Fined 15% of each player's match fee. | J. R. Reid |
| Sri Lanka | SL v. WI 2nd one-day Int. at Colombo, 16.12.93 | Team 1 over short of target. Fined 5% of each player's match fee. | Z. Abbas |
| West Indies | " " | Team 4 overs short of target. Fined 5% of each player's match fee for each over short. | Z. Abbas |

| | | | |
|---|---|---|---|
| South Africa | Aus. v. SA 1st one-day Int. at Melbourne, 21.1.94 | Team 1 over short of target. Fined 5% of each player's match fee for each over short. | J. L. Hendriks |
| South Africa | SA v. Aus. 2nd Test at Cape Town, 17–21.3.94 | Team 2 overs short of minimum target. Fined 10% of each player's match fee. | D. B. Carr |
| West Indies | WI v. Eng. 4th Test at Barbados, 8–13.4.94 | Team incurred penalty of -13 overs. Fined 5% of each player's match fee ($US21,903 overall). | J. R. Reid |
| England | Eng. v. NZ 2nd Test at Lord's, 16–20.6.94 | Team 3 overs short of minimum target. Fined 15% of each player's match fee (£360 per player). | C. H. Lloyd |
| South Africa | Eng. v. SA 1st Test at Lord's, 21–5.7.94 | Team 3 overs short of minimum target. Fined 15% of each player's match fee (R330 each). | P. J. Burge |
| Pakistan | SL v. Pak. 3rd one-day Int. at Colombo, 7.8.94 | Team 2 overs short of target. Fined 10% of each player's match fee. | C. Smith |
| England | Eng. v. SA 3rd Test at The Oval, 18–22.8.94 | Team 6 overs short of minimum target. Fined 30% of each player's match fee (£720 each). | P. J. Burge |
| South Africa | " " | Team 14 overs short of minimum target. Fined 70% of each player's match fee. | P. J. Burge |
| Pakistan | SL v. Pak. 3rd Test at Kandy, 26–28.8.94 | Team 2 overs short of target. Fined 10% of each player's match fee. | C. Smith |

| | | | |
|---|---|---|---|
| Sri Lanka | Zim. v. SL 1st Test at Harare, 11–16.10.94 | Team 4 overs short of target. Fined 20% of each player's match fee. | P. van der Merwe |
| India | Ind. v. WI 2nd one-day Int. at Bombay, 20.10.94 | Team 2 overs short of target. Fined 10% of each player's match fee. | R. Subba Row |
| India | Ind. v. WI 3rd one-day Int. at Visakhapatnam, 7.11.94 | Team 2 overs short of target. Fined 10% of each player's match fee. | R. Subba Row |
| West Indies | " " | Team 2 overs short of target. Fined 10% of each player's match fee. | R. Subba Row |
| England | Aus. v. Eng. 4th Test at Adelaide, 26–30.1.95 | Team 3 overs short of target. Fined 30% of each player's match fee. | J. R. Reid |
| England | Aus. v. Eng. 5th Test at Perth, 3–7.2.95 | Team 3 overs short of target. Fined 30% of each player's match fee. | J. R. Reid |

# APPENDIX II

## Grimmett–O'Reilly Partnership

| | Grimmett–O'Reilly Partnership | | Grimmett pre-O'Reilly | O'Reilly post Grimmett |
|---|---|---|---|---|
| Tests | 15 | 15 | 23 | 10 |
| Wkts | 88 | 81 | 128 | 55 |
| Avge | 20.85 | 21.46 | 26.53 | 21.78 |

## Grimmett and O'Reilly Together

| | | | | Grimmett | | O'Reilly | |
|---|---|---|---|---|---|---|---|
| 4th Test | SA | Adelaide | 1931–2 | 7/116 | 7/83 | 2/74 | 2/81 |
| 5th Test | SA | MCG | | DNB | DNB | DNB | 3/19 |
| 1st Test | Eng. | SCG | 1932–3 | 1/118 | | 3/117 | |
| 2nd Test | Eng. | MCG | | 1/21 | 0/19 | 5/63 | 5/66 |
| 3rd Test | Eng. | Adelaide | | 2/94 | 1/74 | 2/82 | 4/79 |
| 1st Test | Eng. | Trent Bridge | 1934 | 5/81 | 3/39 | 4/75 | 7/54 |
| 2nd Test | Eng. | Lord's | | 1/102 | | 1/70 | |
| 3rd Test | Eng. | Old Trafford | | 1/122 | 0/28 | 7/189 | 0/25 |
| 4th Test | Eng. | Headingley | | 4/57 | 3/72 | 3/46 | 2/88 |
| 5th Test | Eng. | The Oval | | 3/103 | 5/64 | 2/93 | 2/58 |
| 1st Test | SA | Durban | 1935–6 | 2/48 | 3/83 | 3/55 | 5/49 |
| 2nd Test | SA | Johannesburg | | 3/29 | 3/111 | 4/54 | 1/91 |
| 3rd Test | SA | Cape Town | | 5/32 | 5/56 | 1/24 | 4/35 |
| 4th Test | SA | Johannesburg | | 3/70 | 7/40 | 5/20 | 0/26 |
| 5th Test | SA | Durban | | 7/100 | 6/73 | 0/59 | 4/47 |

## Grimmett Before O'Reilly

| | | | | | |
|---|---|---|---|---|---|
| 5th Test | Eng. | SCG | 1924–5 | 5/45 | 6/37 |
| 3rd Test | Eng. | Headingley | 1926 | 5/88 | 2/59 |
| 4th Test | Eng. | Old Trafford | | 1/85 | |
| 5th Test | Eng. | The Oval | | 2/74 | 3/108 |
| 1st Test | Eng. | Exhib. (Bris.) | 1928–9 | 3/167 | 6/131 |
| 2nd Test | Eng. | SCG | | 2/191 | |
| 3rd Test | Eng. | MCG | | 2/114 | 2/96 |
| 4th Test | Eng. | Adelaide | | 5/102 | 1/117 |
| 5th Test | Eng. | MCG | | 0/40 | 2/66 |
| 1st Test | Eng. | Trent Bridge | 1930 | 5/107 | 5/94 |
| 2nd Test | Eng. | Lord's | | 2/105 | 6/167 |
| 3rd Test | Eng. | Headingley | | 5/135 | 1/33 |
| 4th Test | Eng. | Old Trafford | | 0/59 | |
| 5th Test | Eng. | The Oval | | 4/135 | 1/90 |
| 1st Test | WI | Adelaide | 1930–1 | 7/87 | 4/96 |
| 2nd Test | WI | SCG | | 4/54 | 1/9 |
| 3rd Test | WI | Exhib. (Bris.) | | 4/95 | 5/49 |
| 4th Test | WI | MCG | | 2/46 | 2/10 |
| 5th Test | WI | SCG | | 3/100 | 1/47 |
| 1st Test | SA | 'Gabba | 1931–2 | 2/49 | 1/45 |
| 2nd Test | SA | SCG | | 4/28 | 4/44 |
| 3rd Test | SA | MCG | | 2/100 | 6/92 |

## O'Reilly Without Grimmett

| | | | | | |
|---|---|---|---|---|---|
| 4th Test | Eng. | 'Gabba | 1932–3 | 4/120 | 1/65 |
| 5th Test | Eng. | SCG | | 3/100 | 0/32 |
| 1st Test | Eng. | 'Gabba | 1936–7 | 5/102 | 0/59 |
| 2nd Test | Eng. | SCG | | 1/86 | |
| 3rd Test | Eng. | MCG | | 3/28 | 3/65 |
| 4th Test | Eng. | Adelaide | | 4/51 | 1/55 |
| 5th Test | Eng. | MCG | | 5/51 | 3/58 |
| 1st Test | Eng. | Trent Bridge | 1938 | 3/164 | |
| 2nd Test | Eng. | Lord's | | 4/93 | 2/53 |
| 4th Test | Eng. | Headingley | | 5/66 | 5/56 |
| 5th Test | Eng. | The Oval | | 3/178 | |
| Test | NZ | Wellington | 1945–6 | 5/14 | 3/19 |

# Warne–May Partnership

| | Warne with May | Warne without May |
|---|---|---|
| Tests | 17 | 8 |
| Wkts | 105 | 26 |
| Avge | 20.13 | 32.53 |
| Best Bowling | Eng. 8/71, 'Gabba, '94–5 | Eng. 4/51, Old Trafford, '93 |

| | | | | Warne with May | | Warne without May | |
|---|---|---|---|---|---|---|---|
| 4th Test | WI | Adelaide | 1992–3 | 0/11 | 1/18 | | |
| 5th Test | WI | Perth | | | | 0/51 | |
| 1st Test | Eng. | Old Trafford | 1993 | | | 4/51 | 4/86 |
| 2nd Test | Eng. | Lord's | | 4/57 | 4/102 | | |
| 3rd Test | Eng. | Trent Bridge | | 3/74 | 3/108 | | |
| 4th Test | Eng. | Headingley | | 1/43 | 0/63 | | |
| 5th Test | Eng. | Edgbaston | | 1/63 | 5/82 | | |
| 6th Test | Eng. | The Oval | | 2/70 | 3/78 | | |
| 1st Test | NZ | Perth | 1993–4 | | | 1/90 | 0/23 |
| 2nd Test | NZ | Hobart | | 3/36 | 6/31 | | |
| 3rd Test | NZ | 'Gabba | | 4/66 | 4/59 | | |
| 1st Test | SA | MCG | | 1/63 | | | |
| 2nd Test | SA | SCG | | 7/56 | 5/72 | | |
| 3rd Test | SA | Adelaide | | 1/85 | 4/31 | | |
| 1st Test | SA | Johannesburg | 1994 | 1/42 | 4/86 | | |
| 2nd Test | SA | Cape Town | | | | 3/78 | 3/38 |
| 3rd Test | SA | Durban | | | | 4/92 | |
| 1st Test | Pak. | Karachi | | 3/63 | 5/89 | | |
| 2nd Test | Pak. | Rawalpindi | | | | 1/58 | 0/56 |

| 3rd Test | Pak. | Lahore   |        | 6/136 | 3/104 |          |
|----------|------|----------|--------|-------|-------|----------|
| 1st Test | Eng. | 'Gabba   | 1994–5 | 3/39  | 8/71  |          |
| 2nd Test | Eng. | MCG      |        | 6/64  | 3/16  |          |
| 3rd Test | Eng. | SCG      |        | 1/88  | 0/48  |          |
| 4th Test | Eng. | Adelaide |        |       |       | 2/72 2/82 |
| 5th Test | Eng. | Perth    |        |       |       | 2/58 0/11 |

Tim May took 49 wickets (avge 34.91) during this period.

# APPENDIX III

## *Australian Cricketers*

## 10,000 Runs and 500 Wickets in Career

|  | M | I | Runs | HS | Avge | 100 | Wkts | Avge | 5wi |
|---|---|---|---|---|---|---|---|---|---|
| W. E. Alley | 400 | 468 | 19612 | 221★ | 31.88 | 31 | 768 | 22.68 | 30 |
| W. W. Armstrong | 269 | 406 | 16158 | 303★ | 46.83 | 45 | 832 | 19.71 | 50 |
| R. Benaud | 259 | 365 | 11719 | 187 | 36.50 | 23 | 945 | 23.74 | 56 |
| G. Giffen | 251 | 421 | 11758 | 271 | 29.54 | 18 | 1023 | 21.29 | 95 |
| V. E. Jackson | 354 | 605 | 15698 | 170 | 28.43 | 21 | 965 | 24.73 | 43 |
| R. W. Marsh | 257 | 396 | 11067 | 236 | 31.17 | 12 | 803ct/66st. | | |
| C. L. McCool | 251 | 412 | 12420 | 172 | 32.85 | 18 | 602 | 27.47 | 34 |
| M. A. Noble | 248 | 377 | 13975 | 284 | 40.74 | 37 | 625 | 23.11 | 33 |
| F. A. Tarrant | 326 | 539 | 17857 | 250 | 36.37 | 33 | 1489 | 17.66 | 129 |
| G. E. Tribe | 308 | 454 | 10177 | 136★ | 27.34 | 7 | 1378 | 20.55 | 93 |
| A. E. Trott | 375 | 602 | 10696 | 164 | 19.48 | 8 | 1674 | 21.09 | 132 |

## 5,000 Runs and 250 Wickets in Career

|  | M | I | Runs | HS | Avge | 100 | Wkts | Avge | 5wi |
|---|---|---|---|---|---|---|---|---|---|
| W. Caffyn | 200 | 350 | 5885 | 103 | 17.99 | 2 | 577 | 13.46 | 49 |
| G. S. Chappell | 321 | 542 | 24535 | 247★ | 52.20 | 74 | 291 | 29.95 | 5 |
| J. A. Cuffe | 221 | 368 | 7476 | 145 | 22.25 | 4 | 738 | 25.47 | 33 |
| A. K. Davidson | 193 | 246 | 6804 | 129 | 32.86 | 9 | 672 | 20.90 | 33 |
| A. I. C. Dodemaide | 168 | 256 | 5662 | 123 | 29.18 | 5 | 486 | 32.26 | 15 |
| B. Dooland | 214 | 326 | 7141 | 115★ | 24.37 | 4 | 1016 | 21.98 | 84 |
| J. M. Gregory | 129 | 173 | 5661 | 152 | 36.52 | 13 | 504 | 20.99 | 33 |
| T. V. Hohns | 152 | 232 | 5210 | 103 | 27.13 | 2 | 288 | 37.15 | 11 |
| A. J. Y. Hopkins | 162 | 240 | 5563 | 218 | 25.40 | 8 | 271 | 24.40 | 10 |

| | | | | | | | | | |
|---|---|---|---|---|---|---|---|---|---|
| C. Kelleway | 132 | 205 | 6389 | 168 | 35.10 | 15 | 339 | 26.32 | 10 |
| F. J. Laver | 163 | 255 | 5431 | 164 | 25.02 | 6 | 404 | 24.72 | 19 |
| R. R. Lindwall | 228 | 270 | 5042 | 134★ | 21.82 | 5 | 794 | 21.35 | 34 |
| C. G. Macartney | 249 | 360 | 15019 | 345 | 45.78 | 49 | 419 | 20.95 | 17 |
| K. D. Mackay | 201 | 194 | 10823 | 223 | 43.64 | 23 | 251 | 33.31 | 7 |
| G. R. J. Matthews | 159 | 234 | 7570 | 184 | 39.42 | 12 | 432 | 31.50 | 19 |
| K. R. Miller | 226 | 326 | 14183 | 281★ | 48.90 | 41 | 497 | 22.30 | 16 |
| J. Pettiford | 201 | 324 | 7077 | 133 | 25.64 | 4 | 295 | 31.38 | 7 |
| R. B. Simpson | 257 | 436 | 21029 | 359 | 56.22 | 60 | 349 | 38.07 | 6 |
| P. R. Sleep | 174 | 284 | 8122 | 185 | 34.56 | 15 | 363 | 39.36 | 9 |
| G. H. S. Trott | 222 | 393 | 8804 | 186 | 23.54 | 9 | 386 | 25.12 | 17 |
| H. Trumble | 213 | 344 | 395 | 107 | 19.74 | 3 | 939 | 18.44 | 69 |

## Century and 10 Dismissals in a Match by a Wicket-keeper

R. W. Marsh   104 10ct 0st. WA v. SA Perth    1976–7

## Century and 5 Dismissals in an Innings by a Wicket-Keeper in Same Match

| | | | | | |
|---|---|---|---|---|---|
| L. P. D. O'Connor | 160 | 5ct 0st. | Qld v. Vic. | Melbourne | 1928–9 |
| D. Tallon | 193 | 4ct 1st. | Qld v. Vic. | Brisbane | 1935–6 |
| G. R. A. Langley | 141★ | 5ct 0st. | SA v. Qld | Brisbane | 1948–9 |
| B. N. Jarman | 196 | 5ct 0st. | SA v. NSW | Adelaide | 1965–6 |
| J. A. Maclean | 132 | 6ct 0st. | Qld v. Vic. | Melbourne | 1972–3 |
| R. W. Marsh | 104 | 6ct 0st. | WA v. SA | Perth | 1976–7 |
| R. D. Robinson | 120 | 4ct 1st. | Vic. v. SA | Adelaide | 1980–1 |
| T. J. Zoehrer | 136 | 4ct 1st. | WA v. Tas. | Hobart | 1992–3 |

## 500 Runs and 50 Dismissals by a Wicket-Keeper in an Australian Season

| | | Runs | Avge | Ct | St. | Total |
|---|---|---|---|---|---|---|
| R. W. Marsh | 1974–5 | 865 | 37.61 | 58 | 6 | 64 |
| R. W. Marsh | 1975–6 | 631 | 27.43 | 63 | 4 | 67 |
| R. W. Marsh | 1976–7 | 600 | 42.86 | 53 | 0 | 53 |
| R. W. Marsh | 1980–1 | 625 | 29.76 | 59 | 2 | 61 |
| R. W. Marsh | 1982–3 | 538 | 26.90 | 61 | 0 | 61 |

There are some fine allrounders, apart from Marsh, in the wicket-keeping/batting part of Australian cricket, and Ian Healy is the latest of them:

|  | M | I | NO | Runs | HS | Avge | 100s | Cts | Sts | Total |
|---|---|---|---|---|---|---|---|---|---|---|
| W. A. S. Oldfield | 245 | 315 | 57 | 6135 | 137 | 23.77 | 6 | 400 | 262 | 662 |
| D. Tallon | 150 | 228 | 21 | 6034 | 193 | 29.14 | 9 | 302 | 131 | 433 |
| A. T. W. Grout | 183 | 253 | 24 | 5168 | 119 | 22.56 | 4 | 473 | 114 | 587 |
| I. A. Healy† | 140 | 206 | 44 | 5075 | 113★ | 31.37 | 2 | 436 | 39 | 475 |

† Still playing first-class cricket

# INDEX

Aamir Sohail, 233
Adcock, Neil, 245, 246
Adlam, Warwick, 181
AIS Commonwealth Bank Cricket
    Academy, 159–80, 194
Alderman, Terry,66, 69–70, 135, 155,
    221, 224
Allanby, Richard, 181
Allen, G. O. ('Gubby'), 84
Alley, Bill, 207
Alley, Phil, 181
Alliss, Peter, 130–31
Allott, Paul, 98, 223
Ambrose, Curtly, 257
Ames, Les, 84, 85
Angel, Jo, 47, 94, 97, 99, 258
Anil Kumble, 149
Aqib Javed, 37, 255, 256
Arjuna Ranatunga, 258
Armstrong, Warwick, 148
Arnberger, Jason, 181
Asif Ali Abasi, 233
Asif Iqbal, 216
Atherton, Michael, 25, 27–40, 41–2,
    43–4, 47, 48, 49–53, 55, 56, 57–60,
    62, 63–4, 69–71, 72, 73–82, 83–96,
    97–103, 116–17, 133, 146, 153, 159,
    223, 257
Atkinson, Colin, 150
Atkinson, Denis, 128
Atkinson, Mark, 181
Australian Cricket Board (ACB), 2, 7,
    8, 9, 12–13, 106, 109, 114, 116–119,
    151, 152, 165, 166, 171–5, 181, 185,
    225, 232, 257
Australian Golf Club, 132

Australian Institute of Sport see AIS
Australian Sports Commission, 163
Australian Sports Directory, 163
Australian, The, 95
Auty, Clinton, 181

Bacher, Dr Ali, 2, 22
Bailey, Trevor, 143
Ballesteros, Seve, 123–4, 130–31
Bannister, Jack, 20, 23, 125
Barassi, Ron, 183
Barber, Bob, 150
Bardsley, Warren, 203
Barnett, Charlie, 84, 206
Barnett, Kim, 154
Barrington, Ken, 67, 68
Bass, Dr Alan, 196
Battersby, Cam, 9
Bay Hotel, Camps Bay 11
BBC, 30, 207
BBC Television, 32, 36, 110–11, 124,
    130, 216, 219
Beatles, The, 136
Bedford, Ian, 150
Bedser, Alec, 65, 143, 206, 247
Beldham, 'Silver' Billy, 237
Belmore Park, 253
Benaud, Daphne, 122, 123–4, 187
Benaud, John, 194
Benaud, Lou, 208
Benjamin, Joey, 47, 48, 84
Bennett, Bob, 4
Bennett, Murray, 224
Benson & Hedges, Final, 191
    match, 137, 140
    World Series, 106, 159, 185, 194

Bernard, Steve, 194
Berry, Darren, 181
Bevan, Michael, 50–51, 72, 76
Bicknell, Darren, 45
Bird, Dickie, 21, 28
Bishen Bedi, 216
Blewett, Greg, 50, 89–90, 97, 99, 100, 101
Bodenstein, Cobus, 1
Boon, David, 10, 49, 50, 63, 64, 71, 76, 81, 86, 88, 99, 115–16, 223
Booth, Brian, 146
Bophuthatswana, 1
Border, Allan, 6, 7, 8–9, 10, 23, 50, 70, 92, 100–101, 107, 131, 135, 153, 155, 157, 190, 196, 213, 215, 216, 217, 220–26, 232, 244, 255, 256
Botham, Ian, 3–4, 146, 154–5, 156, 189, 215, 221, 223, 226–7, 228, 242
Bowden, James, 254
Boycott, Geoff, 25, 125, 216, 227, 246
Bradman Foundation at Bowral, 251
Bradman, Sir Donald, 54, 57, 60, 74, 203, 206, 246, 251–3
Brearley, Mike, 44, 156, 221
Breasley, Scobie, 234
Brooks, Tom, 206
Brown, Bill, 203
BSkyB, 110, 111
Bucknor, Steve, 21, 80
Bugialli, Guiliano, 187
Burge, Peter, 28–9, 31, 38–9, 40
Burke, Jim, 205

Campbell, Alistair, 77, 152
Campbell, Greg, 224
Campese, David, 75–6
*Cape Times*, 1
Carew, Paul, 181
Carr, Donald, 7, 9
Castle Cup, 106
CBS, 122
Central Cumberland, 206, 208
Channel 4, 124
Channel Nine, 2, 66, 76, 77, 91, 115, 122, 124, 126, 131, 132, 207
Chappell, Greg, 160, 198, 217–18, 225, 226, 251
Chappell, Ian, 23–4, 44, 58, 66, 98, 101–102, 120, 160, 164, 202, 205
Chee Quee, Richard, 181

Chegwyn, Jack, 161
Cheltenham Gold Cup Festival, 124
Chetan Chauhan, 218, 219
Chicago White Sox, 236
Chilvers, Hughie, 208
Chingoka, Peter, 152
Clark, Clive, 133
Clarke, David, 181
Clarke, Sylvester, 216
Compton, Denis, 33, 131, 141
Cook, Simon, 181
Copson, Bill, 84
Corbett, Troy, 181
Cornell, John, 114
Corrigan, Dr Brian, 196
Coulter, John, 236
Covent Garden, 121
Coward, Mike, 95
Cowdrey, Chris, 156
Cowdrey, Sir Colin, 3, 43, 67, 156, 157
Cowper, Bob, 2
Cox, Jamie, 181
Coxon, Alex, 206
Craig, Ian, 117–18
Cranston, Ken, 206
Crawley, John, 71, 83, 90–91, 98, 100
*Cricket, a Social History 1700–1835*, 231
*Cricket Crisis*, 117
*Cricket Reminiscences and Personal Recollections*, 254
Cricketers' Association, 223
*Crocodile Dundee*, 115
Crompton, Alan, 8, 9, 13, 106–7, 185, 186
Cronje, Hansie, 7, 198
Cullinan, Daryll, 8, 13
Currie Cup, 6, 106

Daniel, Wayne, 221
Davidson, Alan, 146, 204, 206
DeFreitas, Phil, 49, 51, 52, 53, 61, 71, 77, 83, 87, 88, 89, 91, 93
de Klerk, F. W., 2
Denness, Mike, 120, 156
Depeiza, Clairmonte, 128
Derby, The, 234
de Villiers, Fanie, 40, 258
Dexter, Ted, 67, 154, 156, 227, 235
Dilip Doshi, 218
Di Venuto, Michael, 181

Diver, E.J., 134
Donald, Allan, 10, 242
Dooland, Bruce, 204–5, 207
Doordarshan, 112
Drinnen, Peter, 181
Duckworth, George, 85
Dujon, Jeff, 221
Dunhill Masters, 130–31
Durrani, Wing Commander S. K., 218
Dwyer, Chappie, 206
Dykes, Andrew, 181

Easton, Neil, 32
Edmonds, Phil, 223–4
Edrich, Bill, 206
Edrich, John, 156
Egar, C.J., 232–4
Emburey, John, 156
Euberoth, Peter, 111
Evans, Godfrey, 235

Fagg, Arthur, 84
Fairbrother, Neil, 39–40, 77–8, 84, 153
Farnes, Ken, 84
Favell, Les, 57
Feherty, David, 122–3
Fingleton, Jack, 117
Fishlock, Laurie, 84
Fitzgerald, David, 181
Fitzpatrick, Kate, 132
Flegler, Shawn, 181
Fleming, Damien, 59, 64, 70, 72–3, 76,
    78, 80, 85, 86, 90, 91, 94, 103, 211
Fletcher, Keith, 42–3, 45, 156, 178, 182
Flower, Andy, 77, 152
Flower, Grant, 76, 77, 81, 152
Fonteyn, Dame Margot, 121
Ford, John, 231, 236–8, 239
Fraser, Angus, 45–7, 48, 56, 71, 72, 74,
    75, 76, 78, 81, 84, 87, 90, 93, 99,
    220
Fredericks, Roy, 229

'Gabba, the, 9, 19, 43, 47, 48, 50, 52,
    77, 123, 131, 207, 222
Gallian, Jason, 181
Garner, Joel, 221
Gatting, Mike, 46, 51, 53, 55, 60, 64, 72,
    79, 83, 85, 87, 90, 93, 98, 154, 155,
    156, 201–2, 207, 222, 223, 244, 250

Gavaskar, Sunil, 2, 3, 190, 216, 217,
    218
George, Shane, 181
Gibbs, Lance, 228
Gibson, Jack, 183
Gilbert, Dave, 224
Gillette, 137
Gladwin, Cliff, 143
Glassock, Craig, 181
Gleeson, John, 205
Gooch, Graham, 3–5, 51, 52, 55, 60–
    61, 62, 64, 67, 70, 76, 77, 78, 79, 83,
    85, 90, 97, 98, 99, 100, 101, 156,
    197, 198, 220, 228, 244
Goodwin, Murray, 181
Goss, Zoë, 132
Gough, Anna, 240
Gough, Darren, 43, 45, 47, 49, 50, 51,
    52, 53, 60, 61, 62, 71, 72, 74, 78, 81,
    83, 91, 101, 239–43
Gough, Liam, 240
Gower, David, 25, 32, 67, 86–7, 155,
    156, 216, 222, 223, 224, 226–8
Grace, W. G., 254
Grand National, The, 124
Graveney, Tom, 67, 196
Gray, Bob, 234
Gregory, Jack, 203
Greig, Tony, 120
Griffith, Charlie, 245
Griffiths, Alan, 125–6, 147
Grimmett, Clarrie, 197, 198–9, 201,
    202, 203, 204, 208–9, 212
*Grimmett on Getting Wickets*, 198
Grobbelaar, Bruce, 236
Grout, Wally, 146, 211
Gundappa Viswanath, 216

Hadlee, Sir Richard, 38, 189, 215, 216
Haigh, Schofield, 134
Hair, Darrell, 76, 81
Halbish, Graham, 233
Hall, Wesley, 127, 245, 246
Hammond, Ashley, 181
Hammond, Walter, 84
Hanif Mohammad, 191
Harden, 105
Hardstaff, Joe, 84
Harper, Laurence, 181
Harrity, Mark, 181

Harvey, Ian, 181
Harvey, Neil, 118, 121, 143, 146, 156, 198, 251
Hassett, Lindsay, 67
Hayden, Matthew, 10, 34, 50, 151, 243
Haynes, Desmond, 241, 256
Hayter, Peter, 36–7, 40
Healy, Ian, 8, 52–3, 54, 60, 61, 70, 71, 72, 76, 86, 89, 93, 98, 99, 101, 195, 210–12
Heine, Peter, 245, 246
Hemmings, Eddie, 220
Hendy, Trevor, 67
Hero Cup, 112, 249
Hick, Graeme, 5, 45, 46, 51, 52, 55, 60, 64, 73, 78, 79, 83, 85, 101, 136, 246
Higgs, Jim, 205
Hill, Jack 'Snarler', 120
Hills, Dene, 181
Hobbs, Robin, 150
Hodge, Bradley, 180, 181
Hogan, Paul, 114
Hohns, Trevor, 155, 205, 224
Holder, Vanburn, 216
Hole, Graeme, 143
Holland, Bob, 205, 224
Homeward Bound, 234
Houghton, David, 77
Howard, Craig, 181
Howard, Rupert, 85
Howell, Gwynne, 32
Hudson, Andrew, 8, 21–2, 115
Hughes, Kim, 66, 217, 221, 222
Hughes, Merv, 7–8, 10, 11–12, 41, 47, 115, 119, 151, 255, 256, 257
Hughes, Simon, 200–201
Humpage, Geoff, 241
Hutton, Len, 63, 141, 228

Illingworth, Raymond, 25, 28, 30–31, 39, 40, 44, 46, 52, 77, 156, 159, 228, 242
Ilott, Mark, 84
Imran Khan, 4, 5, 37, 38, 189, 215–16
Ingleby-Mackenzie, Colin, 247
Insole, D. J., 30, 153–4
Intikhab Alam, 232, 255
Iverson, Jack, 205–6

Jackson, Archie, 245
Jackson, Les, 143

Jackson, 'Shoeless Joe', 236
Jackson, Vic, 207
Jarman, Barry, 147
Javed Miandad, 12, 216, 255
Jenkins, Dan, 231
Jenner, Terry, 205
Johnson, Ian, 127, 143
Johnston, Bill, 206
Johnston, Brian, 131
Jones, Andrew, 256
Jones, Dean, 243
Jugiong, 105
Julian, Brendon, 94, 96

Kanga Cricket, 176
Kapil Dev, 189, 190, 215, 216–21, 226
Karsan Ghavri, 217–18
Kasprowicz, Michael, 181
Keating, Paul, 4, 5
Kenning, David, 187
Kerley, Neil, 183
Kippax, Alan, 245
Kirsten, Peter, 256, 257
Knott, Alan, 144

Laidlaw, Renton, 33
Laker, Jim, 65, 146
Lamb, Allan, 5, 37, 52
Lambson, 8, 21, 22
Langer, Justin, 151
Lara, Brian, 98, 126, 190–94, 195, 197, 198, 212, 215, 258
Launceston Examiner, 115
Law, Stuart, 181
Lawry, Bill, 58, 147, 164, 202
Laws of Cricket, 28
Lawson, Geoff, 224, 245
Lee, Alan, 33
Lee, Michael, 113
Lee, Shane, 181
Lewis, Chris, 5, 8, 84, 90, 93, 94, 99, 100, 101, 259
Lewis, Geoff 'Flipper', 234
Lewis, Joan, 32
Lewis, Tony, 27, 32, 125, 147
Leyland, Maurice, 84
Lillee, Dennis, 12, 42–3, 54, 66, 67, 114, 120, 160, 202, 218, 219, 226, 234, 235, 245
Lindwall, Ray, 40, 67, 206, 245, 246

Lloyd, Clive, 156, 221, 228
Lock, Tony, 65, 118, 146
Longhurst, Henry, 130
Lord's Taverners, 131
Lovell, Guy, 236
Loxton, Sam, 206
Lynam, Desmond, 129

MacGill, Stuart, 181
Mack, Christopher, 181
Mackaness, Miss, 61
Mackay, Ken, 143
Mackenzie, Keith, 27, 32, 124–5, 130
Maher, James, 181
*Mail on Sunday*, 36
Malao, Jacob, 33–4
Malcolm, Devon, 38–9, 40, 42, 43, 45,
    48, 61, 62, 71, 72, 74, 76, 78, 80, 81,
    84, 90, 91–3, 97, 99
Mandela Trophy, 22
Mangope, President Lucas, 1
Manoj Prabhakar, 256
Marsh, Daniel, 181
Marsh, Geoff, 49, 92, 243
Marsh, Rodney, 120, 159, 160, 180,
    196, 207, 226, 234, 235
Marshall, Malcolm, 215, 221
Martyn, Damien, 47, 151
Mascarenhas, Mark, 111, 249
Maskell, Dan, 130
Masters Tournament, Augusta, 122,
    123–4
Matthews, Greg, 224
May, P. B. H. (Peter), 67–8, 141, 156,
    228
May, Tim, 51, 52–3, 54, 55, 72, 73, 78,
    79–80, 149, 202, 203, 204, 207, 210,
    232
McCabe, Stan, 161, 203
McCague, Martin, 47, 51, 52, 53, 56,
    81, 83, 195
McConnon, Jim, 148
McCool, Colin, 204, 207
McCormack, Mark, 122
McDermott, Craig, 8, 10, 48, 52–3, 54,
    60, 61, 64, 66–7, 70, 72–3, 78, 80,
    86, 90–91, 94, 97, 99, 100, 101, 102,
    103, 133, 211, 224
McDermott, Mrs, 4
McDermott, Peter, 4

McDonald, Colin, 143
McGrath, Glenn, 52, 87, 98, 99, 100,
    101, 211
McIntyre, Peter, 87, 92–3, 94, 194
McKenzie, Graham, 146
*Melbourne Herald*, 122
Mercantile Mutual, 186
Miller, Keith, 44, 205, 206, 234, 245, 251
Misson, Frank, 146
Mitchell, Kevin Jnr, 49
Moles, Andy, 241
*Morning Chronicle*, 236–7
Moroney, Jack, 205
Morris, Arthur, 205
Morris, Geoff, 128
Moss, Alan, 143
Murdoch, Billy, 134
Mushtaq Ahmed, 5, 149
Mushtaq Mohammad, 232

Narendra Hirwani, 220
Nash, Dion, 81, 257
National Cricket Coaching Plan, 161–2
National Lottery, 160
NatWest Trophy, 32, 36, 111, 137,
    140, 241
Nayan Mongia, 257
*News of the World*, 27, 29, 30, 38
Newton, Jack, 133
*New York Times*, 1
Nicklaus, Jack, 123–4
*1993–4 Channel Nine Wide World of
    Sports Yearbook*, 10
Noble, M.A., 199–200, 201
Norman, Greg, 123–4, 132–3
Nyren, John, 237

O'Donnell, Simon, 223–4
O'Keeffe, Kerry, 150, 205
Oliver, Stuart, 181
Olympic Games, 26, 111
    Los Angeles, 111
    Winter, 115
O'Neill, Norman, 146
*On Reflection*, 116
O'Reilly, Bill, 54, 150, 197, 198, 202,
    203, 204, 208
Oslear, Don, 37
O'Sullevan, Peter, 130

Packer, Kerry, 114
Palmer, Ken, 39
Pamensky, Joe, 3
Park, Desmond, 122
Parker, Geoffrey, 181
Parramatta High School, 161
Pavarotti, Luciano, 32
Pay TV, 110
Phillip, Norbert, 216
Phillips, Wayne, 223
Philpott, Peter, 205
Playing condition, 78–9, 144, 248–9,
    254
Pollard, Dick, 206
Pollard, Ron, 235
Ponting, Ricky, 151, 181
Potter, Jack, 164
Prestwidge, Scott, 181
Price, Nick, 123–4
*Private Eye*, 129
Pycroft, Rev. James, 238
Pyke, Dr Frank, 43

Queensland Cricketers' Club, 131
Quirk, Trevor, 23–4

Radford, Bob, 79
Radio 2UE, 122
Ramprakash, Mark, 84, 97, 98, 99, 100,
    101, 227
Randell, Steve, 28
Rashid Latif, 255
Ravely Cricket Club, 105
Ravi Shastri, 195, 198, 220
Redpath, Ian, 198
Reid, Bruce, 46, 135, 196
Reid, John, 8, 19, 81–2, 94–5, 117
Reiffel, Paul, 23, 47, 151
Rhodes, Jonty, 39, 49, 52, 61, 64
Rhodes, Steve, 71, 76, 83, 90, 102
Rhodes, Wilfred, 134
Rice, Sir Tim, 157
Richards, David, 19, 233
Richards, Viv, 156, 157, 221, 226–7,
    228–9
Richardson, David, 259
Richardson, Richie, 241
Richardson, Vic, 203
Richie Benaud Oval, 253
Ring, Doug, 204–5, 213

Ritchie, Greg, 245
Robert, Jeffrey, 43
Roberts, Andy, 156
Roberts, Kevin, 181
Robertson, Austin, 114
Robins, Walter, 84
Robson, John, 241
Rothmans, 137
Rothmans Medal for Rugby League, 235
Rothmans National Sport Foundation,
    161, 182
Roxy Theatre, Parramatta, 96
Royal Melbourne Golf Club, 212
Rugby League State of Origin, 115
Russell, Jack, 84
Rutherford, Ken, 81, 198, 259
Ryder, Jack, 206, 251

Sadiq Mohammad, 216
Salim Malik, 22, 198, 233
Salisbury, Ian, 45, 46, 150
Santa Claus, 234
Sarfraz Nawaz, 37
Sawle, Laurie, 49, 224
Scuderi, Joseph, 181
Seccombe, Wade, 181
Seddon, Dudley, 251
Shakoor Rana, 222
Shand, Adam, 233
Shaw, John, 32
Shaw, Tim, 211
Shepherd, David, 8, 21
Shepherd's Restaurant, 33
Shival Yodav, 217
Shrewsbury, John, 125
Simpson, Bob, 9, 146, 181–2, 204, 205
Simpson, Reg, 205
Sims, Jim, 84
Sinrich, Bill, 112
Sky News, 25
Slater, Michael, 10, 49–51, 71, 74, 75,
    81, 86, 87–8, 91, 97, 99, 101, 102,
    239, 242–4
Sledge, Percy, 'When a Man Loves a
    Woman', 119
Small, Steve, 243, 245
Smith, A. C., 30, 157
Smith, Mike, 145–6, 156
Smith, Robin, 154, 202
Snow, John, 245

Sobers, Sir Garfield, 60, 98, 189, 190, 191, 192, 246
South African Broadcasting Corporation, 22, 23
South African RFU, 2
Spence, Peter, 164
Spink, Warren, 236
Spofforth, Fred, 134
Sproat, Ian, 159, 164
Spurling, John, 33
Statham, Brian, 65, 146, 245
Statistics, 269–71
Steele, David, 120
Stewart, Alec, 47, 52–5, 60, 61, 73–4, 83
Stewart, James, 181
Strang, Paul, 152
Streak, Heath, 78, 152
Subba Row, Raman, 9, 10
Sun City Casino, 1
Sunday League, 110, 137, 140, 149
Sunday Telegraph, 201
Sunday Times, South Africa, 1
Swanton, E. W., 157
Sydney Morning Herald, 232
Symonds, Andrew, 181

Taber, Brian, 161, 194
Taylor, Mark, 6, 9, 10, 13, 43–4, 49–50, 52, 54, 58, 59, 60, 62, 64, 69, 72, 74, 75, 76–8, 81, 87–8, 91, 92, 96, 99, 100, 101, 103, 107, 133, 135, 159, 194, 202, 211, 213, 239, 242, 243, 244–5
Te Kanawa, Dame Kiri, 32, 122–3
Tendulkar, Sachin, 190, 191, 195, 213, 215
Test and County Cricket Board (TCCB), 31, 110, 114
Test Series
Australia v. England in Australia, 1954–5, 65
Australia v. England in Australia, 1994–95, 8, 57, 65, 83
Australia v. South Africa in Australia, 1993–94, 6, 7
England v. South Africa in England, 1994, 27–40
South Africa v. Australia in South Africa, 1994, 2, 7–26

The Game's the Thing, 200
The Times, 33
Thomson, Jeff 'Thommo', 42–3, 202, 224, 245, 246
Thomson, Peter, 133
Thorpe, Graham, 55, 60, 64, 70, 72, 73, 83, 90, 98, 100, 101, 102, 103
Tillingfold Cricket Club, 105
Topley, Don, 236
Toshack, Ernie, 206
Trans World International (TWI), 112
Tribe, George, 204, 207
Trueman, Fred, 119–20, 146, 245, 246–7
Trumper, Victor, 254
Tucker, Adrian, 181
Tufnell, Phil, 44, 45, 46, 49, 53, 54, 56, 61–2, 71, 74, 75, 76, 78, 79–80, 83, 93, 97, 258
Tyson, Frank, 40, 65, 146, 245, 246

Udal, Shaun, 44, 46, 83
Underwood, Derek, 145–6
United Cricket Board of South Africa, 2

Verity, Hedley, 84
Vinod Kambli, 256
Vladivar, Fiona, 130
Voce, Bill, 84

Wade, Tommy, 85
Walcott, Sir Clyde, 19
Walker, Alan, 206
Walters, Doug, 161
Wanderers Club, The, 2
Waqar Younis, 29, 242
Ward, Frank, 203
Warne, Shane, 7, 8, 10, 11–12, 13, 15–16, 23, 48, 52–6, 59, 60, 61, 64, 66, 72, 73, 78, 79–80, 90–91, 96, 97, 98, 99, 100, 101, 115, 119, 135, 136, 149, 189–214, 215, 232, 244, 257
Wasim Akram, 5, 29, 153, 190, 215, 242
Watkins, Alan, 206
Waugh, Mark, 34, 49, 50, 51, 61, 62, 71, 73, 76, 85, 88–9, 91, 93, 97, 98, 99, 100, 101, 102, 133, 198, 232, 241, 244
Waugh, Steve, 10, 16, 23, 41–2, 59–60,

62, 71, 72, 76, 87, 90, 91, 97, 98, 99,
  100, 101, 195–6, 197, 224, 246
Waverley Club, 183
Webber, Darren, 181
Wessels, Kepler, 6, 7, 223
Wheatley, Ossie, 155, 222
White, Craig, 47, 52, 83
White, Ted, 203
Whitney, Michael, 224
Whittal, Guy, 258
Wilkinson, 'Slim', 187
Williams, Brett, 181
Williamson, Cameron, 181
Willis, Bob, 108, 146, 155, 156, 221, 228
Wilson, Mark, 33
*Wisden Cricket Monthly*, 41, 106, 252
Wishart, Warren, 181
Wood, Barry, 120

Woodcock, John, 20
Woodfull, Bill, 224
Wooller, Wilf, 148
World Cup
  1983, 219
  1987, 225
  1991, 3, 5, 21
  1996, 111
World Series Cricket, 114, 151
Worthington, Stan, 84
Wright, Gary, 181
Wyatt, Bob, 84

Yallop, Graham, 220
Yardley, Bruce, 218, 219

Zaheer Abbas, 216
Zoehrer, Tim, 232